Targeting Language Delays

Targeting Language Delays

IEP Goals & Activities for Students with Developmental Challenges

Caroline Lee, L.C.S.T

Woodbine House   2014

Library of Congress Cataloging-in-Publication Data

Lee, Caroline, date.
  Targeting language delays : IEP goals & activities for students with developmental challenges / Caroline Lee.
-- First edition.
     pages cm.
  Includes bibliographical references and index.
  ISBN 978-1-60613-198-5
 1. Language disorders in children. 2. Communicative disorders in children. 3. Children with disabilities--Education. 4. Individualized education programs. I. Title.
  RJ496.L35L43 2013
  618.92'855--dc23

                                                    2014000587

Manufactured in the United States of America

10 9 8 7 6 5 4 3 2 1

This book is dedicated to all children for whom learning language is a challenge.

"The limits of my language mean the limits of my world."
—*Ludwig Wittgenstein (philosopher, 1889–1951)*

TABLE OF CONTENTS

Foreword

In the field of education, few would argue that the task of providing meaningful, measureable, and achievable language programming for children with significant developmental challenges is complex and demanding.

Many factors must be taken into consideration in order to achieve success for these students. Skills being taught must be at an attainable level for the student. Each targeted skill must be specific, with increasing challenge added as each step in the sequence of acquisition is mastered by the student. Many repetitions will be required at each step in order for the student to reach the target. And individual skills must be transferred into broader "real world" applications to ensure that the skill is useful to the student.

Few resources exist that discuss and demonstrate ideas for providing this type of instruction for very early language and communication development that can be easily implemented by the teachers, educational assistants, or volunteers who work with the student on a daily basis. This book is the culmination of Caroline Lee's many years of experience working in the school system designing and implementing these types of programs for students with significant developmental and communication difficulties. The suggestions and activities are those that she used to successfully build the early language skills of her students in consultation and collaboration with teachers, educational assistants, and parents. They are shared here to allow others, particularly those with limited experience or limited access to a speech-language pathologist, to benefit from her knowledge and experience.

Targeting Language Delays is a useful resource for all those working with children with significant developmental challenges, including autism spectrum disorders. It includes goals suitable for children with early levels of language skills, and outlines steps to move these children forward in their development of language and communication. The goals are systematic and explain a logical progression of skill development. The activities are straightforward, and can be easily implemented by the school team as presented, or, with simple alterations, to suit the needs of the individual student. Ideas for carryover of skills into practical situations are provided. A strategy for teaching whole word reading is also presented for verbal and nonverbal students who are not yet ready for traditional strategies.

The rewards of helping children with limited language achieve success are immeasurable. With the use of the activities and strategies presented in this book, I believe that your team will find success for your student in attaining stronger language and communication skills.

Susan B. Swirski, M.Sc.(A), CCC-SLP

Preface

When I was creating language programs for students with developmental challenges, first as a speech-language pathologist for the Renfrew County District School Board and later, in private practice, I often used as a reference R. Leaf and J. McEachin's book *A Work in Progress* (DRL Books, 1999). Their book presents many helpful steps for building the foundations of receptive and expressive language.

Once my students had achieved these foundations, they needed to move on further, but I could not find a suitable text that gave me step-by-step guidance toward those next language levels. Each time I developed a program for a student, I felt that I was at risk of omitting important steps either from the overall planning or from my instructions to the support person delivering the program.

This manual is an attempt to provide sequential steps in programming to meet more than 100 Individualized Education Program/Individual Education Plan (IEP)* or equivalent goals for listening, receptive and expressive language, and whole word reading for students with developmental challenges. The manual can be used by speech-language pathologists as they provide therapy directly or indirectly through support personnel. In addition, I hope that the steps are written clearly enough that the manual can also be used by teachers, parents, and others who have no formal training in the speech and language areas.

This is not intended as a "cookie cutter" or "one plan serves all" manual. The activities are experience-based, and what works for one student will not always work for another. Users will want to be selective and present only those goals appropriate to their student. They may also want to add goals and activities from other sources to provide a student-specific program.

I hope that this manual will provide detailed programming and program tracking to enhance therapy goals, save planning time, and increase clarity when the supervising SLP shares her goals with support personnel, teachers, or others. I hope too that it will encourage programming in the language areas for the many students with developmental challenges who do not have access to the services of a speech-language pathologist.

---

* This book will use the abbreviation IEP to refer to both the U.S. and Canadian terms for the individualized education plans required for students receiving special education services at school.

Acknowledgements

I would like to thank the Renfrew County District School Board for the opportunity to work with the dedicated staff in the special education department for seventeen years. Also, I thank the many parents who entrusted their children's language therapy to me throughout my career and particularly during my years of private practice.

Special thanks go to Jennie Mick for her thoughtful editing of an early version of the book and for contributing her own tricks-of-the-trade for me to include, and to Nicola Innes for her early comments and encouragement.

Thank you to friend and colleague, Susan B. Swirski, who gladly wrote the thoughtful foreword. Her valuable perspective early on in the project broadened my thinking and strongly influenced the eventual format for the goals.

I am grateful to the many people who have shared their knowledge with me over the years informally or formally through presentations and print. I have learned so much from them. Of special mention is Theresa Dodwell, whose presentation in 2004 opened my eyes to the possibility of nonverbal children learning to read.

I appreciate Dr. Ronald Leaf granting permission to reproduce the developmental order in which children learn the names of colors and body parts from *A Work in Progress*.

Thank you to Susan Stokes and the staff at Woodbine House for sharing my vision for this book and helping me with the final steps and publishing process.

A big thank you to my husband, David, whose vast collection of books on basketball coaching gave me the initial idea for this book, and to everyone else who encouraged me as my "three-month project" stretched to two years!

Part 1:
Before You Begin Therapy

Who Is This Book For?

This manual is designed to be used with school-age students (ages 5–21 years) who:
- Have been identified by a psychologist or other qualified professional as having mild to severe delays in the cognitive areas, with or without characteristics on the autism spectrum.
- Have been identified by a speech-language pathologist or other qualified professional as having delays in the language areas.

The student may or may not yet have an Individual Education Plan/Individualized Education Program (IEP) or equivalent.

Student Profile

Receptive Language:
- Is able to follow routine instructions and understand some concepts—e.g., put your coat on the hook.
- Has significant "gaps" in listening, language comprehension, and general understanding.

Expressive Language:
- Is able to communicate verbally in single words, phrases, or incomplete sentences.
- Has difficulty asking or answering questions, describing events, or delivering a clear message.

Note: *Nonverbal students who use a voice-output device may benefit from some of the goals and activities, but modifications will be needed.*

Literacy:
- Is able to or is not yet able to read.

Behavior:
- Is compliant and able to attend to table-top tasks for at least a short period of time.
- *The student may have received or be receiving applied behaviour analysis (ABA) programming prior to or concurrent with present language programming.*

Users

This manual is designed to be used by:
- Speech-language pathologists,
- Teachers and other professional educators,
- Support personnel with experience in language therapy,
- Parents and volunteers who have little or no experience in language therapy.

How to Use This Manual

Goals and Prerequisites

1. This manual is divided into sections that reflect the fundamentals for language development. Each section is divided into **goals.** The goals are presented in the order that they would be acquired by a typically developing student and are appropriate for inclusion in the student's IEP or equivalent.

2. Each goal contains:
   - a list of **materials** needed to carry out the activities,
   - an **introduction** advising you how to introduce and model the target goal,
   - **receptive and expressive** steps to achieving the goal (in mainly expressive goals, these components are combined), and
   - **carryover (generalization) activities** that can be used to work on the goal in an informal manner or help the student to generalize the goal at school and at home.

3. Several goals include a form for **tracking progress.** This form will help you to keep track of target vocabulary within the goal that the student understands (receptive), is able to use in a structured setting (expressive), and is eventually able to use in spontaneous language (established/generalized).

   The list **Tracking Goals and Prerequisites** in Appendix 1 will enable you to track when a goal is completed, giving an overall view of the student's progress through the program, either during one school year or from one year to the next, and from one program supervisor to another.

4. The student's daily program should **include goals from several different sections** rather than goals all from one section. For example: he may work on a goal from Chapter 3 (Same and Different), as well as a goal from Chapter 4 (Yes/No) and from Chapter 7 (Verbs). It may sometimes be helpful to work on activities from goals at an earlier level than assessment findings suggest the student is ready for in order to review the student's prior knowledge and build confidence or rapport.

5. Some goals have **prerequisites** listed under the goal title. It is *essential* that the student have this language foundation before the goal is introduced.

6. The goals and activities are intended for individual programming but most could easily be adapted for group work or work with nonverbal students.

Criterion

In most goals, it is recommended that students reach a criterion of 80–90 percent accuracy before progressing to the next goal in a chapter. If the criterion is not met within a reasonable number of sessions, then:

   a. Review the previous goal in the chapter.
   b. Provide more modeling of the goal in therapy sessions and everyday life.
   c. Present the goal in a different way (e.g., a game format).
   d. Use different materials (e.g., pictures instead of objects; black and white pictures instead of colored).
   e. Sub-step to an easier task or try advancing to a more difficult step. Be aware that students with developmental delays often do not follow the same progression in language acquisition as typically developing students.

     f. Leave the goal and come back to it days or months later.

     g. Work on foundation skills necessary for the goal (e.g., auditory memory, visual processing, or increased vocabulary).

12 Tips for Therapy

The following tips are suggested to encourage positive outcomes and fully engage students in the learning process:

1. **Make learning fun.** Make sure that you and your student both laugh many times during each therapy session!

2. G**ive positive feedback.** Give verbal comments and praise to reinforce the correct response; e.g., "good—you gave me the bigger cup." Keep your comments honest so they reflect the student's performance; e.g., "you are almost right"; "that was close"; "good"; "wow, fantastic!" Use material rewards if necessary.

3. **Choose materials that are meaningful.** Use objects, pictures, games, and themes of interest to the student. Adapt the activities accordingly.

4. **Plan the session in advance.** Select the goals, activities, and materials before the session begins so you are well prepared and the session can run smoothly.

5. **Take the lesson into the day.** Find teachable moments throughout the day to generalize skills that were presented in the teaching session.

6. **Teach, don't test.** Use good teaching practices, including demonstrating and modeling; repeating steps and *sub-stepping* (i.e., going back to an easier task within the goal or to a previous goal in the chapter); imitating and prompting (see Appendix 4). Make deliberate errors and have the student correct you. Avoid asking "testing" questions. If you must ask questions, then either be sure that the student already knows the answer or provide him with choice answers.

7. **Work at the student's pace.** You may need to spend many weeks on one step before he is ready to progress to the next. Keep in mind that some students may need 200 or more repetitions before they learn a specific skill.

8. **Be aware of the student's level of competence.** Teach to his attention span, cognitive ability, and receptive and expressive language levels. Do not challenge him with activities that are too difficult or bore him with activities that are too easy or overly familiar.

9. **Allow the student to take some ownership.** Allow him to choose the order of the activities, how many to do, or when to do them (if scheduling permits). Have a visual means for him to see how many tasks still need to be completed or how much longer the session is to last.

10. **Be patient and make every moment of your therapy session count.** Your time in a structured setting with the student is precious.

11. **Support the reader with written words.** Write the target word, phrase, or sentence on a small individual cue card and use the card as a prompt. Show it to the student at the same time as you say the target word or phrase to reinforce his understanding, and show it to him when you are expecting him to say the target without a verbal model. For example, write "he" on a cue card and present it when teaching the understanding and use of the pronoun "he" in Chapter 12 (Pronouns). Gradually fade the use of the cue card so that he comes to understand or use the target without visual support.

Note: *If the student cannot already read, do not try to teach him to read the words on cue cards before you work on language goals with him. Cue cards are suggested only for students who can easily read the words on the cards.*

12. **End each session on a positive note.** Present a task that the student prefers at the end of the session or one that he can manage easily.

Using Games in Language Therapy

Play games during therapy sessions to:
- reinforce the target goal,
- develop auditory skills and visual processing,
- motivate language use,
- encourage joint attention and student/instructor rapport,
- teach turn taking fundamental to conversation,
- encourage group participation and learning through peer modeling.

Games played should be:
a. Simple and easily learned by the student so that time is not wasted on teaching the rules,
b. Appropriate for the target (goal) and provide opportunities for many repetitions of the target within the playing time,
c. Cooperative rather than competitive for students who have difficulty losing (to make a game more cooperative, play against the clock; use wording such as "this card is finished" rather than "this person wins"; have characters or stuffed toys represent the players; keep a running tally of wins and losses so that one loss is not overly significant),
d. Fun!

Multipurpose Games

The following games are included in many of the goals. Substitute other games and/ or play additional games according to the student's preference. The page reference to the description of the game is given the first time that the game is suggested in the book and not on subsequent occasions.
- Barrier Games
- Fishing
- Go Fish
- Hide the Sticker
- Lotto games
- Magic Bag
- Memory
- Simon Says
- Snakes (Chutes) and Ladders
- Snap
- Tim's Game (magnetic wand and bingo chips)

Barrier Games

In barrier games, players carry out a verbal direction without being able to see a visual model. Sit at a table across from the student and place a barrier (such as an upright file folder) between you.

Perform an activity on your side of the barrier using the specific materials listed in the goal. Direct the student to carry out the same activity on his side of the barrier using his duplicate set of materials; e.g., put the red car in the cup.

Lift the barrier so that you can both compare the student's response with your direction. If his response *did not* match your direction, demonstrate the correct response without the barrier. For example, say, "This is 'put the red car in the cup.'" Then return the barrier and materials to their places and repeat the same direction.

Commercial barrier games can be used for additional practice of some goals.

Fishing

Players "fish" for a picture and say the target response for the one that they catch; e.g., the target noun "turtle." Attach a magnet on a piece of string to a piece of doweling to make the fishing rod and attach metal paperclips to picture cards to make the fish.

Go Fish

For this traditional matching game, use 10–20 matched card pairs. Deal 5 random cards to each player and place the remaining cards in a pile on the table. Place any pairs that you now have in your hand (or get during play) face up on the table. To play: take turns to ask the other player for a specific card from his hand to make up a pair with a card already in your hand. If the player does not have the card that you request, he will say "Go Fish," and you must pick up a card off the pile. The winner is the first player to find a match for all of his cards. Each player must use the specific language target when asking for a card. For example, players say the name of the picture or a sentence such as "I want the _____."

Use paired commercial picture cards that are:
- *Identical* for vocabulary building/naming (e.g., dog/dog)
- *Non-identical* but illustrate the same concept (e.g., "under" in different situations; opposites such as "hot/cold"; associations such as "paint/paintbrush").

Hide the Sticker

Play this game to add incentive to a task that requires the use of single-picture cards (e.g., naming verb cards). Spread out the target cards face down on the table and hide a sticker (or a note promising a reward such as extra computer time or an edible treat) under a random card. The student will find and get to keep the sticker when he picks up the card.

Lotto

For this matching game, use a Lotto card of 4 to 8 pictures and a set of identical single picture cards. Each player chooses a Lotto card and the matching pictures are placed face down on the table. Take turns picking up a card and place it on your Lotto card if it matches. If it does not match, give it to the other player to place on his card or return it to the table. Each player must use the specified language target.

Use commercial Lotto games or make your own game to target specific vocabulary and concepts (use cardstock and stickers, digital photos, and/or pictures from catalogs and the Internet).

Alternatively, use 8 to 16 pairs of cards from commercial card sets (e.g., association cards; opposites). Make two Lotto cards (one for each of you) by placing one of each pair closely side by side in two square formations. Place the matching cards face down on the table and play as above.

Magic Bag

Add a little mystery to an activity by placing objects or pictures in a "Magic Bag" such as a decorative cloth gift or shoe bag. Take turns removing each item from the bag and using the target language; e.g., "flower" or "I got a flower."

Memory

In this game of Memory (often called Concentration), players find matching pairs by memorizing where the cards are placed on the table. Use 4–12 pairs of picture cards (depending on the student's ability). Arrange them in random order in rows face down on the table. Take turns to turn up 2 cards. If the cards match, keep them; if they do not match, turn them back face down in exactly the same place. The winner is the player with the most matching pairs. Name the pictures that you turn up using the language target; e.g., nouns such as "dog, horse" or a sentence such as "I found the _____."

Use commercial Memory games, commercial card sets (e.g., singular/plural), or make your own pairs of cards to target specific vocabulary.

Simon Says

Play this listening and motor activity game as a group activity using actions from Chapter 1 (Following Directions), Goal 1, p. **14**). When you preface a direction with "Simon says," then players are to carry it out; when you omit "Simon says," the players are to stand still and not do the action. Players who do the action will be out of the game. For example:

> *Instructor*: Simon says: "Touch your ear" (each player touches his ear).
> *Instructor*: Simon says: "Stomp your foot" (each player stomps his foot).
> *Instructor:* Put your hands on your head (players do not move—those who do the action are "out").

To add interest, instead of saying "Simon," use a name chosen by the students or the name of a character; e.g., Superman says: "Touch your ear."

Snakes (Chutes) and Ladders

In this board game, each player progresses his token from the bottom of a grid to the top (moving as many squares as indicated by the roll of a die). If a player lands on designated squares, he either advances several rows up the board by climbing up a ladder or he goes back to a lower square by sliding down a snake (or chute).

You can use commercial games of Snakes and Ladders (also called Chutes and Ladders) designed to target language goals or you can make you own game to target specific vocabulary by using cardstock, markers, small pictures, and/or stickers. Put a target word relevant to the goal on each square and have each player name the picture that he lands on; e.g., theme "animals"—horse, cow, sheep, etc. Limit the number of squares on the grid and make the ladders and snakes quite short. Lengthy "drop backs" can make the game long and frustrating!

Snap

The first player to respond verbally in this game wins a stack of cards. It is a great game for repetitive practice to improve the quick recall of a target word. Use a regular deck of cards, but remove the kings, queens, and jacks so you will have only red and black numbered cards in the deck. Divide the deck in half and place one-half facedown stacked in front of you and the other half facedown in front of the student.

Choose a target word or sentence relevant to the goal; e.g., "mine" or "I want them." Build a stack of cards in the middle of the table by taking turns to place a card from your own stack face up on top.

When a player places a red card on top of a red card or a black card on top of a black card, players say the target word/sentence. The first player to say the target wins the stack, and then a new stack is started. The winner is the player with the most cards at the end of the game.

Cards of the same color come together frequently, so there are many opportunities to use the language target. You can hesitate before saying the target word to give the student more opportunities to win and more confidence in saying the word. The game can become loud and boisterous, so it is a good "ice-breaker"!

Tim's Game—Wand and Chips

For Tim, using a magnetic wand and bingo chips (plastic disks with metal edging) was the highlight of his therapy session!

Use a wand and chips to add interest to a task or as a reward. For example:

- Place vocabulary cards separately face down on the table and put a bingo chip under the center of each. Have the student pick up the card of his choice by touching it with the wand (the wand attaches to the chip through the thickness of the card—magic!).
- Place chips in different locations when teaching concepts of position and have the student pick them up with the wand after describing their location; e.g., "under the cup"; "beside the pencil."
- Allow the student time to play with the wand and chips at the end of his therapy session.

Part 2:
IEP Goals, Activities, and Carryover

1.
Following Directions

These goals are appropriate for students with one or more of the following characteristics:

- understands routine directions (e.g., "hang up your coat"), but has difficulty following novel directions (e.g., "give your coat to Luke")

- does not always understand concepts in directions (e.g., "put the pen beside the book")

- has difficulty following directions of more than one step (e.g., "open your book and write your name on page 2")

- looks confused and copies peers when directions are given

- has difficulty giving directions or telling people what he wants them to do for him

Following Directions Goals

The student will follow and give one- and two-step directions:

Goal 1: involving body parts with and without props; e.g., touch your hair; put on the hat.

Goal 2: involving selected prepositions—in, on top of, under, beside, between, next to, in front of, behind; e.g., put the ball under the table.

Goal 3: involving colors and prepositions; e.g., put the red car in the bowl.

Goal 1: The student will follow and give one- and two-step directions involving body parts with and without props (e.g., touch your hair; put on the hat) (with 80–90 percent accuracy).

Materials

1. Lists of activities: MOTOR ACTIVITIES WITHOUT PROPS, Table 1, below, and MOTOR ACTIVITIES WITH PROPS, Table 2, below.
2. Blank copies of DIRECTIONS WITH/WITHOUT PROPS, Table 3, below.

Introduction

Introduce the goal by telling the student that he is going to learn to follow directions using his body and some well-known objects. Review the names of the body parts and objects that are to be used. Instruct the student to look at the objects when you name them in a direction.

Tell the student that he is to **Listen** to the direction, **Repeat** it back to you, and then **Do** the direction as requested. Write these key words on a cue card as a visual reminder for the student who can read.

> **Listen:** It is important that the student listen without attempting to join in or say anything. He must be silent at this time.

> **Repeat:** The student must repeat back the direction with 100 percent accuracy before attempting to carry it out. When there is difficulty, repeat the direction as often as is needed and/or have the student say the direction with you until he is able to repeat it independently and confidently.

> **Do:** When the student is able to repeat the direction accurately, have him carry it out.

Activity **Receptive**

Follow the steps below and use the Listen/Repeat/Do format. If the student is unable to carry out a direction, then provide verbal prompts and/or demonstrate the direction as often as needed (e.g., this is "roll the ball"). The student must reach 80–90 percent accuracy on each step before progressing to the next.

Record directions and responses for each session on a blank copy of DIRECTIONS WITH/WITHOUT PROPS.

> **Step 1:** Give the student single-step directions from MOTOR ACTIVITIES WITHOUT PROPS (present in random order) (e.g., "lick your lips"; "stand up"; "hands in the air").

> **Step 2:** Give single-step directions from MOTOR ACTIVITIES WITH PROPS (present in random order) (e.g., "touch the chair"; "roll the ball"; "pick up the book").

Step 3: Present two-step directions joined by "then" from MOTOR ACTIVITIES WITHOUT PROPS.

Vary the combinations; e.g., "clap your hands, then sit down"; "touch your nose, then clap your hands." The student must repeat and carry out the two steps in the same order as presented.

Step 4: Present two-step directions from MOTOR ACTIVITIES WITH PROPS. Vary the combinations. The student must repeat and carry out the two steps in the same order as presented.

1. One action word and two items joined by "and" (e.g., "point to the toothbrush and the chair"; "pick up the spoon and the ball").
2. Two action words and two items joined by "then" (e.g., "open the book, then point to the window"; "show me the ball, then open the book").

Activity **Expressive**

When working on each step, have the student be the teacher and give you directions using the same body parts and props. Prompt as needed. For example, say, "tell me what to do with my hands" (student: "clap your hands"); "tell me what to touch" (student: "touch the brush").

It may be helpful to have the student carry out the direction that he proposes before verbalizing it so that you know his words accurately reflect what he wants you to do. Prompt this by saying "show me first—then tell me what to do so I can do the same."

When working on Steps 3 and 4 above, have the student give directions involving two items joined by "and" and two steps joined by "then."

Carryover

- Encourage the use of the strategy *Listen, Repeat, Do* when you are giving the student directions throughout the day.
- Have the student run errands in school or carry out tasks in the classroom (e.g., "give this note to the secretary"; "take the book to Kyle").
- Increase to two items and two steps when he is ready (e.g., "pick up the crayons and the scissors"; "put your shoes and hat in your backpack"; "take the pencil to Sean and pick up your shoes").
- Give directions that involve physical activities such as "run," "jump," "skip," "walk," and "spin" (e.g., "walk to the table"; "jump three times"; "run to the swing, then stand on one foot").

Table 1: MOTOR ACTIVITIES WITHOUT PROPS

- Stand up
- Close your eyes
- Sit down
- Turn around
- Clap your hands
- Swing your arms
- Stamp your foot
- Stand on one foot
- Cross your arms
- Wiggle your thumb/ fingers
- Lick your lips
- Point to your leg/arm/hair

- Smile
- Wave hello
- Cover your eyes/ears with your hands
- Nod your head
- Open your mouth wide
- Stick out your tongue
- Shake your head/hand/foot
- Hands in the air/behind your head/at your sides
- Kneel down
- Touch your nose/ear/hair/arm/foot/mouth/toes/knee
- Put your hands on your head/tummy/ears/knees

Table 2: MOTOR ACTIVITIES WITH PROPS

Props: toothbrush, hairbrush, book, pencil, spoon, crayon, glove, hat, Kleenex, ball, shoe, bell

Props specific to workplace: e.g., window, door, light, desk, rug, table, chair

Directions applicable to all props:
- Pick up the.........e.g., pick up the pencil
- Show me the......e.g., toothbrush
- Point to the.........e.g., chair
- Touch the...........e.g., glove
- Get the ....e.g., hairbrush
- Give me the........e.g., pencil

Directions appropriate to specific props
- Brush your teeth/hair
- Open/close the book
- Put on/take off the glove/hat
- Wave the Kleenex
- Ring the bell
- Roll/throw the ball
- Write with the pencil/crayon

Table 3: DIRECTIONS WITH/WITHOUT PROPS

Direction	Correct/ Incorrect
1.	
2.	
3.	
4.	
5.	
6.	
7.	
8.	
9.	
10.	
11.	
12.	
13.	
14.	
15.	
16.	
17.	
18.	
19.	
20.	

Goal 2: The student will follow and give one- and two-step directions involving selected prepositions—in, on top of, under, beside, between, next to, in front of, behind (e.g., "put the ball under the cup) (with 80–90 percent accuracy).

Note: This goal involves prepositions that are usually learned first by the typically developing student. Prepositions learned later can be found in Chapter 9 (Concepts), Goal 1, p. 149.

Materials

1. 8–10 pairs of small identical toys, or household or school items (e.g., 2 identical toy cars/dinosaurs/spoons/erasers).
2. 2 identical sets of 5 objects or containers that can be used as "places" (e.g., 2 blue cups, 2 identically patterned plates, 2 small brown paper gift bags, 2 very small cardboard boxes, 2 red plastic cereal bowls).
3. Cardboard barrier for Barrier game (see p. 7).
4. List TRACKING PREPOSITIONS IN BARRIER GAMES, Table 4, below.

Introduction

Introduce the goal by telling the student that he is going to learn words that tell us where to put something. As in Goal 1, he is to **Listen** to the direction, **Repeat** it back to you, and then **Do** the direction. Write these key words on a cue card as a visual reminder for the student who can read.

Model the preposition "in." Use a small object such as a block and two "places" such as a cup and a box. Place the block in relation to one of the places and say, for example, "This is 'put the block <u>in the cup.</u>'" Repeat the direction and have him imitate your action. Then model the direction using the other "place"; e.g., "put the block <u>in the box</u>" and again have him imitate. Repeat these two directions until he is able to place the object in the correct place with 90 percent accuracy. Present a variety of "in" directions using the same object and different places and different objects and the original two "places." Provide prompts and modeling as needed.

Proceed to Activity *Receptive*.

Introduce prepositions "on top of," "under," "beside," "between," "next to," "in front," and "behind" in this way, one at a time, before contrasting one with another in Step 3 (below).

Activity **Receptive**

Note: The following instructions for the Barrier game using concept "<u>in</u>" will be the same for every other concept in this goal.

Erect the cardboard barrier between you and the student. Place one of a pair of small objects on the student's side of the barrier and the other one of the pair on your side along with the same two "places" for each person (e.g., object—dinosaur; places—cup and bag). Have the student name the object and places.

Step 1: Place your object <u>in</u> either of the two places (e.g., <u>in</u> the bag). Direct the student to do the same (e.g., "put the dinosaur <u>in</u> the bag." Have him follow the ***Listen, Repeat,*** and ***Do*** strategy.

Lift the barrier to see if the student followed the direction correctly. Model and correct as needed.

Step 2: When the student is able to follow a single-step direction using "in" and a choice of 2 "places," enlarge the choice of objects to be placed and the number of places until he is able to place any one of the 8 items in any of the 5 different "places" (80–90 percent accuracy).

Keep a record of the student's progress using the list TRACKING PREPOSITIONS IN BARRIER GAMES.

Step 3: Teach a new preposition; e.g., "under" by following Steps 1 and 2 above.

Step 4: Contrast the two prepositions learned (e.g., "in" and "under"), in mixed single-step directions (e.g., "put the dinosaur <u>under</u> the bag"; "put the crayon <u>in</u> the cup)."

Step 5: Increase to 2-step directions joined by "and." Do not use the barrier for this step, as you need to be able to monitor the order in which the student carries out the directions. (He must carry them out in the order given.)
   1. Use the *same* preposition in both steps of the direction; e.g. put the dog <u>in</u> the box and the block <u>in</u> the cup
   2. Use *different* prepositions in each step of the direction; e.g. put the pencil <u>on top</u> of the plate and the dinosaur <u>in</u> the bag.

If the student reverses the order, go through the ***Listen*** and ***Repeat*** format again. Provide modeling and repetition as needed.

Activity **Expressive**

When working on Steps 1–4, play the barrier game with the student as the instructor. Have him put an object in a specific place behind his barrier and tell you to put yours in the same place using the target preposition.

If, because he gave you the wrong direction, yours is not in the same place as his when the barrier is removed, he may want to change the position of his own object to match the position of yours. Tell him not to touch the objects but to tell you how to fix it so that yours is the same as his. This helps the student become aware of how important it is to give accurate information in directions.

If the student denies or is unable to remember what direction he gave, write down his direction as he gives it, so you can both "check back" to see what he said.

When working on Step 5, remove the barrier and have him give you two-step directions joined by "then" or "and."

When the student has reached 95 percent accuracy giving directions using all prepositions and items, then make some deliberate errors when following his directions and have him correct you. This encourages critical thinking and is a great confidence builder, but should be introduced with caution so that the student does not become confused.

Carryover

- Use the target prepositions in real-life situations; e.g., have the student stand or hide in/beside/in front of a large cardboard box or on top of/under a chair.
- Play with felt/magnetic scenes and toys (e.g., garage, farm, doll house), that contain small items or people that can be arranged according to the direction given (e.g., "put the girl <u>beside</u> the swing"; "put the man <u>in</u> the car").
- Give single-step directions that are not routine (e.g., "put your shoes <u>next to</u> your chair"; "put the cars <u>under</u> your desk").
- Have the student hide an object and give directions to a robot (you!) in order to find it.
- Play Simon Says (p. 8) and use prepositions; e.g., on your head; under your chin; behind your back.
- Play commercial games that involve basic prepositions.

Note: *To teach other concepts of position, see Chapter 6 (Concepts), Goal 1, p. 78.*

Table 4: TRACKING PREPOSITIONS IN BARRIER GAMES

Preposition	Receptive	Expressive	Established
In			
On top of			
Under			
Beside			
Between			
Next to			
In front of			
Behind			

Goal 3: The student will follow and give one- and two-step directions involving colors and prepositions; e.g., "put the red car in the bowl" (with 80–90 percent accuracy).

Prerequisite: *Knowledge of colors—Chapter 8 (Descriptors), Goal 1, p. 120.*

Materials

1. 2 matched sets of 4 objects or toys that are identical but ***vary in color;*** e.g., 4 small toy cars of the same size and shape but different colors (red, yellow, blue, green); 4 small blocks of same size and shape but different colors.
2. 2 identical sets of 5 objects or containers that can be used as "places"; e.g., 2 blue cups, 2 identically patterned plates, 2 small brown paper gift bags, 2 small cardboard boxes, 2 red plastic cereal bowls (as for Goal 2).
3. Cardboard barrier for Barrier game (as for Goal 2).

Introduction

Introduce the goal by telling the student that now that he has learned some words that tell him where to put something, he is going to learn to listen for the color of the object and the place to put it. As in Goal 1, he is to **Listen** to the direction, **Repeat** it back to you, and then **Do** the direction as requested. Provide written visual support for the reader as needed.

Begin by reviewing the names of the colors of the objects that you are going to use. Do not proceed with the goal if the student's color naming is not 100 percent accurate.

Erect the barrier between you and use materials #1. Put 2 of the objects on the student's side of the barrier and the same 2 on your side along with 1 "place" (the same for each person). For example, you may use a red car and a blue car and a cup as a "place."

Activity **Receptive**

Step 1: Use the preposition "in." Put one of your objects in relation to a place. Then direct the student to do the same; e.g., "put the <u>blue</u> car in the cup." The student must **Listen, Repeat,** and **Do** the direction.

Lift the barrier to see if the student followed the direction correctly. Model, demonstrate, and correct as needed.

Step 2: Enlarge the choice of colors and increase the choice of places when the student is able to select the correct color from a choice of 2 with 80–90 percent accuracy (but use only one preposition). Eventually the student will be choosing between all 4 colors and all 5 different "places."

Step 3: Repeat Steps 1 and 2 for each of the prepositions taught in Goal 1: "on top of," "under," "beside," "between," "next to," "in front," and "behind" with color and place.

Step 4: When a preposition is established to 80–90 percent accuracy in Step 2, then contrast 2 known prepositions in single-step directions (e.g., "put the red car <u>beside</u> the plate"; "put the yellow block <u>under</u> the bag").

Step 5: Increase to 2-step directions joined by "and" or "then." Do not use the barrier for this step, as you need to be able to monitor the order in which the student carries out the directions. (He must carry them out in the order given.)
1. Use the same preposition in each part of the direction; e.g. put the blue car <u>in</u> the bag and the red car <u>in</u> the box
2. Use different prepositions in each part of the direction; e.g. put the yellow car <u>under</u> the bowl and the red car <u>on top of</u> the plate.

Activity **Expressive**

When working on Steps 1–3, play the barrier game with the student as the instructor. Have him put an object of a specific color in a particular place behind his barrier and tell you to put yours in the same place using the target preposition.

Use the same strategies as for Goal 2 Activity *Expressive* if, because he gave you the wrong direction, you have selected a different color or your object is not in the same place as his when the barrier is removed.

When working on Step 4, remove the barrier and have him give two-step directions joined by "then" or "and."

Carryover

- Pretend to be a robot. Have the student give you directions to carry out a task such as washing your hands or getting lunch items out of your lunch bag (e.g., "turn on the faucet/pick up the soap/rinse your hands/ turn off the faucet/dry your hands"). Do not do the next step unless directed, so leave the faucet running unless told to turn it off.
- Give directions to make an art project using modeling clay, felt, or other materials (e.g., how to make a snake from clay; how to make a paper-bag puppet).
- Give directions for paper/pencil/crayon tasks (e.g., "color the flower blue"; "draw a circle around the tree").
- Start a drawing or picture and have the student tell you how to finish it; e.g., draw a house and have him tell you what parts to add and where; draw a vase and have him tell you how to draw the flowers.
- Use two identical sets of Mr. Potato Head. Have the student make his person and then tell you how to make yours the same as his; e.g., "put the brown hair on top of his head"; "put pink lips between his nose and his chin."
- If the student is familiar with a regular deck of cards, spread 6–10 cards face up on the table. Give directions involving these cards (e.g., "put the 6 of spades under the 5 of diamonds"; "put the 2 of hearts beside the 4 of clubs." Increase to 2- or 3-step directions, but be sure that he carries them out in the order that you gave them. (You can use single object or animal picture cards instead of the deck of cards.)
- Play commercial barrier games that involve directions.

2.
Negative No/Not

These goals are appropriate for students with one or more of the following characteristics:

- has difficulty processing negatives; e.g., give me the ball that is <u>not</u> red [student gives <u>red</u> ball]

- has difficulty solving positive/negative problems; e.g., which one belongs? Which one <u>does not</u> belong?

- is unable to use negative forms in his expressive language; e.g., I do <u>not</u> want the book; this is <u>not</u> a duck

Negative No/Not Goals

The student will understand and use "no" and/or "not" applied to:

Goal 1: names of objects, people, and animals (e.g., this is "dog"; this is "not dog").

Goal 2: concrete/visual parts (e.g., the car has no wheels; the tree does not have leaves).

Goal 3: attributes, actions, and places (e.g., the cat is not brown; the dog is not jumping; the horse is not in the field).

Goal 1: The student will understand and use negative "not" applied to the names of objects, people, and animals (e.g., this is "dog"; this is "<u>not</u> dog.") (with 80–90 percent accuracy).

Materials

- Objects and toys and/or pictures of single objects, people, or animals that are familiar to the student (e.g., cup, ball, toothbrush, photo of mom).

Introduction

Introduce the goal by telling the student that she is going to learn to understand and use the word "not."

Place two objects or object pictures side by side, face up on the table. Label one of them (e.g., this is "car,") and label the other in terms of the first one (e.g., this is "<u>not</u> car"). Emphasize the negative word when it occurs. Present several examples.

Activity **Receptive**

Place pairs of objects or object pictures as demonstrated and ask the student to show you the one that you name. For example, say, "Show me 'dog'; show me '<u>not</u> dog'" Or, "Show me '<u>not</u> mom'; show me 'mom.'"

Mix the order in which you say the name and the negative so that the student cannot anticipate the answer.

Activity **Expressive**

Place pairs of objects or object pictures in front of the student and ask him to tell you about the one that you point to. For example, point to a house and ask, "Is this 'house'?" (Wait for response: "house.") Then point to tree and ask, "Is this 'house?'" (Response: "<u>not</u> house"). To add interest, play Fishing or Hide the Sticker (p. 7).

Carryover

- Label objects and pictures using the real name or "not" before a name in different settings throughout the day; e.g., "I see someone coming—it is not mommy!"
- Play Tim's Game (p. 9). Use a set of Memory cards. Select one pair of cards and turn one of the pair face up on the table; e.g., cat. Mix the other one in with a group of random cards spread out facedown on the table. Place a magnetic bingo chip under each card and have the student select cards with his magnetic wand until he finds the matching one. When he selects a card that does not match the one that is face up, he will say "not _____" (e.g., cat).
- Read books that have "not" in the story such as *Green Eggs and Ham* by Dr. Seuss ("not in a train, not in a tree," etc.) or *Are You My Mother?* by P.D. Eastman ("you are not my mother").

Goal 2: The student will understand and use negative "no" and/or "not" applied to concrete/visual parts (e.g., the car has no wheels; the tree does not have leaves) (with 80–90 percent accuracy).

Materials

1. Identical pairs of toys/objects with and without a specific part (e.g., a cup with a lid/an exact same cup with no lid). See suggested list REAL OBJECTS FOR POSITIVE/NEGATIVE ACTIVITIES, Table 5, below.
2. 10–20 commercial positive/negative pairs of picture cards (e.g., rabbit with tail/with no tail; tree with leaves/with no leaves).

Introduction

Explain to the student that she is going to learn to use the words "no" and "not" when she is talking about the parts of something.

Place a pair of objects side by side on the table. Point to and label the part that makes the objects different (e.g., lid/no lid; tail/no tail). Present several examples.

After completing Step 1 below, model Step 2 using materials #2. Place a pair of commercial pictures face up in front of the student and describe the feature that makes them different (e.g., this cat has ears; this cat has <u>no</u> ears). Present several examples and emphasize the negative words.

Activity **Receptive**

Step 1: Use materials #1. Place a pair of objects side by side in front of the student and have her identify the one that you describe (e.g., find <u>no</u> wheels; find wheels).

Use a variety of wording but make sure that the two opposing directions/statements are the same except for the inclusion of the word "not" or "no." For example: Show me/point to/give me:

The cat with ears/the cat with <u>no</u> ears.

The cat has ears/the cat has <u>no</u> ears.

The cat does have ears/the cat does <u>not</u> have ears.

Emphasize the negative words so that they are easier for the student to hear. Arrange the objects so that the negative one is sometimes on the right and sometimes on the left and mix the order in which you present the positive and negative statements so she cannot anticipate the response.

Step 2: Use materials #2. Place a pair of commercial pictures in front of the student and have her identify the one that you describe (e.g., find "the house has <u>no</u> windows"; find "the house has windows").

Activity **Expressive**

Present pairs of objects or pictures from materials #1 and 2. Point to one of the pair (in random order, positive/negative). Have the student tell you about the one that you point to; e.g., the bowl has a spoon; the bowl has <u>no</u> spoon; this house does <u>not</u> have a chimney/this house does have a chimney.

Carryover

- Give directions and make statements that contain a negative. For example, say, "Pick up the toys that do not have wheels" or "Look at the dog with no collar."
- Ask positive and negative questions about pictures and concrete items during the day. For example, ask, "Are your boots wet or not wet?" (wet). "Is the girl running or not running?" (not running).
- Use modeling clay, felt, paper, or paints/crayons at craft time to create two identical animals or items. Omit a feature from one of them; e.g., make two flowers but omit the leaves from one; make two faces but omit the eyes from one. Describe the differences; e.g., no leaves, no eyes.
- Compare clothing and items in store catalogs; e.g., this jacket has a hood/this jacket has no hood; this chair has cushions/this chair has no cushions.

Table 5: REAL OBJECTS FOR POSITIVE/NEGATIVE ACTIVITIES

Use identical objects, but alter one of the pair (e.g., cut the fingers off one of the gloves; put a ring on one of your fingers).

- Cup with lid/no lid
- Plate with apple/no apple
- Sock with stripes/no stripes
- Toy car with wheels/no wheels
- Pop bottle with pop/with no pop inside
- Bowl with spoon/no spoon or cereal/no cereal
- Book with pencil/no pencil
- Drinking glass with water/no water
- Glove with fingers/no fingers
- Stick with leaf/no leaf
- Shoe with laces/no laces

- Pen with top/no top
- Finger with ring/no ring
- Wrist with watch/no watch
- Hand with glove/no glove
- Foot with shoe/no shoe
- Teddy bear with ribbon/no ribbon
- Doll (or Mr. Potato Head) with hat/no hat, ears/no ears, hair/no hair, etc.
- Pencil with eraser/no eraser
- Paper with writing/no writing
- Picture with colors/no colors
- Toy bus with people/no people

Goal 3: The student will understand and use negative "not" applied to attributes, actions, and places (e.g., the cat is not brown; the dog is not jumping; the horse is not in the field) (with 80–90 percent accuracy).

Materials

1. A collection of paired toys/objects and pictures of toys/objects that are identical except for one attribute such as color, size, or shape (e.g., 2 red blocks—one square and one round; 2 pictures of a blue ball—one with stripes and the other with no stripes).
2. 10 or more paired action pictures of the same animal and/or person carrying out different activities (e.g., a dog running and the same dog jumping; a man sleeping and the same man eating).
3. 10 or more paired pictures of the same object, person, and/or animal in a variety of places (e.g., a girl on a swing and the same girl on a slide; a bird on the ground and the same bird in a tree).

Introduction

Explain to the student that she is going to learn to use the words "no" and "not" when she is talking about how things look, what they do, and/or where they are.

Model each activity listed below before having the student carry it out. For each activity, provide a choice of objects or pictures and describe them using "no" and "not." Vary the order in which you present the pictures and the order in which you request the positive and negative.

Activity 1: Attributes (e.g., show me the big tree; show me the tree that is <u>not</u> big).

Activity 2: Actions (e.g., point to the dog that is <u>not</u> running; point to the dog that is running).

Activity 3: Places (e.g. the cats are in the basket; the cats are <u>not</u> in the basket).

Activity **Receptive**

Activity 1: Attributes

Use the collection of objects and pictures of different colors, sizes, or shapes (materials #1). Have the student show you the object that fits your positive or negative description. For example, say, "Show me a blue block; show me a block that is <u>not</u> blue"; "Show me the cat is wet/is <u>not</u> wet"; "Show me the mouse that is <u>not</u> big/is big."

Activity 2: Actions

Use the action pictures (materials #2). Have the student show you the one that matches the action that you describe (e.g., the boy who is/is <u>not</u> running; the dog that is <u>not</u> sleeping/is sleeping).

Activity 3: Places

Use the pictures of objects, people, and animals in a variety of places. Have the student show you the one that matches the location that you describe (e.g., the frog that is/is <u>not</u> in the pond; the ball is <u>not</u> under the table/is under the table; the cat is/is <u>not</u> on the grass).

Activity **Expressive**

Following each receptive activity (#1, 2, and 3), present pairs of pictures and have the student tell you about the one that you point to. Then have her describe the other one in terms of the first. For example, this box is yellow/this box is <u>not</u> yellow; this horse is <u>not</u> running/this horse is running; this dog is in a doghouse/this dog is <u>not</u> in a doghouse.

It is not essential that the student use full sentence structures at this time, but she must use the negative. Responses such as "not running" or "not doghouse" are acceptable.

Carryover

- Make statements, give directions, and ask positive and negative questions about attributes, actions, and positions in pictures and real-life situations during the day. e.g., say, "Your toy car is not in the box—look under the chair"; "Find a T shirt that is not red to wear today"; "Are the big books in the box or not in the box?"; "There are no girls in your group today."
- Play Simon Says, using positive and negative directions e.g. Simon says "touch your head"; "Simon says "do *not* touch your head." (if a player touches her head she is out).
- Play Snap (see p. 9). As each player puts her card down on top of the pile, she will label it in relation to the color of the card that is already showing; e.g., if the top card is red and she puts a red card on it, she will say "red," but if she puts a black card on it, she will say "not red."
- Play Go Fish (see p. 7). Encourage use of "no" and "not" in response to the card that the player picks up and those in her hand (e.g., "pair/not a pair"; "match/not a match").

For further work on negatives, see:

Chapter 6 (Classification and Categorization), Goal 4: Identify the item that does not belong in a named category, p. 89.

Chapter 7 (Verbs), Goal 6: Name actions that a person, animal, or thing can and cannot carry out, p. 114.

Chapter 9 (Concepts), Goal 3: Concepts of inclusion/exclusion (including "none"), p. 162.

3.
Same and Different

> **These goals are appropriate for students with one or more of the following characteristics:**
>
> - is able to match object to object, picture to picture, and object to picture
>
> - has difficulty understanding and using the words "same" and "different"; e.g., horse and horse (same); horse and cow (different)
>
> - is unable to clearly describe features specific to a person, object, or animal
>
> - is developing visual discrimination skills

Same and Different Goals

The student will understand and use "same" and "different" applied to:

Goal 1: identical and non-identical objects (e.g., cup/cup, cup/pen).

Goal 2: objects of the same name that are identical or non-identical by color (e.g., red car/blue car).

Goal 3: the presence or absence of objects in a physical group (e.g., cow/pig/ sheep compared with cow/pig/sheep/horse).

Goal 4: objects that have the same name but vary by features other than color (e.g., round/square blocks; striped/spotted pillows).

Goal 5: objects that do not have the same name but have some shared features (e.g., orange and apple; sun and moon).

Goal 6: pictures that vary by *one* feature.

Goal 7: picture scenes that vary by *several* features.

Goal 1: The student will understand and use "same" and "different" applied to identical and non-identical objects (e.g., cup/cup, cup/pen) (with 80–90 percent accuracy).

Prerequisite: *Ability to match object to object, object to picture, and picture to picture (not covered in this manual).*

Materials

● 10–20 paired identical toys/objects or pictures of toys/object; e.g., 2 identical dolls, 2 identical pencils (create non-identical pairs by selecting an object from each of 2 identical pairs).

Introduction

Introduce the goal by telling the student that he is going to learn the words "same" and "different."

Use some of the paired identical objects or object pictures. Label paired objects that match as the "same" and paired objects that do not match as "different" (e.g., identical toy cars = "same"; toy car and ball = "different"). Describe the reason that they are the same or different (e.g., these are the same—they are both cars; these are different—this is a car and this is a ball). Provide several examples. Give visual support to the student who can read by presenting the written words "same" and "different" on separate cue cards when appropriate and as needed.

Activity **Receptive**

Place 2–6 paired identical toys/objects or toy/object pictures mixed up on the table. Hold up one object and tell the student to "find same" (e.g., a pencil and an identical pencil). Hold up any object from the collection and tell the student to find "different" (the student is to show any object other than the matched one (e.g., pencil and car). Ask for "same" and "different" objects randomly.

Note: *If the student is having difficulty, work on having him find "same" to 80–90 percent accuracy and then work on "different" to the same level before working on "same" and "different" at random.*

Activity **Expressive**

Present pairs of objects (identical and non-identical) and have the student identify them as the same or different (e.g., sock and identical sock = same; hat and mitt = different).

Ask, "How are they different?" Encourage the student to respond using as much of the sentence structure as he is able (e.g., "This one is a car and this one is a ball"). A reduced structure is acceptable at this stage (e.g., "This car this ball").

Carryover

- Play Lotto, Memory, Fishing, Magic Bag, and Go Fish (pp. 7-9). Point out and label the cards that are the "same" and those that are "different."
- Introduce additional vocabulary that expresses the concepts of "same" and "different" (e.g., match, go together).

Goal 2: The student will understand and use "same" and "different" applied to objects of the same name that are identical or non-identical by color (e.g., red car/blue car) (with 80–90 percent accuracy).

Prerequisite: *Knowledge of color—Chapter 8 (Descriptors), Goal 1, p. 120.*

Materials

- 10 sets of 3 objects or object pictures of the same name—two of which are identical in every way including color and one of which is identical but of a different color; e.g., 3 identical toy cars (2 red and 1 blue); 3 drinking straws (2 yellow and 1 green); 3 pompoms for crafts (2 orange and 1 purple).

Introduction

Explain to the student that sometimes things have the same name and are exactly the same (as in Goal 1) but sometimes things have the same name but are a little bit different. He is going to find the things that are the same or different depending on their color.

Present a set of 3 objects. Label them as having the same name (e.g., they are all pompoms). Describe 2 pompoms of the same color as being the "same"; e.g., both orange. Then describe 2 pompoms of different colors as being different (e.g., orange and purple). Provide several examples, and support students who can read with the written words "same" and "different," as needed.

Activity **Receptive**

Step 1: Use 2–6 sets of 3 objects (materials #1) and mix them up on the table. Have the student find the ones that are the same (give the direction "find same"). For example, the student will group all of the pencils, all of the cars, etc. Use a Magic Bag to add interest.

Step 2: Present each set of objects separately. Have the student "find same" within each group (e.g., cars—2 blue cars).

Step 3: Return the objects to their group and have him "find different" (e.g., blue car and red car).

Activity **Expressive**

Select pairs of objects from the same group and have the student tell you whether they are the same or different (e.g., 2 blue pencils = same; 1 blue pencil and 1 yellow pencil = different).

Ask, "How are they different?" Encourage the student to respond using as much of the sentence structure as he is able (e.g., "This one is blue and this one is yellow"). As in Goal 1, it is acceptable for him to use a reduced sentence structure at this stage.

Carryover

- Discuss objects that are the same/different color throughout the day (e.g., peers wearing same color of clothing; different colors of backpacks; same color work books).
- Play Memory or Magic Bag using pairs of color cards.
- Play Snap. Say "same" when 2 black cards or 2 red cards are placed on top of each other and "different" for black/red on top of each other.
- Give directions that involve discriminating the color of objects within a group; e.g., put all the chairs that are the same (red) around the table; put the different-colored chairs in a stack; give the books that are the same color (green) to the teacher; put your different-colored books in your desk.

Goal 3: The student will understand and use "same" and "different" applied to the presence or absence of objects in a physical group (e.g., cow/pig/sheep compared with cow/pig/sheep/horse) (with 80–90 percent accuracy).

Materials

1. 2 identical paper or plastic plates.
2. 10–20 pairs of identical toys/objects or animals (e.g., cats, blocks, erasers).

Introduction

Introduce this goal by telling the student that he is going to be a detective and learn to notice when things have changed from being the same to being different.

Position the 2 plates 6 inches apart side by side on the table in front of the student. Select 2 pairs of objects and place one of each pair on each plate so that the plates are the same (e.g., cow and pig on each plate). Explain that the plates are "the same." Remove one object from one of the plates and explain how the plates are now different—this one has a cow and a pig; this one has a pig—they are different.

Model use of "has" and "does not have" when describing how the plates are the same/different. Support the reader with the written words "same" and "different" as needed.

Activity **Receptive**

Use the plates and pairs of objects. Have the student make the plates the "same" or "different," as directed. For example, make the plates "different" (dinosaur + horse +

sheep on one plate/and horse + sheep on the other); make the plates the "same" (both plates have the same animals on them).

At first, give the student the specific objects to make the plates the same or different, but as he comes to understand what is required, have him select the objects that he needs from the group.

Activity **Expressive**

Remove objects from and add objects to the plates. Have the student be the "detective" and tell you, after each removal or addition, if the plates are the same or different. Increase to 6 objects on the plate at one time depending on the student's ability. Make a difference of only one object at first; and increase to 2 or 3.

Ask, "How are they different?" Encourage the student to respond using as much of the sentence structure as he is able (e.g., "This one has a dog and cat and this one has a dog, cat, and sheep"). Use of a reduced sentence structure is acceptable at this stage.

Carryover

- At home, have the student look at family members' plates after everyone has been served and say how they are the same or different (e.g., no peas).
- Make up plates of artificial, plastic, or Play-Doh food at playtime and offer peers, dolls, or puppets a plate that is the same or different.
- Create two contrasting groups of objects in real-life situations and discuss how one group is different from the other (e.g., two groups of shoes—one group has a different shoe in it than the other group; groups of shells; groups of leaves).

Goal 4: The student will understand and use "same" and "different" applied to objects that have the same name but vary by features other than color (e.g., round/square blocks; striped/spotted pillows) (with 80–90 percent accuracy).

Prerequisite: *Knowledge of descriptors—Chapter 8 (Descriptors), Goals 2 (p. 125), 3 (p. 127), and 4 (p. 128).*

Materials

- 20 pairs of toys/objects or pictures of toys/objects of the same name that have different features (e.g., big/little teddy bears but otherwise identical; striped/spotted pillows but same size/color/shape; round/square wooden blocks of the same size and color).

Introduction

Explain that now that the student is able to talk about things being the same or different because of their color, you are going to talk about how things can be the same or different in other ways.

Present a pair of toys/objects or pictures of toys/objects and describe how they are the same and different; e.g., both cups (same); this cup has a flower on it, but this cup does not (different); both white socks (same); this sock has a stripe around the top, and this sock is plain (different).

Present several examples. Compare features such as size, pattern, shape, texture, weight.

Activity **Receptive** and **Expressive**

Same Name/One Difference:

Present pairs of objects and discuss with the student how they are the same (both have the same name) and how they are different (one contrasting feature).

Compare features such as size, shape, stripes, spots, what they are made of or how they feel. Prompt by pointing to specific features or saying "tell me more about. . . ."

When the student is able to recognize that the objects have the same name, and he can describe one difference between them with 80–90 percent accuracy, progress to:

Same Name/More Than One Similarity and Difference:

Have the student describe multiple similarities and differences (e.g., both cups/both have handles/ both the same size; this one has a pattern on the handle and this one does not; this one has a chip in the edge and this one does not).

Carryover

- Discuss how items with the same name are the same and different (e.g., different kinds of balls in the gym; different sizes of paint brush during art; different books in the library). Compare people (e.g., Ann and Kaitlyn are both girls, but Ann has long hair and Kaitlyn has short hair).
- Make collections of objects and discuss how they are the same and different (e.g., shells, buttons, leaves, rock samples).
- Play Memory; use pictures of objects of the same name that differ by one or more feature(s).
- Play Snap. Instead of saying "snap," say "same" when two cards of the same color are placed on top of each other.

Goal 5: The student will describe how objects that do not have the same name but have some shared features are the "same" and "different" (e.g., orange and apple; sun and moon) (with 80–90 percent accuracy).

Prerequisite: *Knowledge of classification and categorization—Chapter 6 (Classification and Categorization), Goal 3, p. 81. Also knowledge of noun function—Chapter 5 (Nouns) Goal 2, p. 58.*

Materials

1. List of SAME/DIFFERENT PAIRED ITEMS, Table 6, page 36.
2. Commercial pictures of the items listed on the above list (optional).

Introduction

Introduce this goal by saying that now the student knows how things that have the *same* name are the same or different, you are going to talk about how things that have *different* names can be the same and different.

Select an example from the list of SAME/DIFFERENT PAIRED ITEMS. Identify the category name or class and describe multiple ways in which the pair of items are the same or different. For example, apple/orange are the same because they are both food/fruit; they are both round. They are different because an apple is red and green but an orange is orange; you can eat the skin of an apple, but you cannot eat the peel of an orange.

Activity **Receptive** and **Expressive**

Present paired items from the list of SAME/DIFFERENT PAIRED ITEMS and have the student list same and different characteristics. This can be presented as a collaborative activity with both of you adding characteristics alternately.

Provide pictures of the items you are discussing, if needed.

For the reader: *Print the list on cardstock and cut out each pair. Take turns picking up a pair and describing the similarities and differences. Write a list of the similarities and differences of each pair and see if you can think up more for the next pair that you describe or the next time that you describe the same pair during a subsequent therapy session.*

Carryover

- Compare similarities and differences between objects, places, animals, and people in real life.

Goal 6: The student will recognize and describe features that are the "same" and "different" in pictures that vary by *one* feature (with 80–90 percent accuracy).

Prerequisite: *Understanding of negative no/not—Chapter 2 (Negative No/Not), Goals 1–3, pp. 24-28.*

Materials

1. Drawing materials—colored marker pens and 8 x 11 paper or cardstock.
2. Craft supplies.
3. 2 or more pairs of identical commercial felt or magnetic scenes that have small items and/or people that can be arranged on the scene.

Introduction

Tell the student that now that he is able to describe how *objects* (or use the word *things*) are the same and different, you are going to talk about *pictures* that are the same

Table 6: SAME/DIFFERENT PAIRED ITEMS

1. Orange Apple	2. Tape Glue	
3. Gloves Mitts	4. Hat Sock	
5. Butterfly Bird	6. Marble Soccer Ball	
7. Drum Piano	8. Hot dog Hamburger	
9. Knife Scissors	10. Button Zipper	
11. Milk Juice	12. Bed Couch	
13. Soap Toothpaste	14. Stove Refrigerator	
15. Sun Moon	16. Car Airplane	
17. Cat Dog	18. Rain Snow	
19. Bus Train	20. TV Telephone	
21. Flower Tree	22. Lamp Flashlight	

and different. He will need to look very carefully at the pairs of pictures to see if the same things are in each one.

You are going to create 2 hand-drawn pictures by adding a feature alternately to each (see steps below). Sometimes you will add the same feature to both pictures so they are the same, but other times you will add a feature to only one so the pictures are different. When you add that feature to the other picture, they become the same again.

Possible scenes: "outside" (sky, sun, tree, house, flower); "inside" (furniture, TV, carpet, pet); people (wearing different clothing, limbs in different positions); snow man (hat, face, carrot nose, stick arms, sun, sky).

Note: *If you cannot draw—do not worry! The pictures do not have to be perfect—stick figures and rough outlines are fine.*

When the student understands same/different applied to the hand-drawn pictures in Steps 1–5 with 80–90 percent accuracy, introduce a pair of identical commercial felt or magnetic scenes in Step 6. Demonstrate how you can make the scenes the same/different according to what you add to them.

Activity **Receptive** and **Expressive**

Step 1: Take 2 pieces of paper and write "A" in the corner of one and "B" in the corner of the other. Draw a cloud at the top of each. Discuss with the student that the two pictures are the same.

Step 2: Add a sun to picture "A." The pictures are now different. Ask, "What is different?" (This one has a sun and this one does not.) Model and prompt as needed.

Encourage use of "has/has no," "has got/has not got," "has/does not have," "is/is not."

Step 3: Add a sun to picture B. Ask, "Are the pictures different now?" (No, they are the same.)

Step 4: Add a tree to both pictures. Ask, "Are the pictures the same or different?" (same).

Step 5: Continue in this way, adding a feature to one or both pictures. Vary features by attribute (color, size, shape), position (place), or "has/does not have" (e.g., red hat in one picture and green hat in the other; big flower/little flower; bird up in the tree/bird down on the ground; leaves on the tree/no leaves on the tree).

Be sure that the pictures **only** *vary by* **one** *feature* (e.g., if you drew a bird in a tree in Picture A and a bird on the ground in Picture B so they were different, then add the bird in the other position to each picture so that the scenes are the same again.)

Start a new picture scene when you reach 4–6 items, depending on the student's ability. Avoid having the pictures become too cluttered.

Step 6: Use a pair of identical commercial felt or magnetic scenes (materials #3). Create different scenes by using the small items and/or people. Progress through Steps 1–5, above. Make this fun! Sometimes have the student choose what should go in the scene, whether to make the scenes the same or different, and how to make them the same again when they are different (e.g., this picture needs a yellow sun to make it the same).

Carryover

- Have the student create paired scenes or designs by using stickers, craft items, modelling clay, or building blocks. Keep to only one difference.

Goal 7: The student will recognize and describe features that are the "same" and "different" in picture scenes that vary by *several* features (with 80–90 percent accuracy).

Materials

- Commercial same/different picture scenes showing single and increasing to multiple differences (use clear, uncluttered pictures at first).

Introduction

Tell the student that now he is going to look at pictures that someone else has made and find what is the same and what is different.

Activity **Receptive** and **Expressive**

Use commercial same/different materials, but be careful to start with scenes that are clearly illustrated and contain only one difference. Cartoon characters can be very confusing, so avoid them at first. Have the student gradually work up to searching for multiple similarities and differences.

If necessary, use a piece of cardstock to cover irrelevant parts of the picture and highlight the area in which the student is to look.

Carryover

- Have 2 typically developing students draw a picture of the same object or scene (e.g., car, house, playground, beach). Compare and discuss with your student how the pictures are the same and different.
- Take photos at different times of places and scenes familiar to the student. Compare and discuss them (e.g., trees in summer and fall; playground at recess and after school; tidy desk/untidy desk).
- Play computer games or use apps that require the student to find two or more differences in designs and pictures.

4.
Yes/No Responses

These goals are appropriate for students with one or more of the following characteristics:

- does not use critical thinking/listening so takes everything said to her as being correct/truthful

- gives unclear messages about wants, needs, and events

- is unable to respond reliably to yes/no questions to clarify her message (e.g., she responds "yes" when she means "no")

- uses yes/no inconsistently

Yes/No Goals

The student will respond "yes" or "no" when presented with a statement or question related to:

Goal 1: name of a single object, person, or animal; e.g., this is a pencil (yes); this is a cup (no—pencil)

Goal 2: action carried out by a person or an animal; e.g., is the dog running? (yes)

Goal 3: color of an object or animal; e.g. the pen is red (no—blue)

Goal 4: position of an object, person, or animal; e.g., the fork is on the plate (yes)

Goal 5: general knowledge; e.g., can a bird read a book? (no)

Goal 6: personal information; e.g., is your name X?

Right/Wrong (True/False)

Closely associated with the understanding and correct use of "yes/no" is the understanding and use of the concepts of "right/wrong" ("true/false"). Students use their prior knowledge and vocabulary, auditory processing, critical thinking, and listening to tell what is right from what is wrong.

The following activities may be presented to elicit the response "right/wrong" prior to presenting them to elicit "yes/no" answers. For some students, particularly those who confuse the meaning of the words "yes/no," working on "right/wrong" responses may be an easier step. Work through all goals using "right/wrong," then work through them using "yes/no."

Beware! *During the teaching of "yes/no" responses, it is essential to use only vocabulary and concepts familiar to the student and only questions that the instructor knows the answers to. For example, questions such as "Did you go shopping on the weekend?" should be avoided, even during carryover activities, unless the instructor knows the correct answer.*

Goal 1: The student will respond "yes" or "no" when presented with a statement or question related to the name of a single object, person, or animal; e.g., this is a pencil (yes); this is a cup (no—pencil) (with 80–90 percent accuracy).

Prerequisite: *Understanding of negative "no/not"—Chapter 2 (Negative No/Not), Goals 1 and 2, pp. 24-25.*

Materials

1. 20 toys/objects and/or pictures of toys/objects, people, or animals familiar to the student.
2. Blank copies of TRACKING "YES/NO," Table 7, below.

Introduction

Introduce this goal by telling the student that she is going to learn the words "yes" and "no." Explain that often we nod our heads when we say "yes" and shake our heads when we say "no." Model nodding and shaking your head and have the student imitate you. (It is not essential that the student make the head movements during the following activities, but for some students, they do help to reinforce the verbal responses.)

Model the activity. Present an item or picture and name it correctly followed by the word "yes" and a statement (e.g., pencil—yes, it is a pencil). Present the same item again and name it incorrectly (e.g., book—no, it is a pencil). Give visual support to students who can read by presenting the written words "yes" and "no" on separate cue cards when appropriate and as needed.

Make comments such as, "Oh no, that's silly. It is not a book because I cannot read it," or "Oh no, that isn't a picture of Mom—Mom does not look like that!"

Present a variety of examples until the student is starting to respond "yes" or "no" before you do.

Table 7: TRACKING "YES/NO"

Statement or Question	Student Response	Correct Response	Correct/ Incorrect
1.			
2.			
3.			
4.			
5.			
6.			
7.			
8.			
9.			
10.			
11.			
12.			
13.			
14.			
15.			
16.			
17.			
18.			
19.			
20.			
Total Correct:		Incorrect:	

Activity **Receptive** and **Expressive**

Step 1: Present each item or single item picture and name it either correctly or incorrectly at random. Have the student answer "yes" or "no" (or "right" or "wrong") appropriately. The student may use the full statement (e.g., "Yes, it is a pencil" or only say "yes" or "no").

If necessary, present many positive statements until the student is using "yes" with 80–90 percent accuracy. Then present many negative statements to the same level of accuracy before mixing positive and negative at random.

List the expected responses and the student's responses on a blank copy of TRACKING "YES/NO" and monitor her progress.

Step 2: Present an item or single-item picture and use a question format to elicit a "yes/no" response; e.g., is this a pencil? Correct name: yes; incorrect name: no. Play Fishing (p. 7) and ask questions; e.g., did you catch a dog?" (no); "did you catch a horse?" (yes).

Carryover

- Ask questions about preferred and nonpreferred items throughout the day. Make the nonpreferred choice very obvious; e.g., do you want an apple? (yes); do you want a rock? (no).
- Ask yes/no questions and make correct/incorrect statements related to the identification of familiar items and people in storybook pictures and the everyday environment. Encourage a "yes/no" response; e.g., "Is this a dog?" (yes). "This is a spoon" (no, fork). "Is this mommy?" (yes).

Goal 2: The student will respond "yes" or "no" when presented with a statement or question related to an action carried out by a person or an animal; e.g., is the dog running? (with 80–90 percent accuracy).

Prerequisite: *Ability to understand and name the action shown in a picture—Chapter 7 (Verbs), Goal 2, p. 103.*

Materials

1. List of COMMON ACTIONS from below.
2. Pictures of single people or single animals carrying out an action that is familiar to the student (e.g., a man eating; a baby sleeping; a dog running).
3. Blank copies of Table 7, TRACKING "YES/NO," at end of Goal 1, p. 41.

Introduction

Tell the student that now that she can use "yes" and "no" when you name things, she is going to learn to use "yes" and "no" when you name an action.

Carry out one of the actions from the list COMMON ACTIONS and label what you are doing correctly or incorrectly, followed by "yes/no" (e.g., I am standing—yes, I am standing. I am standing—no, I am sitting).

Present some of the action pictures and label them in the same way; e.g., he is jumping (no, eating); she is running (yes—running).

Support readers with the written words "yes" and "no" as needed.

Activity **Receptive** and **Expressive**

Step 1: Perform an action from the list of COMMON ACTIONS and name it correctly or incorrectly at random. Ask the student for a "yes/no" response; e.g., I am walking (yes); I am running (no). The student may use the full statement ("yes, you are walking") or only say "yes" or "no."

If necessary, present many positive statements until she is using "yes" with 80–90 percent accuracy. Then present many negative statements to the same level of accuracy before mixing positive and negative at random.

Step 2: Name the action in a picture correctly or incorrectly at random and have the student respond "yes" or "no," as appropriate; e.g., the dog is eating (yes); the girl is playing [sleeping] (no).

Step 3: Perform an action or present a picture of an action. Use a question to elicit a "yes/no" response; e.g., is this jumping? Correct name for action: yes; incorrect name for action: no.

Carryover

- Ask questions that require a "yes/no" answer related to the identification of familiar actions in stories and the student's everyday activities; e.g., Are we running? (no); Is the rabbit sitting? (yes); Is the cat is barking (no).
- Play Lotto. Use cards of any theme. Ask, "Does this picture go on your card?" Response: yes/no.

Table 8: COMMON ACTIONS

• Blowing	• Running	• Walking
• Clapping	• Sitting	• Waving
• Jumping	• Standing	

Goal 3: The student will respond "yes" or "no" when presented with a question or statement related to the color of an object or animal; e.g., the pen is red (no—blue) (with 80–90 percent accuracy).

Prerequisite: *Ability to recognize and name colors—Chapter 8 (Descriptors), Goal 1, p. 120.*

Materials

1. Familiar toys/objects and/or pictures of toys/objects or animals in a variety of primary colors (e.g., red car, green ball, brown horse).
2. Blank copies of Table 7, TRACKING "YES/NO," at end of Goal 1, p. 41.

Introduction

Tell the student that she is going to learn to use "yes" and "no" when you name the color of an object or animal.

Present an object or a single-color picture of a single toy, object, or animal. Name the color either correctly or incorrectly, followed by "yes" or "no"; e.g., This is a red car—yes; This is a blue (red) car—no.

Activity **Receptive** and **Expressive**

Present the familiar toys/objects and/or pictures of single toys, objects, or animals one at a time:

Step 1: Make statements related to their color and model the use of "yes" or "no" (e.g., The pen is blue—yes; The dog is black—no). Gradually encourage the student to supply "yes" or "no" following your statements. Support the reader with the written words "yes" and "no" as needed.

Step 2: Ask questions related to their color and answer "yes" or "no"; e.g., Is this pen red? (yes); Is the block yellow? (no). Gradually encourage the student to supply the answer. She may respond with "yes" or "no" or use a full statement; e.g., "Yes, the pen is red."

Carryover

- Make statements and ask "yes/no" questions related to the color of objects in view throughout the day (clothing, materials in art class and craft projects). For example, "Are these pompoms blue?" (yes). "The paint is black" [orange] (no).
- Misname colors and have the student correct you; e.g., "I am wearing a red sweater today" ("no, it's green").
- Play Snap. Say "yes" if cards of the same color are placed on top of each other and "no" if cards are a different color.
- Expand your statements to include other descriptors such as size and shape; e.g., I am holding the big cup (yes); You are threading the round beads (no, square beads).

Goal 4: The student will respond "yes" or "no" when presented with a statement or question related to the position of an object, person, or animal; e.g., the fork is on the plate (with 80–90 percent accuracy).

Prerequisite: Understanding and use of prepositions "in," "on," "under," "beside," "in front of," "behind"—Chapter 1 (Following Directions), Goal 2, p. 18.

Materials

1. 10 familiar toys/objects or pictures of toys/objects (e.g., toy car, dinosaur, fork, eraser).
2. 5 objects or containers that can be used as "places" (e.g., cup, plate, paper gift bag, small cardboard box, plastic cereal bowl).
3. Commercial felt or magnetic scene that has people, animals, or objects that can be arranged on the scene.
4. Blank copies of Table 7, TRACKING "YES/NO" at end of Goal 1, p. 41.

Introduction

Tell the student that she is going to learn to use "yes" and "no" when you say where an object is.

Use one of the familiar objects or toys (materials #1) and an object that can be a "place" (materials #2). Position the object in relation to the place and model a correct statement (e.g., put a dinosaur on a plate and say, "on the plate—yes, the dinosaur is on the plate"). Use other objects and places and model correct and incorrect statements (e.g., "The car is under [on] the plate. No, the car is on the plate").

Activity **Receptive** and **Expressive**

Step 1: Use materials #1 and 2 and the prepositions "in," "on," "under," "beside," "in front," and "behind." Place an object in relation to one of the "places" and have the student respond to your yes/no statements and questions about its position; e.g., "The fork is beside the bag" (yes); "Is the eraser under the plate?"(no, on the plate).

Step 2: Use a felt or magnetic scene (materials #3). Place one of the small items or people in a specific place on the scene (e.g., the girl on the swing). Make statements or ask "yes" or "no" questions; e.g., "The girl is on the grass" (no); "Is the girl on the swing?" (yes).

Carryover

- Make statements about what you and the student are doing or where you have been during the day. Have her correct you when you are wrong; e.g., "We are in the gym" (no, we are in the classroom); "We are eating lunch" (yes, we are eating lunch).
- Ask yes/no questions related to the place of objects and people in stories and pictures; e.g., "The children in the story are in a boat" (yes); "Are the monkeys on the ground?" (no, in a tree).
- Play Hide and Find. Take turns hiding an object. The other player asks questions in order to find it, and the player who hid the object answers "yes" or "no"; e.g., "Is it on the shelf?" (yes); "Is it behind the blue book?" (no).

Goal 5: The student will respond "yes" or "no" when presented with a statement or question related to her general knowledge; e.g., can a bird read a book? (with 80–90 percent accuracy).

Note: *Be aware of the student's understanding of subjects and events and only ask yes/no format questions about familiar topics.*

Materials

1. List YES/NO "CAN" QUESTIONS, Table 9, below.
2. YES/NO STATEMENTS, Table 10, below.

Introduction

Tell the student that she is going to learn to use "yes" and "no" when you give her some information or ask her a question related to things that she knows about.

Give some examples; e.g., If I said that a cow can bark, you would say no. If I asked, "Can you eat a cookie?" you would say yes, but if I asked, "Can you eat a tree?" you would say no.

Activity **Receptive** and **Expressive**

Step 1: Ask the student questions from the list YES/NO "CAN" QUESTIONS and have her give "yes/no" responses as appropriate. Discuss and explain as needed.

Step 2: Present statements from the list YES/NO STATEMENTS and have her give "yes/no" responses. Discuss why the incorrect statements are "silly."

For the reader: *Both lists can be presented as a game. Print the lists onto 8 x 11 cardstock and cut them into individual statements/questions. Take turns turning over a statement/question, reading it, and responding or direct the question to the other person. (This is excellent practice for turn taking and asking questions during conversation.)*

Carryover

- Throughout the day ask questions and make statements related to the student's general knowledge that require a "yes" or "no" response; e.g., I can sit on a chair (yes); Can a dog sing? (no).

Table 9: YES/NO "CAN" QUESTIONS

Question	Student Response	Correct Response	Correct/ Incorrect
1. Can you wear a jacket?		Y	
2. Can you eat a chair?		N	
3. Can you cut paper with scissors?		Y	
4. Can you go to sleep in the bathtub?		N	
5. Can a fish sing a song?		N	
6. Can you slide down a slide?		Y	
7. Can you hear with your ears?		Y	
8. Can you drink your pajamas?		N	
9. Can you peel a banana?		Y	
10. Can a baby drive a car?		N	
11. Can you unwrap a present?		Y	
12. Can a bird read a book?		N	
13. Can you write with a toothbrush?		N	
14. Can you eat soup with a fork?		N	
15. Can you open a door?		Y	
16. Can you climb a stove?		N	
17. Can you jump on a ladder?		N	
18. Can you play on a swing set?		Y	
19. Can you wash with soap?		Y	
20. Can you listen to music?		Y	

10 Answers each "yes" and "no"

Table 10: YES/NO STATEMENTS

Statement	Student Response	Correct Response	Correct/ Incorrect
1. Children go to school.		Y	
2. We drink water.		Y	
3. Cats bark.		N	
4. Horses say "moo."		N	
5. The sun is in the sky.		Y	
6. The moon shines in the daytime.		N	
7. A blanket feels soft.		Y	
8. We sleep in a bed.		Y	
9. Fish can fly.		N	
10. Scissors cut paper.		Y	
11. I wear a coat when it's cold out.		Y	
12. I eat soup with a fork.		N	
13. Fire is hot.		Y	
14. I clean my teeth with soap.		N	
15. We clap our ears.		N	
16. It is my birthday every day.		N	
17. We play with a ball.		Y	
18. A frog sits on a nest.		N	
19. We can eat rocks.		N	
20. A doctor helps us if we are sick.		Y	

10 Answers each "yes" and "no"

Goal 6: The student will respond "yes" or "no" when presented with a question related to her personal information; e.g., is your name X? (with 80–90 percent accuracy).

Note: *The instructor must know the correct answer prior to asking the questions.*

Materials

1. List PERSONAL YES/NO QUESTIONS, Table 11, below.
2. List 20 PERSONAL QUESTIONS FOR USE IN TURN-TAKING GAME, Table 12, below.

Introduction

Tell the student that she is going to learn to use "yes" and "no" to answer questions about herself. Give some examples; e.g., If I ask you, "Do you go to this school?" you would say "yes," but if I ask you, "Do you go to St. John's High school?" you would say "no."

Give other examples and model use of "yes" and "no" as needed.

Activity **Receptive** and **Expressive**

Step 1: Ask questions in random order from the list PERSONAL YES/NO QUESTIONS and track the student's answers. Ask the questions again at this time or during a subsequent therapy session, but change them by inserting a different incorrect name, age, school name, etc.

Step 2: Ask questions from the list 20 PERSONAL QUESTIONS FOR USE IN TURN-TAKING GAME and track the student's answers.

For the reader: *Make Step 2 into a game. Print the questions from the list onto 8 x 11 cardstock and cut into individual questions. Take turns picking a question and reading/answering it or direct it to the other person.*

Carryover

- Ask the student "yes/no" questions related to personal information in her everyday environment. For example, "Are you in Mrs. Smith's class?" (no); "Does your sister go to this school?" (yes).

Table 11: PERSONAL YES/NO QUESTIONS

Note: *Present the questions in random order. Ask the same questions again in a different order during subsequent work sessions, but insert a different incorrect name/age, etc.*

Question specific to the student	Student Response	Correct Response	Correct/ Incorrect
Is your name _____? (student's name)			
Is your name _____? (incorrect name)			
Are you ____ years old? (student's age)			
Are you ____ years old? (incorrect age)			
Is your school called _____? (correct name)			
Is your school called _____? (incorrect name)			
Is your teacher's name _____? (correct name)			
Is your teacher's name _____? (incorrect name)			
Are you a boy/girl? (correct gender)			
Are you a boy/girl? (incorrect gender)			
Are you in grade ____? (correct grade)			
Are you in grade ____? (incorrect grade)			

Table 12: 20 PERSONAL QUESTIONS FOR USE IN TURN-TAKING GAME

Note: *Before working on this activity, find out the answers to questions 5, 6, 7, 14, and 18 from a reliable source or omit these questions.*

1. Are you wearing a hat?
2. Are you wearing shoes?
3. Are you 100 years old?
4. Is this your home?
5. Do you have a cat at your house?
6. Do you have a brother?
7. Does your mom drive the car?
8. Do you watch TV at your house?
9. Did you get your hair cut today?
10. Do you like to eat rocks?
11. Do you go to school?
12. Can you drive the car?
13. Do you come to school on the bus?
14. Did you have breakfast today?
15. Do you have three ears?
16. Are you a grandfather?
17. Do you have short hair?
18. Do you go to a babysitter after school?
19. Are you a baby?
20. Is your shirt blue?

5.
Nouns

These goals are appropriate for students with one or more of the following characteristics:

- has a limited knowledge of the names of things

- has weak understanding of what he hears or reads resulting in difficulty following directions and acquiring new information

- delivers an unclear message due to limited word choices and use of vague words

- uses simple or immature words; e.g., "woof-woof" for "dog"

- has word finding difficulties that interrupt the flow of communication (word searching, false starts, misnomers, or use of non-specifics; e.g., "thing")

Noun Goals

The student will:

Goal 1: Build a basic vocabulary of nouns.

Goal 2: Describe object function; e.g., what do we do with a toothbrush?

Goal 3: Develop understanding of association:
1. Object to object; e.g., paintbrush/paint.
2. Object to location; e.g., bathtub/bathroom.
3. Object to occupation; e.g., fire truck/fireman.
4. Object to activity; e.g., comb/fix hair.
5. Part to whole; e.g., steering wheel/car.

Goal 4: Develop understanding of classification and categorization (discussed further in Chapter 6, Classification and Categorization).

Goal 5: Define nouns using a Word Web.

Teaching Nouns in Different Contexts

For a student to fully understand and use a noun effectively, it is essential that he be taught the word in many different contexts. Before starting Goal 1, view the Word Web in Goal 5, p. 73, and throughout the learning process, present nouns in the context of other words. Teach function, association, and classification and categorization.

For example: A <u>dog</u> is an animal; it barks; it lives in a house with people or in a dog-house; it has a collar, leash, dog food bowl, and dog bed; it has a tail, ears, and nose; it is brown, black, or white.

Goal 1: The student will build a basic vocabulary of nouns (each target word to 80–90 percent accuracy).

Materials

1. Real-life experiences, objects, pictures, storybooks, games, educational TV, videos, and conversation relevant to the target.
2. List NOUN VOCABULARY, Table 13, below.

Introduction

Introduce this goal by saying that the student is going to learn to understand and use a new word or words.

Choose target nouns from the list NOUN VOCABULARY that are relevant to the student's environment and interests and that he is likely to hear and need to use frequently. Tie your selection in with current classroom themes and vocabulary lists recommended for the student's grade level and curriculum.

Activity **Receptive**

Model and teach the target word using:
  a. Real-life experiences—e.g., to teach target word "kitchen," go into a kitchen and discuss what we do in the kitchen; involve the student in preparing snacks or meals, cleaning dishes, and putting food items away after grocery shopping.
  b. Real objects or realistic miniatures—e.g., to teach target word "glove," present gloves of many different colors and sizes.
  c. Photos and realistic pictures—e.g., mom preparing supper in the kitchen; mom sitting in the living room.
  d. Word choices (objects and/or pictures)—e.g., given a choice of two objects or pictures (glove and hat), say, "Show me the glove."
  e. Story books— read a story in which the target word is the main subject or occurs frequently. Have the student hold up a picture of the target word each time the word occurs in the story; e.g., target word "tiger." If necessary, change the words of the story so that the target word occurs more often.

    f. Educational TV or videos—say the name of the target each time it appears on the screen.

    g. Games—play commercial games that include the target word in their theme; e.g., zoo animals, tools.

    h. Imaginative play—e.g., play "house" with kitchen toys (toy stove, utensils, pots and pans, etc.).

Present the target word as part of a whole as the student comes to understand function, association, and categorization. Present the word frequently and in more than one situation during the therapy session and during the course of the day.

Activity **Expressive**

Have the student use the target word to:

    a. Name items immediately after hearing the model—e.g., "This is a <u>frog</u>. What is it?" (frog). Prompt as needed by providing the first sound of the word; e.g., "ffff…" (frog).

    b. Make word choices—e.g., Instructor: "Is this a <u>frog</u> or a butterfly?" (frog). At first emphasize the correct word in your question.

    c. Answer direct questions—e.g., "What is this?" (spoon); "Where are we?" (kitchen).

    d. Complete a sentence—e.g., Instructor: "After lunch, we are going to the _____." Student: "Playground."

    e. Answer a guessing game—e.g., Instructor: "I am thinking of an animal that can hop. It is green and says 'ribbit'—what is it?" Student: "Frog."

    f. Make conversation—include the target noun frequently in conversation with the student.

After the student has worked on function, association, and categorization (Goals 2–4):

    g. Answer questions related to function—e.g., "What do I eat my cereal with?" (spoon).

    h. Answer questions related to association—e.g., "What goes with a fork?" (spoon).

    i. Answer questions related to category name—e.g., "A dog is an animal—tell me another animal" (frog).

Carryover

- Inform parents and caregivers of target nouns, and encourage relevant activities, stories, songs, and games.
- Make a collection of real items or a collage of pictures of items of the same name; e.g., dogs, shoes.
- Play Picture Dominoes with target vocabulary as the theme. Match and name the pictures.
- Play Go Fish, Hide the Sticker, Magic Bag, Memory, Snakes/Chutes and Ladders, Tim's Game, and Fishing using pictures of target vocabulary.
- Discuss opposite nouns (antonyms); e.g., girl/boy, night/day, sister/brother.

Table 13: NOUN VOCABULARY

Real Names	Animals	Food/Drink
Own name Family—siblings'/relatives' Pet's Peers' Caregiver's Teacher's Characters' in/on TV, movies, books Favorite toys'	Pets Specific to where student lives Farm Zoo Forest Ocean Pond Jungle Bugs Birds	Favorite foods Snacks/treats Fruit/vegetables Meat Dairy Desserts Sandwiches BBQ Foods that animals or other people eat Breakfast, supper, lunch
Home/School	**Vehicles**	**Clothing**
Rooms and contents; e.g., kitchen, gym, rug, lights Furniture Appliances and tools Items used for everyday activities; e.g., spoon, pencil Playground/yard Musical instruments Subjects; e.g., math, art Outside; e.g., trees, flowers	Car, van, taxi Truck School bus Boat Motorbike Bicycle Snowmobile Four wheeler Airplane, helicopter Scooter	Girl's wear Boy's wear Outerwear Footwear For specific weather or season; e.g., rain, hot sun For specific activities; e.g., riding a bike, playing a sport
Body Parts*	**Place of Significance**	**Places in Community**
Mouth, eyes, nose, feet Hair, tongue, head, ears, hands, legs, arms, fingers, stomach, back, teeth, toes Chin, thumbs, knees, neck, fingernails Heel, ankle, jaw, chest Wrist, shoulder, hip, elbow Waist	Home address School name Caregiver's address Park Mall, stores, restaurants Facility for out-of-school activities; e.g., gym, pool, ball park, arena, rink Religious institution Doctor's office Dentist's office	Parents' workplace Fire station Hospital Police station Post office Grocery store Bank Library Train station Airport Museum

*Body parts are presented in developmental order from *A Work in Progress*, edited by Ron Leaf and John McEachin (New York, NY: DRL Books, 1999). Used with permission.

(Table 13 continued)

Sports	Signs	Time
Played by student Played by family members Seen on TV Played on video games	On road—traffic lights, stop sign, yield, etc. On stores and restaurants	Days of week Day/night Months of year Seasons Morning/afternoon/evening

Places	Occupations	Weather
Own town Own street Own province/state Town/province/state where significant family members live; e.g., grandparents Country Earth Sky Universe Planets	Parents' jobs Babysitter Teacher Principal Secretary Janitor Mailman/carrier Doctor Dentist Fireman Policeman Astronaut	Sun Rain Clouds Wind Snow Frost Temperature Weather specific to student's region; e.g., tornado, hurricane, drought

Feelings	Vacation	Leisure Activities
Angry Happy Mad Sad Scared/afraid Sick Tired/sleepy Surprised	Place name Beach Lake Motel Tent/trailer/camper Campground Ocean Mountains	Toys and games Equipment; e.g., computer, bat, trampoline Titles of preferred books, TV shows, videos, movies Songs and rhymes Beach Backyard pool/hot tub

Shapes	Medical	Special Occasions
Triangle Square Circle Rectangle Heart Star	*(as pertains to the student or people close to him)* Wheelchair Hearing aid Medicine Thermometer Stethoscope	Holidays; e.g., Christmas Thanksgiving, Hanukkah Special days; e.g., Valentine's day, Halloween Birthday/party Wedding

Goal 2: The student will understand and describe object function; e.g., What do we do with a broom? What are gloves for? (each target word to 80–90 percent accuracy).

Materials

1. Collection of familiar objects and/or pictures of familiar objects—see list OBJECTS FOR DESCRIPTION OF FUNCTION (TABLETOP SIZE), Table 14, below.
2. List DESCRIBE THE FUNCTION OF AN OBJECT, Table 15, below.

Introduction

Introduce this goal by telling the student that you are going to talk about what we do with things.

Place a familiar object or object picture on the table and describe its function; e.g., "This is a pencil—we write with a pencil." Present several examples.

Activity **Receptive**

Use materials #1. Place two objects or pictures of familiar objects side by side, face up on the table, and have the student show you the one that you describe. For example, "Show me the one that we wash with" (soap); "Show me the one that we write with" (pencil). Model and teach as needed.

Activity **Expressive**

Step 1: Use materials #1. Have the student name the function of the object or object picture presented. For example, "What do we do with a toothbrush?" (brush our teeth); "What do we do with a ball?" (throw/catch).

Step 2: Read the questions from DESCRIBE THE FUNCTION OF AN OBJECT and have the student describe the function of the object. Provide choice answers if necessary. For example, "What do we do with a toothbrush—drink it or clean our teeth with it?"

For the reader: *Print the list on cardstock and cut into individual questions and answers. Have the student match the answers to the questions. Provide choice answers if necessary.*

Carryover

- Discuss the function of objects throughout the day; e.g., objects in picture books, store catalogs, around the school.
- Discuss what we can do with body parts; e.g. eyes, ears, and hands.
- Play Lotto, Memory, Hide the Sticker, Snakes/Chutes and Ladders, and Go Fish using object picture cards.

Table 14: OBJECTS FOR DESCRIPTION OF FUNCTION (TABLETOP SIZE)

Ask: What is it for? What do we do with it?

Object	Function	Student Response Correct/Incorrect
Toothbrush	Clean teeth	
Washcloth	Wash face/body	
Spoon	Eat cereal/soup	
Sock/shoe	Put it on foot	
Cup	Drink	
Towel	Dry hands/face/body	
Ice cream cone	Put ice cream in	
Coat/jacket	Wear outside	
Comb/brush	Fix hair	
Brush/dustpan	Clean up mess	
Scissors	Cut paper	
Pen or pencil	Write	
Paper	Draw on it	
Crayons	Color	
Book	Read	
Apple	Eat	
Ball	Throw/catch	
Blocks	Build	
Toy cars	Play with	
Shampoo	Wash hair	
Tissues	Blow/wipe nose	
Pajamas	Wear in bed	
Soap	Wash hands	
Umbrella	Put up (to keep dry)	
Gift	Open it	
Money	Buy things	
Flashlight	Turn on (to see in the dark)	

Table 15: DESCRIBE THE FUNCTION OF AN OBJECT

Question	Answer
1. What do we do with a chair?	Sit on it
2. What do we do with a bus?	Ride on it to school
3. What do we do with a bed?	Sleep in it
4. What is a house for?	Live in
5. What is a telephone for?	To talk to someone
6. What do we do with a TV?	Watch it
7. What do we do with water?	Drink it or wash with it
8. What are teeth for?	Bite things
9. What do we do with a table?	Put things on it
10. What does a zipper do?	Zip up a coat
11. What do we do with our ears?	Hear
12. What does a clock do?	Tells time
13. What do we do with our nose?	Smell
14. What is a lawnmower for?	Cut grass
15. What does an airplane do?	Fly
16. What do we do with a bicycle?	Ride it
17. What do we do with a shovel?	Dig
18. What does a bell do?	Ring
19. What is a book for?	Read
20. What do we do with a hammer?	Hit nails

Goal 3: The student will develop understanding of ASSOCIATION (each target word to 80–90 percent accuracy).

1. **Object to object; e.g., paintbrush/paint.**
2. **Object to location; e.g., bathtub/bathroom.**
3. **Object to occupation; e.g., fire truck/fireman.**
4. **Object to activity; e.g., comb/fix hair.**
5. **Part to whole; e.g., steering wheel/car.**

Association 1: Object to object (e.g., paintbrush/paint)

Materials

1. Objects that are associated in pairs; e.g., toothpaste/ toothbrush—see list OBJECTS FOR ASSOCIATION (TABLETOP SIZE), Table 16, below.
2. Commercial Association picture cards (use only the object-to-object cards).

Introduction

Tell the student that you are going to talk about things that go together. Some objects go together because we use them for the same activity.

Use paired objects or pictures from materials #1 and 2 and describe how they go together (are associated). For example, toothbrush and toothpaste go together because we use them both to clean our teeth.

Activity **Receptive**

Step 1: Use the associated objects (materials #1). Have the student sort the objects into their associated pairs. Prompt, "What goes with the _____?" Provide choices as needed.

Step 2: Use the commercial association picture cards (materials #2). Have the student sort them into their associated pairs and/or present three or four cards and have the student find the associated pair; e.g., <u>dog</u>, apple, <u>bone</u>, car.

Activity **Expressive**

Following each of the receptive steps above, have the student describe how the two objects are associated. Example: Why does the sandwich go with the lunchbox? (because we keep the sandwich in the lunch box).

The student does not need to give a full sentence answer at this time. It is more important that he identify the reason than use the conjunction "because." For activities to stimulate use of "because," see Chapter 10, "General Suggestions for Developing Reasoning Skills to Understand and Answer Why? Questions," p. 200.

When the student is able to describe why the objects are associated with 80–90 percent accuracy, select two cards that are *not* associated and ask why they do *not* go together. For example, "Why does the dog *not go* with the paintbrush?" (because a dog can't paint). Have fun with this—make these combinations silly!

Carryover

- Play Memory, Hide the Sticker, Snakes/Chutes and Ladders, Tim's Game, or Go Fish using commercial association picture cards.
- Discuss and ask "why?" questions about associated pairs in real life. For example, why does the janitor need a broom and dustpan? Why do you need mittens and a hat when you go outside?
- Give the student one half of an associated pair in real-life situations and ask him what he needs to go with it e.g., "here is your jacket. What do you need to go with it?" (hat or gloves). "Here is your cereal bowl. What do you need to go with it?" (cereal or spoon).

Table 16: OBJECTS FOR ASSOCIATION (TABLETOP SIZE)

• Toothbrush/toothpaste	• Paint brush/paint	• Cup/plate
• Spoon/knife/fork	• Pencil/paper	• Pencil/eraser
• Spoon/bowl	• Paper/scissors	• Coloring book/crayon
• Soap/washcloth/towel	• Cereal/bowl	• Flower/vase
• Shoe/sock	• Hammer/nail	• Lunch box/sandwich
• Hat/mitts/gloves	• Brush/comb	
• Jacket/hat	• Broom/dustpan	

Association 2: Object to location (e.g., bathtub/bathroom)

Materials

1. Objects, object miniatures, and/or object pictures that are associated with a specific place and a picture of the place they are associated with; e.g., horse, cow, pig plus farm picture; stove, fridge, sink plus kitchen picture. Select object-to-location pictures from a commercial association card set.
2. List OBJECT-TO-LOCATION ASSOCIATION, Table 17, below.

Introduction

Tell the student that some objects go together with a particular place.

Use samples from materials #1 and describe how two or more objects are found together in the same place; e.g., swing, sandbox, climber are all found at a playground.

Activity **Receptive**

Use materials #1. Have the student sort the objects and/or object pictures into groups according to the place that they are found. At first, prompt by giving the name of the place; e.g., find all the things in the <u>kitchen</u>; find all the things on a <u>farm</u>. Later, have him find the associated items and place without you giving him the place name. Provide modeling and assistance as needed.

Activity **Expressive**

Step 1: Use materials #1. Select an object or object picture and ask where we would find it; e.g., where would we find a fire truck? (at the fire station); where would we find a bathtub? (in the bathroom).

Step 2: Use the list OBJECT-TO-LOCATION ASSOCIATION:
   a. Read a list of objects from the list and have the student identify the place where they are found; e.g., leaf, twig, bird nest are found in a tree.
   b. Read the name of a place and have the student name objects that could be found there; e.g., playground has swing, climber, sandbox. Encourage the student to think of additional items that are not on the list.

For the reader: *Present the list as a matching activity. Print the list on cardstock and cut it into lists of objects and individual places. Have the student match the objects to the places or the places to the objects with the assistance of choices as needed; e.g., what would we find in the bedroom—stove, fridge, toaster, and pots or bed, blanket, dresser, and lamp? Where would you find a monkey, an elephant, and a tiger—at the mall or in the zoo?*

Carryover

- Discuss associated items in themed storybooks; e.g., all the things you would find on a farm (including animals, tools, etc.).
- Take a walk in the school or at home. Discuss what you might expect to find in different locations. Examples: What would we find in the office? What would we find on the playground? Ask the location of specific items: Where would we find your shoes? Where do we find the bathtub?
- Include absurdities; e.g., would we see a cow on the playground?

Table 17: OBJECT-TO-LOCATION ASSOCIATION

Objects	Place
1. Sun, moon, stars, clouds	Sky
2. Knife, fork, plate, cup	Dinner table
3. Bed, blanket, dresser, lamp	Bedroom
4. Bathtub, toilet, sink, towel, soap	Bathroom
5. Stove, fridge, toaster, pots	Kitchen
6. Couch, TV, carpet, coffee table	Living room
7. Leaf, twig, bird nest	Tree
8. Cow, pig, horse, hay	Farm
9. Monkey, elephant, tiger	Zoo
10. Desk, chalk, ruler, books	School
11. Swings, slide, monkey bars	Park
12. Sand, waves, bucket, shovel	Beach
13. Water, diving board, lifeguard, swimsuit	Swimming pool
14. Fire truck, boots, helmets	Fire station
15. Doctor, nurse, thermometer, bandages	Hospital
16. Books, movies, shelves, check out card	Library
17. BBQ, food, plates, people	BBQ
18. Stores, cashier, people, shopping bags	Mall
19. Menu, table, food, waitress	Restaurant
20. Gas pumps, cars, attendant	Gas station

Association 3: Object to occupation (e.g., fire truck/fireman)

Materials

1. Toy people and associated toy objects and/or object pictures that are associated with a person who carries out a specific job/activity and a picture of the person; e.g., mail and mailman, stethoscope and doctor. Select object-to-person pictures from a commercial association card set.
2. List OBJECT-TO-OCCUPATION ASSOCIATION, Table 18, below.

Introduction

Tell the student that some things go with a particular person (or occupation) because the person needs them to do his or her job.

Explain examples that will be familiar to the student. For example, a fireman uses a fire truck to go to a fire, so a fire truck and a fireman go together; a doctor uses a stethoscope to listen to your chest, so a doctor and a stethoscope go together. Model other examples from materials #1.

Activity **Receptive**

Use materials #1. Have the student pair the objects and/or pictures with the person who uses them; e.g., boy standing on long grass and lawnmower. Simplify the task by providing a choice of pictures; e.g., <u>fireman</u> and car, bus, <u>fire truck</u>. Prompt and assist as needed.

Activity **Expressive**

Step 1: Use materials #1. Have the student name the person who would go with the object, and/or name the object that would go with the person.

Step 2: Use the list OBJECT-TO-OCCUPATION ASSOCIATION:
   a. Read a list of objects from the list and have the student identify who might use them.
   b. Read the name or job description of a person and have the student generate a list of objects that he/she might use; e.g., teacher uses desk, books, chalk.

For the reader: *Present the list as a matching activity. Print the list on cardstock and cut it into lists of objects and individual people. Have the student match the objects to the person and/ or the person to the objects with the assistance of choices as needed. For example, who would use books, shelves, and library cards—a librarian or a bus driver? What would the janitor use—a bucket, mop, and garbage can or cows, chickens, and corn?*

Carryover

- Discuss people and their associated items in real-life situations, pictures, movies, and story books; e.g., Mom is holding a frying pan—what other things would she use in the kitchen?
- Include absurdities; e.g., would a fireman use a frying pan?

Table 18: OBJECT-TO-OCCUPATION ASSOCIATION

Objects	Occupation
1. Toy car, teddy bear, doll	Child
2. Bandages, stethoscope, thermometer	Doctor or nurse
3. Books, chalkboard, ruler	Teacher
4. Police car, police hat, notebook	Police officer
5. Letter, parcel, mailbox	Mail carrier
6. Cow, chickens, corn	Farmer
7. School bus, stop sign, school	Bus driver
8. Spaceship, helmet, spacesuit	Astronaut
9. Bucket, mop, garbage can	Janitor
10. Scissors, brush, comb, hair clippings	Hairdresser
11. Books, shelves, library card	Librarian
12. Boxed and canned food, fruit and vegetables, cash register	Cashier
13. Sick animal, stethoscope, bandages	Vet
14. Crib, highchair, stroller	Baby
15. Birthday cake, balloons, gifts	Person having a birthday
16. Teeth, recliner chair, instruments	Dentist
17. Lawnmower, rake	Person cutting the grass
18. Swimming pool, whistle, lifesaving ring	Lifeguard
19. Meat, vegetables, pot, stove	Person cooking (cook)
20. Hammer, nails, screwdriver, pliers	Person fixing something (carpenter)

Association 4: Object to activity (e.g., comb/fix hair)

Prerequisite: *Understanding of object function—Goal 2, above, p. 58.*

Materials

1. Objects, object miniatures, and/or object pictures that are associated with a specific activity that a person can carry out and a picture of the person performing the activity; e.g., "toothbrush," "toothpaste," "cup of water," go with "clean teeth." Select object-to-activity pictures from a commercial association card set.
2. List OBJECT-TO-ACTIVITY ASSOCIATION, Table 19, below.

Introduction

Tell the student that we need particular things when we are going to carry out an activity. Explain examples; e.g., "when I clean my car, I need water, soap, polish, rags, and a vacuum cleaner"; "when someone has a birthday cake, balloons, and gifts, you know that he or she is having a birthday."

Activity **Receptive**

Use materials #1. Have the student pair the objects and/or pictures with a person carrying out the associated activity; e.g., shovel, wheelbarrow, flowers in pots go with planting a garden.

Activity **Expressive**

Step 1: Use materials #1. Have the student name the person who would go with the object(s), and/or name the objects that would go with the person.

Step 2: Use the list OBJECT-TO-ACTIVITY ASSOCIATION:
   a. Read a list of objects and ask what activity they would be used for. Example: "What do we use a hockey stick, a hockey puck, and a helmet for?" (play hockey).
   b. Read the name of an activity and have the student generate a list of objects that would be needed for it. Example: "What would I need to wash my dog?" (soap, water, tub, towel).

For the reader: *Present the list as a matching activity. Print the list on cardstock and cut it into lists of objects and individual activities. Have the student match the objects to the activities and the activities to the objects with the assistance of choices as needed. Example: "Do we use soap, a washcloth, and a towel to take a bath or draw a picture?"*

Carryover

- Discuss what will be needed for a routine or special activity during the day. For example, "What do we need to paint a picture?" "What do we need to make cookies?"
- Guess what someone is going to do in view of the things that he is carrying or buying; e.g., "suitcase, pillow, stuffed toy means a sleepover."
- Include absurdities; e.g., "do I need a paintbrush when I bake cookies?"

Table 19: OBJECT-TO-ACTIVITY ASSOCIATION

Objects	Activity
1. Brush, comb, barrettes, hair band	Fix hair
2. Shovel, wheelbarrow, watering can, flowers, seeds	Plant a garden
3. Vacuum cleaner, duster, broom, garbage can	Clean a room
4. Detergent (soap), washing machine, laundry basket	Do laundry
5. Crayons, markers, pencils, paints, stickers, paper	Make a picture
6. Pillow, blanket, sheets, comforter	Make a bed
7. Soap, washcloth, towel	Take a bath or shower
8. Shoes, jacket, hat, mitts	Get dressed to go outside
9. Ball, bat, racket, hockey stick, puck	Play a game (sport)
10. Birthday cake, balloons, gifts, party hats, food	Have a birthday party
11. Helmet, bike, training wheels	Ride a bike
12. Guitar, drums, piano	Make music
13. Water, soap, polish, rags, vacuum cleaner	Clean a car
14. Dog food, bowl, water	Feed a dog
15. Paper, pen, envelope, stamp	Write a letter
16. Flour, eggs, butter, spoon, mixer, bowl	Make cookies
17. Fishing rod, bait (worm), boat, line	Catch a fish
18. Swimsuit, sun block, hat, toys, towel	Play at the beach
19. Glass, juice, water, ice cubes, lemon	Make a cold drink
20. Toothbrush, toothpaste, water	Clean your teeth

Association 5: Part to whole (e.g., steering wheel/car)
Materials

1. Objects or pictures of objects familiar to the student that have clearly shown parts; e.g., house with roof, chimney, windows, door; dog with ears, tail, nose, legs. See suggested objects in PART-TO-WHOLE OBJECTS, Table 20, below.
2. List SAMPLE OBJECTS THAT HAVE PARTS, Table 21, below.

Introduction

Tell the student that some things go together because they are parts of the same thing. Show the student a picture of a house and name its parts; e.g., roof, chimney, windows, door. Then say that all these parts together make the house. Provide other examples.

Activity **Receptive**

Use materials #1. Have the student point to the parts of the object as you name them; e.g., car— show me the steering wheel; show me the door; show me all of the windows.

Activity **Expressive**

Step1: Present an object or object picture from materials #1:
   a. Point to a specific part and have the student name it.
   b. Have the student generate a list of parts without you pointing to specific ones. Example: "Tell me the parts of a jacket"—sleeves, collar, pockets, zipper.

Step 2: Use the list PART-TO-WHOLE ASSOCIATION:
   a. Read a list of object parts and have the student name the object that they make up; e.g., window, steering wheel, seats—car.
   b. Read the name of an object and have the student list its parts; e.g., a tree— leaves, branches, trunk, bird-nest. Encourage him to think of other parts besides those listed. Provide verbal prompts and choices if needed.

For the reader: *Present the list as a matching activity. Print the list on cardstock and cut it into lists of object parts and individual whole objects. Have the student match the parts to the whole and the whole to the parts. Provide choices as needed. Example: Are seat, handlebars, bell, and wheels part of a bike or part of a computer?*

Carryover

- Cut off or cover part of a large single-item picture; e.g., the front wheel of a bike. Have the student identify what part is missing. Increase the level of difficulty by cutting large single-item pictures into many parts and have the student put them back together (like a jigsaw puzzle) while naming the parts; e.g., horse—tail, front leg, back leg, ears, eyes, nose.

Note: *the ability to connect pictures of parts into a whole may be difficult for the student with visual perceptual challenges.*

Table 20: PART-TO-WHOLE ASSOCIATION

Parts	Whole
1. Roof, chimney, windows, door	House
2. Sleeves, zipper, collar, hood	Jacket
3. Eyes, nose, mouth, cheeks	Face
4. Mattress, sheets, blanket, pillow	Bed
5. Doors, windows, steering wheel, windshield wipers	Car
6. Leaves, branches, trunk, bird nest	Tree
7. Seat, handlebars, bell, wheels	Bike
8. Pages, words, cover, title	Book
9. Skin, core, stalk, seeds	Apple
10. Cheese, crust, pepperoni, sauce	Pizza
11. Mouse, screen, games	Computer
12. Thunder, lightening, rain	Storm
13. Tall hat, broomstick, black dress	Witch
14. 8 legs, web, beady eyes	Spider
15. Feathers, wings, beak, eyes, legs, feet	Bird
16. Sun, moon, stars, clouds	Sky
17. Bun, meat, pickle, ketchup, mustard, cheese	Hamburger
18. Straps, fasteners, pockets, flap	Backpack
19. Wings, body, propellers, wheels	Airplane
20. Heel, laces, Velcro, strap, sole	Shoe

- Make a line-drawing on a chalk- or whiteboard; e.g., a house, car, teddy bear. Have the student tell you which part to erase until it has all gone; e.g., draw a flower—erase the leaves, stalk, flower, and bud as the student directs.
- Play Guess What I Am Thinking Of. Think of an object and give the student clues by naming its parts; e.g., I am thinking of something that has a seat, legs, and a cushion (chair).
- Include absurdities. For example, is my toe part of my face?

Table 21: SAMPLE OBJECTS THAT HAVE PARTS

• Car	• Bed	• Tree	• Toothbrush
• House	• Turtle	• Swing set	• Jacket
• Person	• Bird	• Book	• Bike
• Face	• Computer	• Bathtub	
• Dog	• Flower	• Saucepan	

Goal 4: The student will develop understanding and use of classification and categorization (each target word to 80–90 percent accuracy).

Due to the many steps required in the learning of classification and categorization, this goal has been placed in a separate chapter (Chapter 6: Classification and Categorization).

Goal 5: The student will define words using a Word Web (each target word to 80–90 percent accuracy).

Materials

1. Blank copies of WORD WEB LEVEL 1, Table 22, below.
2. Blank copies of WORD WEB LEVEL 2, Table 24, below.
3. WORD WEB GAME Level 1, Table 23, below.
4. WORD WEB GAME Level 2, Table 25, below.

Introduction

Tell the student to think of a spider web and imagine that the word that you are going to talk about is in the center of the web and questions about that word are around the edge. Show WORD WEB LEVEL 1 to the student (even if he is not able to read).

Choose a noun that is familiar to the student and write it in the center of the web. Model how to ask and answer the questions around the edge of the web. For example—target word pencil—"what does it do?" (it writes); "where do we find it?" (on our desk); "what things are associated with it?" (pencil case, crayons, eraser, paper); "what parts does it have?" (sharp point, eraser, part to hold onto); "what color and shape is it?" (yellow, long and thin); "what category does it belong in—things to write with or animals?"

Activity **Receptive** and **Expressive**

Present a familiar noun, or have the student choose one, then together define it using the questions on the branches of WORD WEB LEVEL 1. Write your answers on a blank copy of the WORD WEB (be aware that not all questions are appropriate for every noun).

Advance to WORD WEB LEVEL 2 and WORD WEB Game Level 2 when the student is able to respond to the questions around the target word with 80–90 percent accuracy.

For the reader: *Print WORD WEB Game Level 1 on cardstock and cut out the questions. Take turns asking the other person a question in relation to the target word.*

Carryover

- Apply WORD WEB questions to vocabulary in everyday life.

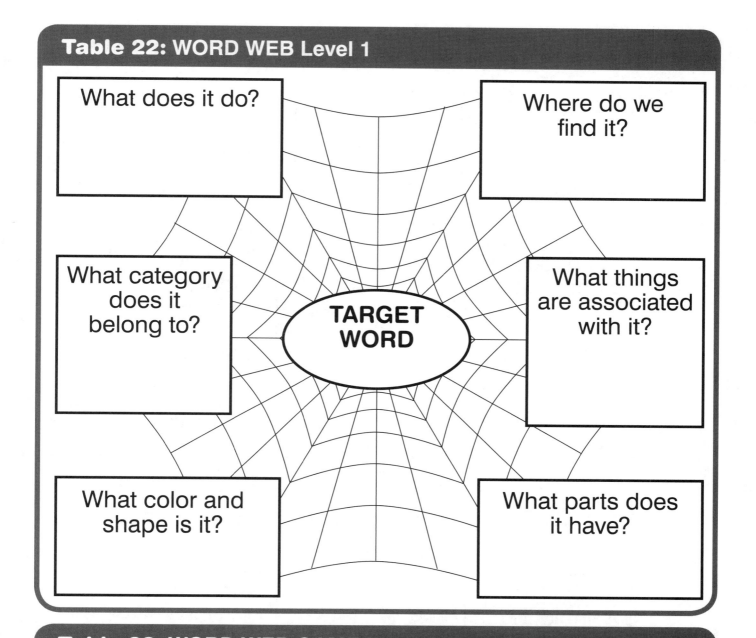

Table 22: WORD WEB Level 1

What does it do?

Where do we find it?

What category does it belong to?

TARGET WORD

What things are associated with it?

What color and shape is it?

What parts does it have?

Table 23: WORD WEB GAME Level 1

What does it do?	Where do we find it?	What category does it belong to?
What things are associated with it?	What color and shape is it?	What parts does it have?

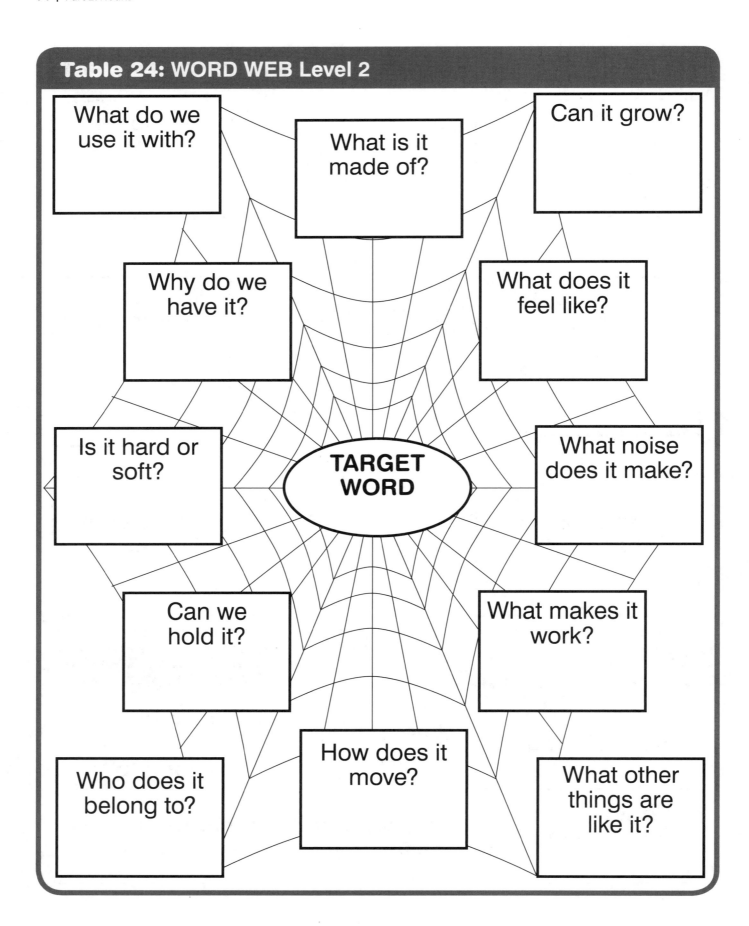

Table 24: WORD WEB Level 2

What do we use it with?

What is it made of?

Can it grow?

Why do we have it?

What does it feel like?

Is it hard or soft?

TARGET WORD

What noise does it make?

Can we hold it?

What makes it work?

Who does it belong to?

How does it move?

What other things are like it?

Table 25: WORD WEB GAME Level 2

What do we use with it?	What is it made of?	Can it grow?
Why do we have it?	What does it feel like?	Is it hard or soft?
What noise does it make?	Can we hold it?	What makes it work?
Who does it belong to?	How does it move?	What other things are like it?

6.
Classification and Categorization

These goals are appropriate for students with one or more of the following characteristics:

- stores words unsystematically, limiting her ability to relate words one to another and retrieve words when needed

- has weak understanding of language

- has a limited understanding and use of category names; e.g., fruit, tools

- delivers a slow and/or unclear message due to word searching and false starts

Classification and Categorization Goals

The student will:

Goal 1: understand group classification through sorting shapes—circle, square, and triangle.

Goal 2: understand exclusion from a group through sorting shapes—circle, square, and triangle.

Goal 3: understand and use a category name (collective noun); e.g., dog, cat, horse, lion = animals.

Goal 4: identify the item that does not belong in a named category (exclusion); e.g., animals—cow, <u>apple</u>, rabbit.

Goal 5: generate an item or a list of items that belong in the same category; e.g., food—cookie, cereal, soup, pizza.

Goal 6: identify and generate a list of items that belong in a subcategory; e.g., animals that live in the ocean (whale, starfish, shark).

Goal 1: The student will develop understanding of group classification through sorting shapes—circle, square, and triangle (with 80–90 percent accuracy).

Prerequisites: *Understanding and use of words "same" and "different"—Chapter 3 (Same and Different), Goals 1–5, pp. 30-38. Names of colors—Chapter 8 (Descriptors), Goal 1, p. 120.*

Note: *Omit Goals 1 and 2 if the student does not already understand and use color and shape names.*

Materials

1. 4 sheets of cardstock (8 x 11 size) of different colors; e.g., red, blue, yellow, purple.
2. Set A: Place all sheets of cardstock together and cut through all layers (or cut out individually) so there are 4 squares/circles/triangles, one each of each color; e.g., red, blue, yellow, and purple (total 12 shapes).
3. Set B: Place all sheets of cardstock together and cut out two more sets of shapes, giving another 24 shapes (keep Set B separate from Set A until directed to use both sets).

    Set A and B together will total 36 shapes—12 of each shape (all colors), within which are 3 of each shape of the same color; e.g., 3 blue squares.

Introduction

Introduce this goal by telling the student that you are going to talk about shapes and colors that belong together in groups. Remind her that she knows the word "same." You are going to find shapes and colors that are the same.

Use Set A, colored cardstock shapes. Demonstrate sorting them by color—e.g., all yellows in a group regardless of shape; by shape—e.g., all circles in a group regardless of color. Use Set A and Set B together to demonstrate sorting by shape and color—e.g., all red triangles together; all blue squares together.

Model use of the word "same." For example: These are the <u>same</u>—they are all red—they belong together. These are the <u>same</u>—they are all squares—they belong together. Support the reader with the written words "same" and "belong" as needed.

Activity **Receptive**

Present assortments of the cardstock shapes (circles, squares, and triangles) and have the student sort them as directed. Limit the number of shapes/colors to be sorted according to the student's ability level.

Work through the following progression:

Step 1: Use Set A to *sort by color.* Have the student start by sorting 8 random shapes of 2 different colors into their color groups. Gradually increase the number of shapes and colors until she is sorting all of the shapes into the 4 color groups; e.g., put all reds in one group and all blues in another regardless of shape. Add a choice of more colored shapes by including some or all from Set B.

Step 2: Use Set A to *sort by shape.* Have the student start by sorting 2 different shapes of any color into their shape groups from a total of 8 shapes; e.g., put all squares in one group and all circles in another regardless of color. Gradually increase to sorting all 3 shapes of all 4 colors. Add a choice of more shapes of the 4 colors by including some or all from Set B.

Step 3: Use Set A and B to *sort by shape and color.* Have the student start by sorting 3 identical shapes of the same color from 8 random shapes of random colors; e.g., put all the blue circles in a group; put all the red squares in a group. Gradually increase to sorting all 3 shapes of the 4 colors from all of the colors and shapes.

Activity **Expressive**

Arrange groups of shapes/colors as for the Activity *Receptive,* Steps 1–3. Or, immediately after the student has completed each step, have her describe why the shapes/colors belong together. For example, these belong together because they are all blue/the <u>same</u> color; these belong together because they are circles/all the <u>same</u> shape; these belong together because they are all yellow squares/all the <u>same</u> shape and color.

Encourage the use of the words "same" and "belong." It is not necessary for the student to use full sentence structures at this time, but her meaning must be apparent.

Carryover

- Find things that match in color and/or shape in everyday life; e.g., hat and mittens—"both red"; sun and dinner plate—"both circles." Find all of the green vegetables in the fridge; find all of the blue toys in the box; find all of the round yellow blocks.
- Play with preschool shape sorters.
- Arrange peers into groups by color; e.g., all those with brown hair, red t-shirts, or white shoes.

Goal 2: The student will develop understanding of exclusion from a group through sorting shapes—circle, square, and triangle (with 80–90 percent accuracy).

Prerequisite: *Understanding of negative "no" and "not"—Chapter 2 (Negative No/Not), Goals 1–3, pp. 24-27.*

Materials

- Squares, circles, and triangles cut from cardstock in 4 different colors already made (see materials Goal 1). Set A: 12 shapes; Set B: 24 shapes.

Introduction

Explain that the student is going to find shapes and colors that do not belong in the group that they have been put in. Remind her that she knows the word "different." You are going to find the shape or color that is different from the other ones in the group.

Review: Use Set A or Sets A and B of the colored cardstock shapes. Review how to sort them by color—e.g., all yellows in a group regardless of shape; by shape—e.g., all circles in a group regardless of color; by shape and color—e.g., all red triangles in a group.

Demonstrate the new goal by making a group of *varied shapes of the same color* and add one that does not belong because it is a different color; e.g., purple square, purple triangle, purple circle, and red triangle. Model the use of the word "different." For example, "These are the <u>same</u>—they are all purple—but this one is <u>different</u>—it is red. The red one does not belong because the others are all purple."

Model other examples using the *same shapes of different colors* and add one that does not belong because it is a different shape; e.g., blue triangle, red triangle, yellow triangle, and purple circle. "Which one is different/does not belong? The circle is <u>different</u> because it is not a triangle. It does not belong with the triangles."

Support the reader with the written words "different" and "does not belong" as needed.

Activity **Receptive**

Present groups of 4 of the cardstock shapes/colors (circles, squares, and triangles in 4 colors) and have the student identify the one that is different. Within each group have 3 shapes or colors that are the same and 1 that is different.

Work through the following progression:

Step 1: Use Sets A and B to *exclude by color* (same shapes). Arrange 4 identical shapes—3 of the same color and 1 of a different color in a line with the different color placed at random; e.g., 1 red circle, 1 purple circle, and 2 red circles. Have the student point to the one that is <u>different</u>/does not belong (purple circle).

Step 2: Use Sets A and B to *exclude by shape* (same colors). Arrange 4 shapes of the same color—3 of the same shape and 1 different shape in a line with the different shape placed at random; e.g., 2 blue triangles, 1 blue circle, and 1 blue triangle. Have the student point to the one that is <u>different</u>/does not belong (blue circle).

Step 3: Use Sets A and B to *exclude by shape from mixed colors.* Arrange 4 shapes of different colors—3 of the same shape and 1 different shape in a line with the different shape placed at random; e.g., 1 purple triangle, 1 blue triangle, 1 red triangle, and 1 yellow circle. Have the student point to the one that is <u>different</u>/does not belong (yellow circle).

Activity **Expressive**

Arrange groups of shapes/colors as for the Activity *Receptive,* Steps 1–3, or immediately after the student has completed each step, have the student describe which one does not belong in the group and why. For example, this one does not belong because the squares are all blue but this one is red—it is a <u>different</u> color; this one does not belong because these are all circles and this one is a triangle—it is a <u>different</u> shape.

Encourage the use of the words "different" and "does not belong." It is not necessary for the student to use full sentence structures at this time, but his meaning must be clear.

Carryover

- Carry out sorting activities that have an "error" and discuss why the "odd one out" does not belong. For example, sort groceries into "cans" and "boxes" and identify which one does not belong when a can is put in with the boxes; sort pencils and crayons of different colors; sort books or decorative erasers of different colors; sort "lost and found"—put a t-shirt in with the socks.

Goal 3: The student will understand and use a category name (collective noun); e.g., dog, cat, horse, lion = animals (with 80–90 percent accuracy).

Materials

1. Toys and objects and/or pictures of toys, objects, and animals that belong in the same category (at least 3 of each). See CATEGORY LISTS, Table 26, below.
2. SORT PERSON AND THING, Table 27, below.
3. List IDENTIFY THE CATEGORY, Table 28, below.
4. List IDENTIFY THE CATEGORY – FOR PRINTING ITEMS and CATEGORY NAMES, Table 29 and 30, below.

Introduction

Introduce this goal by telling the student that you are going to talk about things that belong in groups. When things are the same, they belong in the group; when things are different, they do not belong in the group. Each group has a name.

Use an assortment of toys, objects, or pictures that belong in categories (materials #1). Sort them into their categories and explain why you sorted them that way; e.g., the sheep, the pig, and the cow belong in the same group—they are all "animals." Provide several examples, and support the reader as needed with the individual category names and the key words "same" and "belong" written on cue cards; e.g., animals, food, furniture.

Activity **Receptive** and **Expressive**

Step 1—Objects/Pictures (Receptive): Use toys, objects, or object pictures from materials #1. Select 3 from 2 categories and mix them up on the table; e.g., animals (cow, horse, pig) and food (pizza, cheese, apple). Have the student sort the objects or pictures into their respective categories. Gradually add more items/pictures and more categories so she is eventually sorting into 6 or 8 categories. Provide the reader with the name of the category written on a cue card.

Step 1—Objects/Pictures (Expressive): As the student sorts the items in Activity *Receptive,* Step 1, have her name the category and use the words "same" and "belongs"; e.g., the horse belongs with the mouse—they are animals. Provide written support for the reader, as described in the Introduction.

Discuss what all these things in the category have in common. For example, what do all animals have? What can they all do? How are they all the same? Ask "yes/no" questions; e.g., do all animals have fur? Do all animals breathe? Do all animals live in trees? Ask absurd questions; e.g., is an elephant food?

Step 2—Sort Person and Thing (Receptive): Print the activity on cardstock. Cut out the individual words (or substitute the equivalent pictures), but leave the sorting card intact. Have the student sort the written words into "Person" and "Thing" categories (read the words aloud for the non-reader). Discuss and explain as necessary.

Step 2—Sort Person and Thing (Expressive): As the student assigns each item or person to a category, have her use the group name "person" or "thing."

Step 3—IDENTIFY THE CATEGORY (Table 28) (Receptive and Expressive): Read a list of items to the student and have her name the category in which they

Table 26: CATEGORY LISTS

Animals	Clothing	Furniture	Food
Dog	Jacket	Bed	Cereal
Cat	Hat	Bookshelf	Eggs
Horse	Socks	Chair	Juice
Cow	Shoes	Chest of drawers	Cheese
Fish	Pajamas	Couch	Cookies
Frog	Gloves/mitts	Crib	Apple
Mouse	Pants	Rocking chair	Carrots
Elephant	Underwear	Table	Popcorn
Giraffe	Shirt	Desk	Pizza
Rabbit	Boots	Footstool	Ice cream

School Items	Toys	Transportation (Vehicles)	Body Part
Book	Ball	Car	Head
Chair	Jump rope	Bicycle	Arm
Teacher	Drum	Bus	Ear
Paper	Blocks	Airplane	Eye
Pencil	Balloons	Train	Fingers
Scissors	Bubbles	Van	Hand
Crayons	Kite	Motorbike	Foot
Eraser	Doll	Rowboat	Mouth
Clock	Teddy bear	Helicopter	Nose
Flag	Xylophone	Sailboat	Leg

belong; e.g. cat, dog, horse are _____ (animals). Offer a choice of category names as a preliminary step, if necessary.

For the reader: *Copy the lists ITEMS and CATEGORY NAMES from IDENTIFY THE CATEGORY—FOR PRINTING (Table 30) onto different-colored cardstock. Cut each into individual lines or words. Have the student match the category name to each list (offer a choice, if necessary) or play as a turn-taking game.*

Carryover

- Model category names in everyday situations. Example: Dad is using a saw—a saw is a <u>tool</u>.
- Look around the room and name things that are in the same category; e.g., desk, table, chair = furniture.
- Use catalog pictures to make category-based collages and scrapbooks.
- Incorporate categories into playtime. For example, play "store" using boxed, canned, or real food; play "garage" using a variety of vehicles; play "farm" and "zoo."
- Play Lotto, Memory, or Go Fish, using pictures that match if they are in the same category. Create Lotto cards by placing individual cards in groups. The groups can then easily be changed so the student does not learn the category by rote.
- Hide toys and objects in a large tub of rice or sand. Have the student use her sense of touch to find the ones in the same category.
- Spread a variety of single-item pictures out on the table, and, together with the student, find pairs or groups that do not have the same category name but can be classified together; e.g., an airplane and a chicken—things with wings; a car and skateboard—things with wheels; a snowman and an ice cream—things that are cold.
- Play commercial categorizing computer games and apps.

Table 27: SORT PERSON AND THING

Dad	Man	Shoe
Mom	Lady	Picture
Father	Girl	House
Mother	Boy	Book
Sister	Neighbor	Tree
Brother	Car	Boat
Cousin	Chair	Computer
Aunt	Door	Telephone
Uncle	Bed	Flower
Teacher	Cookie	Juice
Friend	TV	Sun

(Table 27 continued)

Person	Thing

Table 28: IDENTIFY THE CATEGORY

Items	Category Name	Correct/Incorrect
1. Cat, dog, horse	Animals	
2. Orange, apple, grapes	Fruit	
3. Yellow, red, blue	Colors	
4. Train, motorbike, airplane	Vehicles/transportation	
5. Balls, blocks, puzzles	Toys	
6. 9, 4, 8	Numbers	
7. Bread, peanut butter, pizza	Food	
8. Bus driver, doctor, fireman	People's jobs / Occupations	
9. Chair, bed, dresser	Furniture	
10. Broccoli, lettuce, peas	Vegetables	
11. Jacket, pants, underwear	Clothes	
12. Arm, foot, head	Body parts	
13. Hot chocolate, milk, juice	Drinks	
14. Hammer, screwdriver, wrench	Tools	
15. Bee, wasp, spider	Bugs	
16. Kitchen, living room, bathroom	Rooms in house	
17. Backpack, pencil, lunch bag	Things for school	
18. Triangle, rectangle, square	Shapes	
19. D, M, T	Letters of the alphabet	
20. Drum, guitar, tambourine	Musical instruments	

Table 29: IDENTIFY THE CATEGORY—FOR PRINTING

Items

Cat, dog, horse	Orange, apple, grapes
Yellow, red, blue	Train, motorbike, airplane
Balls, blocks, puzzles	9 4 8
Bread, peanut butter, pizza	Bus driver, doctor, fireman
Chair, bed, dresser	Broccoli, lettuce, peas
Jacket, pants, underwear	Arm, foot, head
Hot chocolate, milk, juice	Hammer, screwdriver, wrench
Bee, wasp, spider	Kitchen, living room, bathroom
Backpack, pencil, lunch bag	Triangle, rectangle, square
D M T	Drum, guitar, tambourine

Table 30: IDENTIFY THE CATEGORY—FOR PRINTING

Category Names

Animals	Musical instruments
Colors	Vehicles/transportation
Toys	Numbers
Food	People's jobs
Furniture	Vegetables
Clothing	Body parts
Drinks	Tools
Fruit	Bugs
Rooms in house	Things for school
Shapes	Letters of the alphabet

Goal 4: The student will identify the item that does not belong in a named category (exclusion); e.g., animals—cow, <u>apple</u>, rabbit (with 80–90 percent accuracy).

Prerequisite: *Understanding of negative "no" and "not"—Chapter 2 (Negative No/Not), Goals 1–3, pp. 24-27.*

Materials

1. Toys and objects and/or pictures of toys, objects, and animals that belong in the same category (3 of each). See CATEGORY LISTS, Table 26, above.
2. List CATEGORY EXCLUSION, Table 31, below.

Introduction

Tell the student that sometimes we put things in the wrong group. They are different and do not belong with the others. She is going to find the things that do not belong.

Use some of the toys, objects, or pictures (materials #1) and make up groups of 4 items of which 3 belong in the same category and 1 does not belong; e.g., pig, horse, <u>apple</u>, cow. Tell the student which one does not belong and describe why; e.g., the apple does not belong (it is different) because it is not an animal (it is a food). Present further examples as needed.

Support the reader with the written words "different" and "does not belong," as needed.

Activity **Receptive**

Place 3 objects (or pictures) from one category and 1 object (or picture) from a different category (pictures face up) on the table in front of the student. Have her point to the object/picture that does not belong; e.g., apple, <u>bed</u>, cereal, ice cream.

Activity **Expressive**

Step 1: Immediately after the student has pointed to the item that does not belong in Activity *Receptive* (or arrange groups of 4 objects with 1 that does not belong) have her tell you which one does not belong and explain why. For example, the bed does not belong because these are all <u>food</u> and the bed is <u>furniture</u>; or the bed does not belong because it is <u>not food</u>.

Step 2: Read each list of items from CATEGORY EXCLUSION and ask, "Which one does not belong?" Have the student identify the item that does not belong and explain why. Change the order of the words or substitute a different item that does not belong when you present the activity during a subsequent work session.

It is not necessary for the student to use full sentence structures at this time, but her meaning must be clear.

Table 31: CATEGORY EXCLUSION

Items	Student Response	Correct/ Incorrect
1. Cat, dog, apple, horse (animals)		
2. Pizza, monkey, cereal, ice cream (food)		
3. Book, green, red, orange (colors)		
4. Triangle, tree, square, circle (shapes)		
5. Teddy bear, doll, ball, sun (toys)		
6. Table, couch, elephant, chair (furniture)		
7. Door, nine, two, seven (numbers)		
8. Milk, water, pencil, juice (drinks)		
9. Bedroom, car, bathroom, kitchen (rooms in house)		
10. Bus, airplane, boat, doll (vehicles)		
11. Green, foot, neck, hand (body parts)		
12. Ant, bee, bird, mosquito (bugs)		
13. H, M, P, orange (letters of the alphabet)		
14. Computer, lettuce, corn, potato (vegetables)		
15. Jacket, hat, pants, cake (clothing)		
16. Piano, crayon, guitar, drums (musical instruments)		
17. Policeman, doctor, dinosaur, bus driver (people's jobs)		
18. Blanket, hammer, saw, screwdriver (tools)		
19. Backpack, pencil, baby, homework (things for school)		
20. Apple, banana, grape, mouse (fruit)		

Carryover

- Sort items and find the "odd one out"; e.g., fruits/vegetables; summer clothes/winter clothes; toys made of plastic/toys made of wood.
- Deliberately put an item in a place where it does not belong. For example, put a toy truck in a lunchbox and say, "Oh no! It is not food"; put a pencil in the sandbox, and say, "It is not a toy; it is something to write with."
- Play Lotto using category-themed cards.

Goal 5: The student will generate an item or a list of items that belong in the same category; e.g., food—cookie, cereal, soup, pizza (with 80–90 percent accuracy).

Materials

1. Toys and objects or pictures of toys, objects, or animals that belong in the same category (4 of each). See CATEGORY LISTS, Table 26, above.
2. List ADD TO THE CATEGORY, Table 32, below.
3. List CATEGORIZATION AND CLASSIFICATION, Table 33, below.

Introduction

Introduce this goal by saying that now the student knows the names of groups (categories) and some of the things that belong in the groups, she is going to learn the names of more things that belong in the same group.

Set out 3 objects or pictures in the same category on the table; e.g., car, boat, plane. Place an additional 2 objects/pictures on the table—1 that belongs in the category and 1 that does not belong; e.g., a bus and an apple. Label the category "vehicles" (transportation) and explain that the bus belongs with the car, boat, and plane because it is also a vehicle.

Introduce Steps 2 and 3 by modeling the activity immediately prior to working on the step.

Activity **Receptive** and **Expressive**

Step 1—With Choice: Set out 3 objects or pictures in the same category in front of the student; e.g., coat, hat, socks. Provide a choice of an additional 2 items (one that does and the other that does not belong in the category); e.g., glove and pencil. Have the student name the category and then identify the additional item that belongs in the category; e.g., clothing—the glove is clothing—it belongs.

Step 2—Without Choice: Set out 3 objects or pictures in the same category in front of the student; e.g., horse, cow, pig. Have the student name the category and generate the name of another item that belongs in the same category; e.g., animals—chicken. She may name another object/picture that was previously presented in that group or she may generate a new one that has not previously been mentioned (a more difficult step). As she becomes more proficient, request that she name more than one item.

Step 3—No Visuals: Present lists of items from ADD TO THE CATEGORY (Table 32) and have the student name the category and add items to the list. Start by requiring one item and increase to 3 or more depending on the student's ability and the category named. (Some are easier than others!)

Step 4: Use the list CATEGORIZATION AND CLASSIFICATION (Table 33): Explain that we group things not only by a category name but also in other ways such as by a description of what we do with the items, where we find them, or what they look like. For instance, we can talk about groups of things that are all "red"; e.g., tomato, crayon, art paper; things that we can sit on; e.g., chair, stool, couch; things that grow; e.g., baby animal, a seed, a child.

For the nonreader: *Give the name of a category or classification and have the student list as many items as possible in the group. Simplify or vary the task by taking turns to add items to the list.*

For the reader: *Print the list on cardstock and cut into individual words. Play as a turn-taking game in which players pick a category or classification and generate as many items as possible.*

Both readers and non-readers can play competitively or non-competitively as a race against the clock (egg timer or hourglass) to name as many items in the specific category as they can within a timeframe. Keep a written list of the items and try to make each new list longer than the previous one now or during a subsequent therapy session.

Carryover

- Draw attention to items and objects throughout the day and name their category or classification, then think of other items that belong in the same category; e.g., a bird can fly—what other things can fly? (airplane, bumble bee, kite).
- Discuss and list groups of items that the student needs or does not need for a specific activity; e.g., what things do you need for gym class? (running-shoes, ball, jump ropes). Include absurdities; e.g., do you need your toothbrush for gym class?
- Write the name of a category on each square of a game such as Snakes and Ladders or Hopscotch. Each player must name one or more items in a category as specified when she lands on a designated square.
- Play Category Snap. Choose a category or classification and say a new item in it each time red or black cards come together.
- Discuss other ways in which an item could be classified/categorized. Example: An apple is a food, a fruit, a snack, a thing that grows on trees, a thing that is round, a thing that tastes sweet.

Table 32: ADD TO THE CATEGORY

Category	Student Response
1. Cookie, cereal, soup…….. (food)	
2. Hand, foot, eye……..(body parts)	
3. Mouse, cow, cat……(animals)	
4. Yellow, green, white…….(colors)	
5. Couch, table, dresser……..(furniture)	
6. Lego, doll, ball……….(toys)	
7. Apple juice, tea, milk……(drinks)	
8. Living room, bathroom, dining room…. (rooms in house)	
9. S, B, K………(letters of alphabet)	
10. Airplane, taxi, sailboat…..(vehicles)	
11. Potato, squash, carrot……(vegetables)	
12. Pants, sweater, jacket….(clothing)	
13. Sunday, Tuesday, Friday….(days of week)	
14. Balloons, gift, party…….(birthday)	
15. 4, 3, 9……….(numbers)	
16. Janitor, teacher, mailman……(people's jobs)	
17. Banana, grapefruit, pear……(fruit)	
18. Ladybird, housefly, ant……(bugs)	
19. August, June, December…….(months)	
20. Cookie, pie, Jello……(dessert)	

Table 33: CATEGORIZATION AND CLASSIFICATION

Food	Things that go in the water
Things that have wheels	Animals
Things that are cold	Things that fly
Things that are hot	Fruit
Things that are hard	Vegetables
Things that are soft	Things that are big
Things that are round	Things that are little
Things that grow	Things on a farm
Things that float on water	Tools
Things to sit on	Things we keep in the fridge
Things we buy at the grocery store	Snacks
Things that are orange	Things that a baby needs
Things that melt	Things we can use
Things that make a noise	Things that are furry
Things that we must not get wet	Things that are heavy
Pets	Things made of wood
Things we keep inside the house	Things made of metal
Birds	Flowers
Things we can hold in our hands	Things to ride on
Things that have four legs	Things that are green
Things that are yellow	Things that are red

Goal 6: The student will identify and generate a list of items that belong in a subcategory; e.g., animals that live in the ocean (whale, starfish, shark) (with 80–90 percent accuracy).

Materials

1. Toys/objects or pictures of toys/objects and animals that belong in subcategories (at least 4 of each) and a picture of the subcategory; e.g., zoo animals, farm animals, furniture for a living room; a picture of a zoo, a farm, and a living room. For suggestions, see SUBCATEGORIES, Table 34, below.
2. Magic Bag
3. List of SUBCATEGORIES printed on cardstock, Table 34, below.

Introduction

Tell the student that some groups (categories) are very big and we find it helpful to break them down into smaller groups (subcategories). You are going to talk about things that fit into big groups but also into smaller groups.

Use some of the toys, objects, or pictures to demonstrate. Explain, for example, that whales, tigers, starfish, snakes, sharks, and elephants all belong in the big group "animals." Then show a picture of the ocean and the jungle and sort the animals into their appropriate subcategory (whales, starfish, and sharks go in the ocean; tigers, elephants, and snakes go in the jungle).

Activity **Receptive** and **Expressive**

Step 1: Place toys and objects or pictures of items that belong in 2 or more subcategories into the Magic Bag. Place a picture of each of the subcategories on the table. Take turns to take a toy/picture out of the bag and put it on the appropriate subcategory picture.

Step 2: Use the list SUBCATEGORIES:

For the nonreader: *Present the name of a subcategory and have the student list as many items as possible in the group. Provide word choices and discussion as needed. To simplify the task or for variety, take turns adding to the list.*

For the reader: *Print the list on cardstock and cut into individual subcategories. Take turns to pick up a subcategory and generate a list of items. Play also as a turn-taking game.*

Both readers and nonreaders can play competitively or noncompetitively as a race against the clock. The players are under pressure to name as many items in the subcategory as they can within a timeframe.

When the student is confidently able to list items in subcategories and it is your turn to list an item, suggest an item that would *not* belong in that subcategory. Have the student correct you and explain why it would not belong. For example, a swimsuit belongs in "clothes we wear at bedtime." Response: no, we wear a swimsuit to go in the water, not to wear in bed.

Carryover

- Play Lotto and Memory. Use pictures of objects and animals in subcategories.
- Write the name of a subcategory on each square of a game such as Snakes (Chutes) and Ladders or Hopscotch. Each player must name one or more items in that subcategory when she lands on that square.
- Read themed story/picture books; e.g., animals in the ocean/forest/zoo/desert/trees.
- Make a collage of items/pictures in the same subcategory; e.g., food to eat for snacks.
- Classify by description such as big, little, striped, round; e.g., a horse is a big animal. What other big animals can we think of? (elephant, rhinoceros).
- Provide category examples and ask questions. Example: I bought food that comes in cans at the grocery store (beans, soup). What food could I have bought that comes in boxes?

TARGETING LANGUAGE DELAYS | 97

Table 34: SUBCATEGORIES

Animals that live in the zoo	Animals that live in the forest
Animals that live in a pond	Animals that live in the dessert
Animals that live in the jungle	Animals that live in the ocean
Animals that can swim	Animals we can have as pets
Animals that can jump	Animals that have stripes
Animals that can climb trees	Animals that we can ride on
Furniture in the house	Furniture in school
Furniture we can sit on	Furniture in the living room
Food we eat for breakfast	Food we eat for snacks
Food we eat for supper	Food we eat for lunch
Drinks that are hot	Food we keep in the freezer
Clothes we wear in Winter	Clothes we wear in Summer
Clothes we wear at bedtime	Body parts that we have two of
Clothes that keep us dry	Vehicles that fly
Vehicles that go on the road	Vehicles that go on or under water
People (real names) we meet at school	People (real names) at home
Toys that have wheels	Toys to play with outside
Toys to play with at the beach or pool	Toys that need batteries
Places to go that you can walk to	Places to go that you need a ride to
Plants that grow in the garden	Plants we can eat

7. Verbs

Verbs Goals

The student will:

Goal 1: imitate and name modeled actions; e.g., walking.

Goal 2: understand and name the action shown in a picture; e.g., sleeping.

Goal 3: sort and match pictures of different people and animals carrying out the same action and name the action; e.g., find all "sitting."

Goal 4: describe and perform the action shown in a picture; e.g., a girl holding up her hand.

Goal 5: name an action that a person, animal, or object can carry out; e.g., a frog can jump. Also, given the name of an action, state who or what can carry out that action; e.g., who or what can walk?

Goal 6: identify the reason why we carry out specific actions; e.g., why do we sweep the floor? Why do we wash our hands?

Goal 7: define verbs using a Verb Word Web.

Teaching Verbs in Different Contexts

For a student to fully understand and use a verb effectively, it is essential that the verb be taught in many different contexts. Before starting Goal 1, view the Word Web in Goal 7, p. 117. and throughout the learning process present verbs in relation to other words such as: Who can carry out the action? Where? When? Why? For example: A dog can <u>jump</u> to catch a ball; <u>run</u> in the dog park; <u>sleep</u> in a dog bed; <u>walk</u> on a leash; <u>roll over</u> to be petted.

Note: *To teach verb tense, see Chapter 11 (Word and Sentence Structure), Goal 5, p. 215.*

Goal 1: The student will imitate and name modeled actions; e.g., walking (with 80–90 percent accuracy).

Materials:

1. List EARLY DEVELOPING VERBS FOR IMITATION AND NAMING, Table 35, below.
2. Props: drum, hairbrush, pencil and paper, 2 bottles or cups of water, small crackers or cereal, ball, toy doll or stuffed toy, small box with lid, sand or water in container and a cup or bowl to pour into, book.
3. List TRACKING EARLY DEVELOPING VERBS, Table 36, below.

Introduction

Introduce this goal by saying that the student is going to learn new "doing" or "action" words. Perform and name actions from the list EARLY DEVELOPING VERBS FOR IMITATION AND NAMING; e.g., "I am standing/waving/clapping" (use present progressive "ing" verb ending). Encourage the student to imitate your action. ***Be aware of any physical limitations that the student may have and adapt the actions accordingly.***

Activity **Receptive** and **Expressive**

Step 1: Perform an action from the list EARLY DEVELOPING VERBS FOR IMITATION AND NAMING and have the student imitate your action; e.g., sit on the floor—student sits on the floor. Model the name of the action and have the student imitate the name; e.g., sitting (encourage the use of "ing" ending). Provide the props for the actions as needed.

Step 2: When the student has completed Step 1 to 80–90 percent accuracy, perform an action and have the student name it, but do not model the name for him. For example, say, "Tell me what I am doing/what am I doing?" Response: "waving." Prompt by using sentence completion or verb choice if necessary; e.g., "you are _____" (waving); "am I waving or clapping?"

Step 3: Name an action from the list and have the student perform it without a model; e.g., show me "standing"; show me "hugging."

Record the student's progress on form TRACKING EARLY DEVELOPING VERBS.

Table 35: EARLY DEVELOPING VERBS FOR IMITATION & NAMING

Verbs (no props)	Verbs (with props)
Blowing	Banging (drum)
Clapping	Brushing (hairbrush)
Crawling	Drawing (pencil and paper)
Crying	Drinking (bottles or cups of water)
Dancing	Eating (small crackers or cereal)
Jumping	Hugging (toy doll or stuffed toy)
Peeking (through fingers)	Kicking (ball)
Running	Kissing (toy doll or stuffed toy)
Singing	Opening (box)
Sitting	Pouring (sand or water)
Sleeping	Reading (book)
Standing	Tickling (toy doll or stuffed toy)
Walking	
Waving	

Props:
- Drum
- Hairbrush
- Pencil and paper
- 2 bottles or cups of water
- Small crackers or cereal
- Ball
- Toy doll or stuffed toy
- Small box with lid
- Sand or water in a container and a cup or bowl to pour into
- Book

Table 36: TRACKING EARLY DEVELOPING VERBS

Verb	Receptive	Expressive	Established
Banging			
Blowing			
Brushing			
Clapping			
Crawling			
Crying			
Dancing			
Drawing			
Drinking			
Eating			
Hugging			
Jumping			
Kicking			
Kissing			
Opening			
Peeking			
Pouring			
Reading			
Running			
Singing			
Sitting			
Sleeping			
Standing			
Tickling			
Walking			
Waving			

Carryover

- Name actions that the student is carrying out throughout the day and encourage him to associate the action with the spoken verb.
- Play Copy Cat. Take turns copying exactly what the other person is doing (pretend the other person is your reflection in a mirror).
- Play a turn-taking game in which one student tells another student to perform a specific action; e.g., crawling, running.

Goal 2: The student will understand and name the action shown in a picture; e.g., sleeping (with 80–90 percent accuracy).

Materials

1. 20 photos or pictures of single people and/or single animals carrying out an action from EARLY DEVELOPING VERBS FOR IMITATION AND NAMING, Table 35, above, that are familiar to the student; e.g., a man eating; a baby sleeping; a dog running. If possible, take photos of the student himself or his peers (with permission) carrying out the actions.
2. Photos or pictures of single people and/or animals carrying out actions *that the student has not been previously taught* selected from TRACKING LATER-DEVELOPING VERBS, Table 37, below.

Introduction

Tell the student that he is going to learn more "doing" words. You are going to show him photos and pictures, and he is going to learn the name of the action that the person or animal is carrying out.

Present a choice of 2 photos/pictures and model the names of the verbs shown; e.g., this is "eating"; this is "running" (point to each one as you label it). Provide more examples as needed.

Activity **Receptive**

Step 1: Present photos/pictures of the actions that the student is *already familiar with* from EARLY DEVELOPING VERBS FOR IMITATION AND NAMING, Table 35, above. Provide a choice of 2 pictures and have the student point to the action that you name; e.g., show me "eating."

Increase to a choice of more than 2 pictures as the student becomes more confident with the task.

Step 2: When the student is able to identify the *familiar* verbs in picture form, introduce *new verbs* from the list TRACKING LATER-DEVELOPING VERBS. Teach these new verbs using real-life activities. Example: Teach "dropping" by deliberately dropping small unbreakable items. Then provide a choice of 2 pictures and have the student point to the new action; e.g., show me "dropping." (If possible, use pictures of the same real-life action as you used to demonstrate it.)

Activity **Expressive**

Either during Steps 1 and 2 or as a separate activity, present single-action pictures and have the student name them. Example: What is/are you/he/she doing? (running).

Use Tim's Game or Hide the Sticker to add incentive.

It is not necessary for the student to use a full sentence structure, but it will be helpful for him to hear you model the complete structure after his response.

Carryover

- Model short sentences about the student's actions. For example, say, "Kyle, you are walking." Shortly after, present a fill-in-the-blank sentence for the student to complete using the same verb. Example: "You are _____" (walking). Then ask, "What are you doing?" (walking).
- Play Lotto, Go Fish, and Memory. Use paired pictures of a variety of verbs; e.g., match "boy running" with the duplicate picture of the boy running.
- Play Fishing, Magic Bag, Tim's Game, and Hide the Sticker using individual verb cards. Play Snakes/Chutes and Ladders using a different verb on each square.
- Take photos of the student and his peers (with permission) carrying out actions during everyday routines and talk about what he/they is/are doing.
- Talk about actions in picture books, videos, TV shows, etc.
- Talk about opposite action words (antonyms); e.g., hold/drop, throw/catch, turn on/turn off, do up/undo, lose/find, push/pull.
- Encourage the student through modeling and prompts to use more linguistically mature verbs during everyday language. For example—Student: "He is getting the ball." Instructor models: "He is *catching* the ball"; Student: "Tom is going." Instructor: "Is there a better word that you could use for 'going'?" Student: "Tom is running."

Table 37: TRACKING LATER-DEVELOPING VERBS

Verb	Receptive	Expressive	Established
Bite			
Bounce			
Break			
Buy			
Catch			
Chase			
Clean			
Climb			
Color			
Comb			
Cook			
Count			
Crawl			
Cut			
Dig			
Drop			
Dry			
Fall			
Feed			
Find			
Fly			
Get			
Give			

(Table 37 continued)

Go			
Have			
Help			
Hide			
Hit			
Hold			
Hop			
Knock			
Laugh			
Lick			
Like			
Listen			
Lose			
Love			
Mail			
Make			
Mix			
Nod			
Paint			
Pick/pick up			
Play			
Pull			
Push			

(Table 37 continued)

Race			
Remember			
Ride			
Roll			
Scratch			
Shout			
Shut			
Skip			
Smile			
Spill			
Stop			
Sweep			
Swing			
Talk			
Thank			
Throw			
Turn			
Wait			
Want			
Wash			
Watch			
Wear			
Write			

Goal 3: The student will sort and match pictures of different people and animals carrying out the same action and name the action; e.g., find all "sitting" (with 80–90 percent accuracy).

Materials

1. 5 pictures of the same verb. Each picture showing the action being carried out by a different person or animal in a different situation; e.g., a cow <u>eating</u> grass, a boy <u>eating</u> a hamburger, a girl <u>eating</u> cereal, a horse <u>eating</u> an apple, a baby <u>eating</u> a cookie.
2. At least 4 different verbs should be targeted; e.g., sleeping, eating, sitting, running.

Note: *Pictures can be downloaded and printed from the Internet or "borrowed" from several different sets of commercial action picture cards.*

Introduction

Introduce the goal by saying that now that the student is able to name what one person is doing in a picture, you are going to show him pictures of people and animals carrying out actions, and he is going to find the ones who are doing the same thing.

Use one set of the 5 pictures of one verb (as described in materials). Name the verb in each picture; e.g., eating. Emphasize that they are each doing the same thing so they are all <u>eating</u>.

Activity **Receptive**

Place the 5 pictures of 2 different verbs in a Magic Bag or mixed up on the table face up. Have the student select a picture from the bag or table and place it in the appropriate pile according to the verb; e.g., all of the pictures of "eating" together and all of the pictures of "running" together.

Activity **Expressive**

When the student is able to sort the pictures, have him name the action in each picture in one pile and then the other. Then have him name them as you hold up a picture or point to one in a pile at random. It is not necessary for the student to use a full sentence structure at this time. Play Magic Bag or Tim's Game to add interest.

Carryover

- Play Lotto games that have multiple pictures of the same verb being carried out by different people or animals. Start with just two verbs; e.g., one card has pictures of people and animals "eating" and another card has pictures of people and animals "sleeping."
- Play "Match the Action" Memory, in which the players are to match the same action but carried out by different people or animals; e.g., a picture of a boy running is matched with a picture of a dog running.

- Play Simon Says.
- Go on assignment. Provide the student with a camera or other digital device for taking photos, and with as much assistance as he needs, have him (or you if he is not capable) take photos of a variety of people and animals carrying out the same action in different settings; e.g., teacher drinking coffee; dad drinking pop; baby drinking milk from a bottle; sibling drinking juice; dog drinking water from a bowl.

Goal 4: The student will describe and perform the action shown in a picture; e.g., a girl holding up her hand (with 80–90 percent accuracy).

Note: *This goal depends on the student's physical ability, his ability to process picture information, and an awareness of his own body. It should be omitted if found to be too challenging.*

Materials:

1. 10–20 photos/pictures that show individual children carrying out an action; e.g., a girl sticking out her tongue; a boy sitting on the floor with his legs crossed.
2. A mirror large enough to show the student's whole body.

Introduction

Tell the student that you are going to play Copy Cat. You are going to look at photos and pictures of children carrying out actions and you are going to do what they are doing. Show a picture, copy the action shown, and describe what you are doing. For example, say "This girl is holding up her hand—I can do that" (demonstrate: hold up your hand). "Look, I am holding up my hand." Present several examples.

Activity **Receptive** and **Expressive**

Take turns performing and describing the action shown in the picture (use Tim's Game to add interest). Use the mirror for the student to compare his action with that shown in the picture.

Carryover

- Name and imitate actions shown in books, on TV, and by other people in real life.

Goal 5: The student will name an action that a person, animal, or object can carry out; e.g., a frog can jump. Also, given the name of an action, state who or what can carry out that action; e.g., who or what can walk? (with 80–90 percent accuracy).

Prerequisites: *Understanding of "who?" and "which?" question words—Chapter 10 ("Wh" Questions), Goals Who?, p. 184 and Which?, p. 193. Chapter 2 (Negative "No/Not"), Goals 1–3, pp. 24-27; reliable use of "yes/no" response—Chapter 4 (Yes/No), Goal 2, p. 42.*

Note: *the change of verb tense for this activity.*

Materials

1. 20 photos/pictures of individual people, animals, or objects able to carry out an action but not actively involved in doing so; e.g., boy, bird, frog, stove, pencil.
2. List of nouns with associated verbs WHAT CAN A PERSON, ANIMAL, OR OBJECT DO? Table 38, below.
3. Activity WHO OR WHAT CAN DO IT? Table 39, below.

Introduction

Tell the student that now that he is able to name lots of "doing" (action) words when he sees them in pictures, you are going to talk about what people, animals, or objects can do, *but the pictures are not going to show the action.*

Present two photos/pictures from materials #1. Ask a question about what one of them can do and model the answer. For example, show a picture of a stove and a pencil, and ask, "Which one can cook?" (stove). Provide several examples.

Activity **Receptive**

Present a choice of two photos/pictures from materials #1. Have the student point to the person, animal, or object that can carry out the action that you name. Example: "Show me the one that can jump" (frog); "show me the one that can dig" (shovel).

Gradually increase the number of pictures from which the student must choose.

Activity **Expressive**

Step 1: Use materials #1. Present individual pictures and ask what the person, animal, or thing can do; e.g., what can a pencil do? (write). To make this more fun, use Tim's Game or a Magic Bag.

Step 2 (for students with reliable yes/no response): Present materials #1 and ask a "can" question related to the verb to which the answer will be either "yes" or "no." For example: "Can a pencil write?" (yes). "Can a pencil sleep?" (no). "Can a frog fly?" (no). "Can a frog jump?" (yes).

When the answer is "no," point out how silly that would be. (This will tie in later with recognizing absurdities in Chapter 13, Advanced Expressive Language, Goal 4, p. 215). For example, a frog cannot fly—it does not have wings— that is silly!

Step 3: Present WHAT CAN A PERSON, ANIMAL, OR OBJECT DO?

For nonreaders: *Read the questions and have the student answer (provide choice answers if necessary). Example: "What can soap do? Soap can wash or sleep?" Record his responses.*

For the reader: *Print the list onto cardstock. Use only the columns of items and actions (discard "student response" and "correct/incorrect"). Cut into individual items and actions. Have the student match items to actions; e.g., soap can—wash. Assist as needed by providing a choice; e.g., "can a dog bark or fly?"; "Can a stove cook or roll?"*

Step 4: Present the activity WHO OR WHAT CAN DO IT?

Print the activity onto cardstock and cut into individual verbs. Put the cards in a Magic Bag or mix them up on the table. Take turns to select a card and ask who or what can carry out the action (read the card for the non-reader). For example: "Who or what can <u>sleep</u>?" (a baby, a dog, Dad); "who or what can <u>mix</u> something?" (mom can mix cookie dough; teacher can mix paint).

Discuss also who or what *cannot* carry out that action and why.

Carryover

- Talk about what people, animals, and things in real-life situations can and cannot do, particularly those who can do more than one action; e.g., a boy can jump, run, sit, catch a ball; a boy cannot drive a car or fly.
- During story time, read an action sentence and ask what other person, animal or thing could have done the same action; Examples: "The dog crawled under the fence"— "who or what else can crawl under a fence?" (a boy, a rabbit). "The fish swam in the pond"—"what other animal can swim in a pond?" (a duck, a beaver).
- Play Alphabet Verbs. Tell a story in which each sentence contains a verb beginning with the next alphabet letter. For example: "Paul <u>a</u>te an apple. After lunch he <u>b</u>aked cookies. Paul <u>c</u>alled to his mom." Take turns making up the sentences or work on them collaboratively.

Table 38: WHAT CAN A PERSON, ANIMAL, OR OBJECT DO?

Items	Actions	Student Response	Correct/Incorrect
A pen can	write		
A fish can	swim		
An airplane can	fly		
Soap can	wash		
A door can	open and close		
A towel can	dry		
Ears can	hear		
A shovel can	dig		
A clock can	tell time		
A rabbit can	hop		
A baby can	cry		
A stove can	cook		
A child can	play		
Grass can	grow		
Teeth can	bite		
Scissors can	cut		
A dog can	bark		
A bell can	ring		
A duck can	say quack		
The wind can	blow		

Table 39: WHO OR WHAT CAN DO IT?

Bite	Bounce	Break	Chase
Climb	Crawl	Cut	Dry
Hit	Hop	Help	Hold
Lick	Listen	Make	Mix
Paint	Pick up	Play	Pull
Push	Ride	Roll	Scratch
Shut	Spill	Stop	Swim
Turn	Wait	Watch	Wear

Goal 6: The student will identify the reason why we carry out specific actions; e.g., why do we sweep the floor? Why do we wash our hands? (with 80–90 percent accuracy).

Prerequisite: *Understanding of "why?" questions—Chapter 10 ("Wh" Questions), Goal Why?, "B," p. 203 and use of conjunctions "because" or "so/so that"—Chapter 10 ("Wh" Questions), Why? General Suggestions, p. 200-01.*

Materials

1. 20 pictures of individual people and/or animals each carrying out an action with the reason for his/her/its action obvious in the picture; e.g., a cat running up a tree to get away from a dog; a girl putting on a jacket to go outside.
2. List WHY? QUESTIONS RELATED TO ACTIONS, Table 40, below.

Introduction

Tell the student that you are going to talk about why people and animals carry out actions. Show an action picture (materials #1) and model a "why?" question and answer involving the action shown. Example: Why is the girl running? (She is running because she wants to catch the school bus.) Present several examples.

Activity **Receptive** and **Expressive**

Step 1: Present materials #1, one at a time, and ask the student a "why?" question related to the action; e.g., why is the dog barking? Provide a choice answer if necessary; e.g., because it is chasing the cat or because it is sleepy?

Encourage the student to use "because" or "so/so that" when responding. However, this is not essential at this stage as long as he is able to give an appropriate reason; e.g., why is the cat climbing the tree? (so/so that it can get away from the dog).

Step 2: Present WHY? QUESTIONS RELATED TO ACTIONS:

For non-readers: *Ask "why?" questions and encourage the student to answer using "because," "so/so that," or "to." Example: "Why do we wash our hands?" Student: "[because] they are dirty" or "[so] they are clean" or "to get them clean." Model the complete structure after the student has responded if he has omitted words. Write down his responses and compare them with those that he gives when you repeat the activity during a subsequent therapy session.*

For the reader: *Print the questions on cardstock and cut them out. Take turns to pick a question and answer it, or read it to the other person and have him answer it (this is excellent practice for conversational turn taking).*

Table 40: WHY? QUESTIONS RELATED TO ACTIONS

Question	Student Response	Correct/ Incorrect
1. Why do we wear a jacket?		
2. Why do we brush our hair?		
3. Why do we wash our hands?		
4. Why do cars stop?		
5. Why do we put ice cream in the freezer?		
6. Why do children go to school?		
7. Why do we eat food?		
8. Why do we talk on the phone?		
9. Why do we turn on the TV?		
10. Why do we use an umbrella?		
11. Why do we turn on the light?		
12. Why do we laugh?		
13. Why do we sit at the table?		
14. Why do dogs bark?		
15. Why do babies cry?		
16. Why do we cut the grass?		
17. Why do we need money?		
18. Why do we visit the doctor?		
19. Why do we close our eyes?		
20. Why do we wave?		

Carryover

- Ask "why?" questions related to activities that the student, other people, or animals are carrying out during the day. Examples: Why are you putting on your boots? Why are we going outside?
- Ask "why?" questions about actions in stories and movies. Examples: Why is the man climbing the ladder? Why did the boy go into the cave?

Goal 7: The student will define verbs using a Verb Word Web (with 80–90 percent accuracy).

Materials

1. Blank copies of VERB WORD WEB, Table 41, below.
2. VERB WORD WEB GAME, Table 42, below, printed on cardstock.
3. List TRACKING LATER-DEVELOPING VERBS, p. 105.

Introduction

Tell the student to think of a spider web and imagine that the action word that you are going to talk about is in the center of the web and questions about that word are around the edge. Show VERB WORD WEB to the student (even if he is not able to read).

Choose an action word (verb) familiar to the student and write it in the center of the web. Then model asking and answering the questions around the edge. Example: target verb "jump." Who can <u>jump</u>? (frog, boy, horse). Why do we <u>jump</u>? (for fun, to get away from something). What do you need to <u>jump</u>? (nothing—just your feet).

Activity **Receptive** and **Expressive**

Present a familiar verb, or have the student choose one, then together define it using the questions on the branches of VERB WORD WEB. Write your answers on a blank copy of the WORD WEB (be aware that not all questions are appropriate for every verb).

For the reader: *Print VERB WORD WEB GAME on cardstock and cut out the questions. Take turns asking the other person a question in relation to the target word.*

For variety, print the questions on cardstock and glue them onto the sides of a cube. Roll the cube ("dice") and ask the question that lands face up.

Carryover

- Discuss action words in settings through the day; e.g., Darryl is painting—what else could he do in free playtime? Why is he painting? Do you get to paint sometimes?

Table 41: VERB WORD WEB

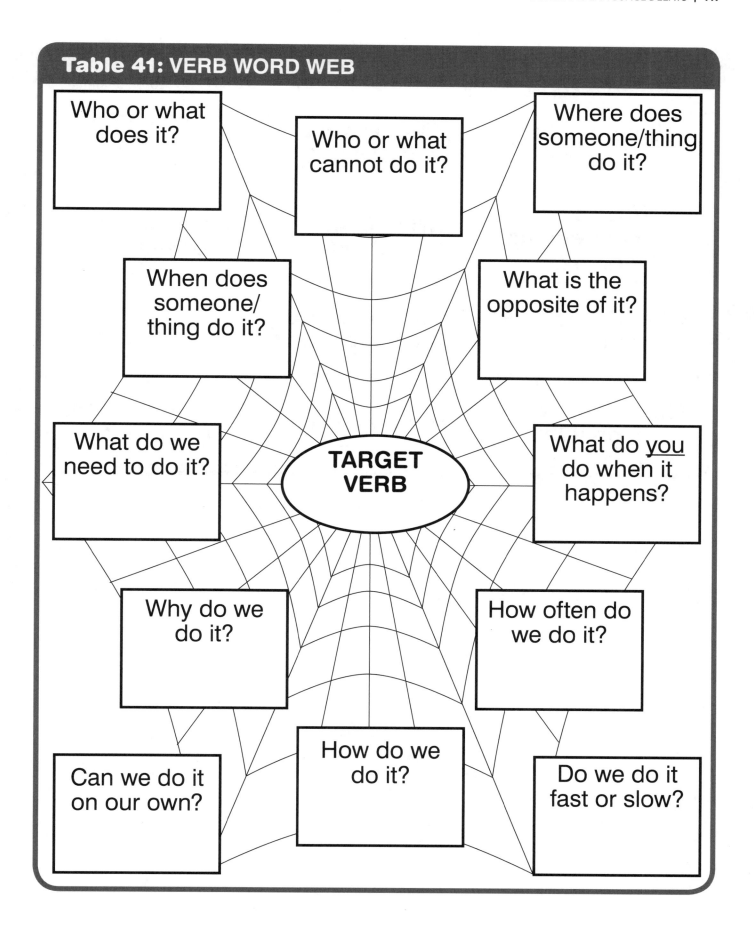

Who or what does it?

Who or what cannot do it?

Where does someone/thing do it?

When does someone/thing do it?

What is the opposite of it?

What do we need to do it?

TARGET VERB

What do <u>you</u> do when it happens?

Why do we do it?

How often do we do it?

Can we do it on our own?

How do we do it?

Do we do it fast or slow?

Table 42: VERB WORD WEB GAME

Who or what does it?	Who or what cannot do it?	Where does someone/thing do it?
When does someone/thing do it?	What is the opposite of it?	Do we do it fast or slow?
What do we need to do it?	What do you do when it happens?	Why do we do it?
How often do we do it?	How do we do it?	Can we do it on our own?

8.
Descriptors

> **These goals are appropriate for students with one or more of the following characteristics:**
>
> - does not understand descriptors in directions and oral and/or written information; e.g., give me the bag that is full
>
> - uses nouns and verbs but does not augment them with descriptors; e.g., big dog; run fast
>
> - uses expressive language lacking in information
>
> - has difficulty comparing one person, animal, or thing to another; e.g., which animal is spotted?

Descriptors Goals

The student will understand and use:

Goal 1: names of primary colors.

Goal 2: size—big/little.

Goal 3: color and size together; e.g., big red apple.

Goal 4: a variety of descriptors; e.g., long, easy, smooth, full.

Goal 5: names of feelings and emotions; e.g., happy, angry, thirsty.

Goal 6: descriptors that are opposites (antonyms); e.g., hard/soft.

Goal 1: The student will understand and use the names of primary colors (with 80–90 percent accuracy).

Prerequisite: *Ability to use words "same" and "different" applied to identical and non-identical objects—Chapter 3 (Same and Different), Goal 1, p. 30.*

Materials

1. *Identical* objects; e.g., blocks, beads, buttons, pom-poms. 8 of each primary color; e.g., 8 square blue blocks, 8 square red blocks, 8 square green blocks, etc.
2. Groups of *non-identical* objects of each primary color (6 of each color in a group); e.g., red pen, red ribbon, red plastic flower, red mitt, red toy car, red ball; blue crayon, blue hat, etc. The objects must be predominately one color but may have small amounts of other colors on them too. The shade and depth of the primary color will vary somewhat from one object to another.
3. Cardboard barrier for Barrier game (p. 7).
4. List TRACKING UNDERSTANDING AND USE OF PRIMARY COLORS, Table 43, below.

Assess Knowledge of Color Names

Prior to the start of this goal assess the student's knowledge of color names to determine the order in which to teach the colors.

This can be carried out through a standardized test or on an informal basis. The SLP may have the student try to name spontaneously the color of one example of each of the groups of identical and non-identical objects in materials #1 and #2. Or she may have the student try to name the color after a model and a short time delay. The student may have been observed using a color name correctly in a different situation, or she may be particularly attracted to one color; e.g., the color of the marker pen that she chooses when offered a choice of multiple colors.

Introduction

Decide on a target color and introduce the goal by telling the student that she is going to learn the color; e.g., blue.

If the student was unable to name *any* colors during the assessment start to teach using Teach a Single Target Color, in the next section.

If the student is able to name *one or more* color(s), start teaching with Teach a New Color Contrasted with a Known Color, p. 122. Use the known color(s) as the contrast when teaching the new color.

Provide support as needed to the student who can read by presenting the target color name written on a cue card preferably of the same color; e.g., "blue" written on blue cardstock.

Teach a Single Target Color

Choose a target color—either the preferred color that the student indicated or in developmental order selected from TRACKING UNDERSTANDING AND USE OF PRIMARY COLORS, Table 43.

Activity **Receptive**

Step 1: Use the objects that are *identical* except for color (materials #1). Have the student sort and match objects of the target color from groups of 4–8 objects (depending on the student's ability).

Make up the groups from objects of:
  a. Target color and 1 other color; e.g., sort target "blue" from a group of red and blue otherwise identical objects.
  b. Target color and 2 or more other colors; e.g., sort target "blue" from a group of red, yellow, green, and blue otherwise identical objects.

Use the name of the target color only and omit the noun; e.g., find "blue" *not* "find the blue dogs."

Step 2: Use the groups of *non-identical objects* of primary colors (materials #2) and have the student sort and match as for Step 1. This is a more difficult task because the student is required to generalize the color over a dark and light spectrum and a variety of shapes and sizes.

Model the name of the target color at every opportunity and encourage the student to imitate it.

Activity **Expressive**

Have the student name the target color when presented with:
  a. Objects that are identical in every way except color.
  b. Non-identical objects of primary colors.

To assist:
  ○ present a choice of color name; e.g., blue or red? (blue)
  ○ use sentence completion; e.g., the pen is _____ (blue);
  ○ provide the first sound of the target color; e.g., the block is bl_____";
  ○ show the color cue card to the student who can read.

Gradually fade the assistance and have the student generate the color name independently. Once the student becomes competent at naming the target color model, encourage her to add the noun; e.g., red t-shirt; red hat, red socks.

When the student is able to select the target color and use its name with 80–90 percent accuracy, progress to Step 2. Track progress using list TRACKING UNDERSTANDING AND USE OF PRIMARY COLORS.

Carryover

● See 24 COLOR ACTIVITIES, below.

Teach a New Color Contrasted with a Known Color

Use the color that the student knew before working on this goal or the one that she has just learned (established); e.g., blue and <u>red</u>. Either choose a color preferred by the student or select the next color in the developmental order as the new target color.

Activity **Receptive**

Step 1: Use the *objects that are identical in every way* (materials #1). Have the student sort and match objects of the old and new target colors from groups of 4–8 objects (depending on the student's ability). Make up the groups of objects from:

    a. The established color and the new target color; e.g., sort new target "red" from blue (established) and red objects.

    b. The new target color and several other colors; e.g., sort new target "red" from a group of green, brown, red, and purple objects.

Use only the names of the new target and established colors and omit the nouns; e.g., find "red" not "find the red dog." Support students who can read with the written color words as needed.

Step 2: When the student has completed Step 1 to 80–90 percent accuracy, use the *objects that are identical in every way* again (materials #1). Name the new and established colors at random and have the student give you an object of the color that you name; e.g., give me blue; give me red.

Step 3: Use the *non-identical objects* of primary colors (materials #2). Have the student sort and match as for Step 1. This is a more difficult task because the student is required to generalize the color over a dark and light spectrum and a variety of shapes and sizes.

Step 4: When the student has completed Step 3 to 80–90 percent accuracy, use the *non-identical objects* of primary colors (materials #2). Name the new and established colors at random and have the student give you an object of the color that you name (as for Step 2).

Step 5: Play a barrier game (p. 7). Use the objects that are *identical* (materials #1). Use 2 objects of the original target color and 2 of your chosen contrasting color; e.g., 2 identical red buttons and 2 identical blue buttons. Place one from each pair on either side of the barrier. Pick up an object on your side of the barrier and tell the student to pick up the same color; e.g., pick up "blue." Remove the barrier and check that you are both holding the same color.

Activity **Expressive**

Step 1: Have the student name the established and the new target colors when presented with:

    a. Objects that are identical in every way except color (materials #1).

    b. Non-identical objects of primary colors (materials #2).

The student should be naming the established target color independently but may need prompts, modeling, choices, or the written color names (for the reader) to assist with generating the new target color.

Gradually fade the support and have the student name both colors independently.

Step 2: Play the barrier game as already described in Activity *Receptive,* Step 5. Use the objects that are *identical* (materials #1), but have the student be the teacher. Have her tell you which color to pick up to match the one in her hand. Be careful that she does not try to change her color for the other one if she has named it incorrectly when giving the direction and she finds that the one in her hand is not the same as the one in yours.

When two colors are understood and used to 80–90 percent accuracy, repeat the steps above for each new target color until all primary colors are learned.

Carryover: 20 COLOR ACTIVITIES

1. Name the color of food at meal/snack times and offer color choices; e.g., "do you want the green grapes or the red ones?"
2. Name the color of clothing that people are wearing. Sometimes dress completely in the target color. Offer color choices; e.g., "do you want to wear the blue t-shirt or the red one?"
3. Have only the target colors available for craft or painting activities (crayons, paints, pom-poms). Have the student ask for the color she wants.
4. Put craft supplies, treats, or other desirable items in different-colored containers—have her name the color correctly to get the contents.
5. Go on a Color Walk—name everything you see that is of the target color.
6. Read storybooks that refer to target colors; e.g., *Brown Bear, Brown Bear, What Do You See?* by Bill Martin Jr. and Eric Carle.
7. Package separate work or tabletop leisure activities in Zip-lock bags and color code them using colored electrical tape. Ask, for example, "Shall we do the green or the yellow activity next?"
8. Tape dinosaur footprints cut out of cardstock on the floor and have the student follow the ones of the target color to a destination or reward; e.g., "follow the orange footprints to the trampoline."
9. Fix a paper square of the target color to the doorframe of the classroom—have the student touch it and name the color each time she goes in or out.
10. Sort items by color into containers labeled with the color name—foam shapes, Lego pieces, pegs for a pegboard, bingo chips, pipe cleaners, pom-poms, crayons, and markers.
11. Make a color collage of pictures from magazines and catalogs.
12. Create a verbal or written list of things that are of the target color; e.g., "green—peas, grass, leaves, lizard, frog."
13. Play Bowling using pins of different colors made from milk cartons or plastic water bottles (tie colored ribbon around them). Each player must say which colors she knocked over; e.g., "I knocked over a red one and a brown one."
14. Play Tiddlywinks—using counters of the target and contrasted colors.
15. Have the student follow directions during crafts or baking that involve color; e.g., "put the orange modeling clay in the bag"; "put the red sprinkles on the cookies."

16. Paint by numbers. Write numbers on areas of an ability-appropriate coloring sheet; e.g., picture of a flower or car. Write out a key; e.g., 1 = blue, 2 = green, etc. Have the student color the picture using the designated colors; e.g., blue for wheels; yellow for body of car.
17. Play Lotto, Memory, Go Fish, Fishing, and Snakes/Chutes and Ladders using colors.
18. Play Snap to work on the colors red and black or make cards of other target colors.
19. Make a collection of things that have 2 colors on them; e.g., leaf—yellow and red; T shirt— blue and brown.
20. Play commercial color sorting/matching games, computer programs, and apps.

Table 43: TRACKING UNDERSTANDING AND USE OF PRIMARY COLORS

Color*	Receptive	Expressive	Established
Red			
Blue			
Green			
Purple			
Yellow			
Orange			
Brown			
Black			
Pink			
Gray			
White			

*Colors are presented in developmental order from *A Work in Progress,* edited by Ron Leaf and John McEachin (New York, NY: DRL Books, 1999). Used with permission.

Goal 2: The student will understand and use descriptors "big" and "little" (with 80–90 percent accuracy).

Materials

1. 2 sets of 10 paired toys and objects that are *identical in every way* except for size; e.g., big red ball/little red ball; big plastic cup/little plastic cup of same design and color. The size variance must be sufficient to easily identify them as "big" or "little."
2. Cardboard barrier for Barrier game.

Introduction

Introduce the goal by telling the student that she is going to learn the words "big" and "little."

Use one of the pairs of toys and objects that are big and little (materials #1). Draw attention to the size difference by comparing the objects side by side, and describe them as "big" and "little." Present more examples.

Provide support as needed to the student who can read by presenting the target words "big" and "little" written on individual cue cards.

Note: *In the activities below, it may be necessary to work on only "big" at first to 80–90 percent accuracy before introducing and working on only "little" to 80–90% accuracy before then working on both "big" and "little" together.*

Activity **Receptive**

Step 1: Present individual pairs of identical big/little objects (materials #1). Have the student select the "big" one of each pair (model and assist as needed). Then, put the pairs back together and have her select the "little" one of each pair.

Present several pairs at the same time and have her put all the little toys/objects together and all of the big toys/objects together.

When she is able to select "big" and "little" in this way with 80–90 percent accuracy, put the pairs back together and request "big" and "little" at random.

Throughout Step 1, name the size and omit the noun; e.g., Say, "show me 'big'" rather than "show me 'big cup.'" Add the noun when the student is able to select "big" and "little" as requested at random with 80–90 percent accuracy.

Step 2: Play a barrier game using 2 sets of the paired objects that are identical in every way except size (materials #1); e.g., 2 big red balls and 2 little red balls. Place one of each pair on either side of the barrier. Pick up either a big or little object on your side of the barrier and direct the student to pick up the object of the same size without her being able to see which one you are holding; e.g., pick up "big." Remove the barrier and check that you are both holding the object of the same size.

Increase the number of object choices and add the noun as the student becomes more competent; e.g., pick up big pencil.

Step 3: Use the pairs of identical objects (materials #1). Make statements and have the student show you the toy/object that you describe; e.g., show me "the cup is <u>big</u>"; show me "the dog is <u>little</u>."

Activity **Expressive**

Step 1: Place a pair of matched big and little toys/objects (materials #1) on the table in front of the student and point to one of them. Have the student tell you the size; e.g., <u>big</u>. Present each of the other pairs and point to big and little at random.

Step 2: Play the barrier game as already described but have the student be the teacher. Have her pick up 1 of a pair of objects and tell you which size to pick up to match the one in her hand; e.g., pick up <u>little</u>. Be careful that she does not try to switch her object for the other one if she has named it incorrectly when giving the command and finds that the one in her hand is not the same as the one in yours.

Increase the number of object choices and have the student add the noun as she becomes more competent at stating the size; e.g., <u>big</u> car, <u>little</u> block.

Step 3: Place a pair of matched big and little toys/objects (materials #1) on the table in front of the student and have her tell you about the toy/object that you point to. Example: "Tell me about this ball." Response: "The ball is big." Example: "Tell me about this cup." Response: "The cup is little." Add interest by using a Magic Bag (have her compare the one she takes out of the bag with the other one of the pair that you have on the table).

Carryover

- Compare the size of everyday objects that have the same name but are not otherwise identical; e.g., big shoe/little shoe; big can/little can of food in the grocery store; big car/little car parked in the parking lot.
- Offer foods or portions of different sizes; e.g., do you want the big cookie/sausage/potato or the little cookie/sausage/potato?
- Use big and little identical items for crafts and activities; e.g., pom-poms, googly eyes, stickers, paintbrushes, marker pens. Have the student request the size that she wants to use.
- Use pictures from a catalog or magazine to make a collage of things that are either big or little.
- Compare baby and adult animals; e.g., big cow/little cow.
- Play Tiddlywinks using big and little counters.
- Read stories that have size as a theme; e.g., the fairy tale *Goldilocks and the Three Bears*.
- Ask questions such as "Can a grown-up wear that shoe?" "No, it's too little." "Can an elephant live in our house?" "No, an elephant is too big."
- Play commercial card games, computer games, and apps that have big and little as a theme.

Goal 3: The student will understand and use color and size together; e.g., the big blue car (with 80–90 percent accuracy).

Materials

1. 2 sets of paired toys/objects that have the same name but vary by size and color and are otherwise identical; e.g., 2 big white socks/2 little red socks; 2 big blue cars/2 little yellow cars. The size variance must be sufficient to easily identify them as "big" or "little."
2. Cardboard barrier for Barrier game.

Introduction

Explain to the student that now that she is able to tell you the color and the size of an object, she is going to put both of these words together.

Present a pair of small toys or objects that have the same name but vary by size and color. Describe each of the pair according to its size and then its color followed by both size and color together. Example: This is a <u>big</u> sock and this is a <u>little</u> sock. This one is <u>white</u> and this one is <u>red</u>. This is a "<u>big white</u> sock" and this is a "<u>little red</u> sock." Model other examples.

Activity **Receptive**

Step1: Use the paired toys and objects (materials #1). Have the student find the one that you describe; e.g., find the <u>big brown</u> crayon.

Step 2: Play a barrier game. Use the paired toys and objects and place one of each pair on either side of the barrier. Direct the student to pick up the same object as you pick up. Remove the barrier and check that you are both holding the same object; e.g., <u>little yellow</u> car.

Activity **Expressive**

Step 1: Place paired toys and objects on the table in front of the student and point to one of them. Have the student name the object and describe its size and color; e.g., <u>big blue</u> block.

Step 2: Play the barrier game as already described but with the student as the teacher. Have her tell you which toy or object to pick up to match the one in her hand; e.g., pick up "<u>big red</u> crayon."

Carryover

- Encourage the use of size and color descriptors throughout the day. For example, sort through the "Lost and Found" for the small brown shoe; big blue shoe.
- Have the student follow directions; e.g., give your big blue book to the teacher; put your little red crayon in your desk.

- Talk about flowers and birds in books and real life; e.g., little yellow bird; big white flower.
- Play "Beanbag Toss" using big and little bags of different colors. Describe which bean bag hit the target; e.g., the big orange bag.

Goal 4: The student will understand and use a variety of descriptors; e.g., long, easy, smooth, full (with 80–90 percent accuracy).

Materials

1. Toys, objects, pictures, and real-life experiences (as suggested in list below).
2. List OPPORTUNITIES FOR TEACHING DESCRIPTORS, Table 44, below.
3. List TRACKING DESCRIPTORS, Table 45, below
4. List TELL ME ABOUT…. , Table 46, below.

Introduction

Select target descriptors from the list OPPORTUNITIES FOR TEACHING DESCRIP-TORS that are relevant to the student's environment and interests and that she is likely to hear and need to use frequently. Tie your selection in with current classroom themes and vocabulary lists recommended for the student's grade level and curriculum.

Use 20 SUGGESTIONS FOR TEACHING A VARIETY OF DESCRIPTORS (below) and the recommendations for specific descriptors listed in OPPORTUNITIES FOR TEACHING DE-SCRIPTORS. Also look for teachable moments unique to the student's situation and interests.

Tell the student that she is going to learn a new word to describe (talk about) things. Model the descriptor before starting formal or table top activities; e.g., today we are going to use the word "wet." Model and use target descriptors frequently in non-structured activities; e.g., talk about heavy/light when packing/unpacking the student's school bag.

Track the student's progress using TRACKING DESCRIPTORS and support the reader with target words written on cue cards.

20 SUGGESTIONS FOR TEACHING A VARIETY OF DESCRIPTORS

1. Use real-life examples and situations; objects or realistic miniatures; photos and pictures that illustrate the descriptor.
2. Present paired items and have the student identify the one that you describe; e.g., show me the one that is "dry"; show me the one that is "wet."
3. Read story books and rhymes that contain target descriptors; e.g., *Old Hat, New Hat* by Stan and Jan Berenstain.
4. Encourage the use of a descriptor:
   a. immediately after hearing it modeled (imitation)
   b. in response to a direct or choice question (e.g., how does it feel? Do you want the thick marker or the thin marker?)

    c. in sentence completion; e.g., this box is full and this box is _____ (empty)

    d. when comparing and contrasting items; e.g., this one is wet [given wet and dry items to compare]

    e. in statements and conversation; e.g., I saw a fluffy kitten. The pillow is soft.

5. Play "What Things Are _____?" Complete the question with a descriptor; e.g., what things are tall? What things are cold? Make a list of things, animals, or people that match that description; e.g., tall—tree, building, Dad, flagpole.

6. Go on a walk in the school or outside and find things that match the target descriptor. For example, let's find all the things that are "rough."

7. Make collections of things that have the same group name or category but vary in texture, size, or shape; e.g., collection of balls—soft, hard, furry, smooth; leaves—big, small, rough. Other collections: buttons, small pieces of fabric, animals, vehicles.

8. Play Go Fish. Players must describe the picture that they want to match the card in their hand without saying the name of it. For example, when playing with animal cards: "I want the animal with the long neck."

9. Play I Spy. Describe an object and have the student guess what you are thinking of. Keep the game simple by describing items within sight; e.g., it is hard (chair). When it is the student's turn to describe something caution her to give a description only and not name the item.

10. Teach negative descriptors using "not." Play a game of elimination. Place a choice of toys, objects, or pictures of single items on the table and have the student guess which one you are thinking of when you describe its negative attributes; e.g., it is *not* round; it does *not* run fast.

11. Put a toy or object into a Touch Bag. Without looking at the toy/object, take turns to put your hand into the bag and describe how it feels; e.g., eraser, cotton ball, rock, comb, piece of sandpaper.

12. Blow bubbles and describe how they look; e.g., big, small, round, shiny.

13. Play a Descriptive Barrier game. Use commercial paired cards of the same object presented with different features; e.g., teddy bears—brown with curly hair; yellow with a red bow; skinny with a brown nose. Pick up one of the cards on your side of the barrier then describe it and have the student select the same one from her side of the barrier; e.g., pick up the brown bear with the curly hair. Remove the barrier and check to see that you both picked up the same one.

14. Play Mrs. Mumpy's Cat. Take turns describing the cat (or substitute any other item) using a different descriptor as you progress through the alphabet. For example, Mrs. Mumpy's cat is <u>a</u>dorable; Mrs. Mumpy's cat is <u>b</u>eautiful, <u>c</u>ute, <u>d</u>ull, etc.

15. Play Descriptive Memory. Name an item and take turns describing it by adding a descriptor; e.g., a car—a big car; a big shiny car; a big shiny red car; a big, shiny, red, fast car (excellent practice for auditory memory!).

16. Give directions that include a descriptor; e.g., put the heavy book on your desk; take the wet towel to the sink.

17. Do a floor-puzzle. Lay all of the pieces face up on the floor within sight but out of reach of the student. Have her describe the puzzle piece that she wants you to pass to her so that she can put it into the puzzle.

18. Decorate a tree for a season or event such as winter, Halloween, or Christmas. Have the student describe the decoration that she is putting on; e.g., a shiny silver snowflake; a small red heart; a scary ghost.

19. Play Snakes/Chutes and Ladders. Create a board that has a picture of a different item on each square. Players must describe the item that they land on.
20. Play commercial games, computer programs, and apps that involve descriptors as their theme.

Activity **Receptive** and **Expressive**

When the student has developed a varied vocabulary of descriptors, present the activity TELL ME ABOUT…. Have the student describe items that are not in sight. Take turns adding a descriptor or describe the complete item. Include color, size, texture, and shape as well as what the object does, what it is used for, and where it lives or is kept.

For the reader: *Print the activity TELL ME ABOUT…. on cardstock and cut the list of items into individual cards (discard the other two columns). Take turns to pick up a card (use a Magic Bag or Tim's Game). Describe the items and use several descriptors.*

Carryover

- Inform parents, teachers, and other caregivers of the target descriptor(s) and suggest carryover activities from the list of General Suggestions (above) or OPPORTUNITIES FOR TEACHING DESCRIPTORS.

Goal 5: The student will understand and use the names of feelings and emotions; e.g., sad, hungry, tired (with 80–90 percent accuracy).

Materials

1. Real-life situations, pictures, and photos showing emotions experienced by the student, other people, and animals (as suggested in list below).
2. List OPPORTUNITIES FOR TEACHING FEELINGS AND EMOTIONS, Table 47, below.
3. List TRACKING FEELINGS AND EMOTIONS, Table 48, below.

Introduction

Introduce this goal by telling the student that you are going to talk about words that tell us how we or someone else feels.

Name and discuss feelings and emotions experienced by people and animals in real-life situations, particularly events and situations that pertain to the student; e.g., explain that right now we feel "happy," but soon it will be close to lunchtime and we will feel "hungry." If we don't get to eat lunch when we want to, we might feel "angry."

Choose a target feeling or emotion that is frequently experienced by the student from TRACKING FEELINGS AND EMOTIONS. Teach its name through the general activities below and the activities listed in OPPORTUNITIES FOR TEACHING FEELINGS AND EMOTIONS.

Table 44: OPPORTUNITIES FOR TEACHING DESCRIPTORS

Descriptors can be targeted in any order depending on the student's interests.

Descriptors	Opportunities
Wet/Dry	Wash/dry hands; paper towel; towel after shower or bath; paint; laundry in washer/dryer; condensation on window; pavement, leaves, windows after rain; water play; e.g., water guns, sponges.
Hot/Cold	Hands; hot/cold taps at sink; containers; e.g., bottles of hot/cold water; winter/summer weather and hot/cold clothing; sun/snow; soup/popsicle; stove/fridge; heating pad in microwave/cold pack in freezer.
Clean/Dirty	Before/after washing hands, teeth, fingernails, floor, clothes, shoes, car; water; mud; food or paint on clothing or hands. Read *Harry the Dirty Dog* by Gene Zion.
Tall/Short	People, animals (giraffe/pig); trees (Christmas trees); buildings; tower of blocks; flagpoles; play equipment (slide).
Heavy/Light	Fill identical containers with different substances—compare weight (puff balls, marshmallows, sand, rocks); compare weight of books, backpacks, lunch bag before/after lunch; brick/feather. Use balance weight scales— watch to see which side goes down with the heavy item on it. Use electronic weigh scales and compare items. Play Bowling— fill the bottles with heavy/light items and find out which are the easiest to knock over.
Empty/Full	Compare identical containers of liquids or solids; e.g., water, juice, sand; lunch bag before/after meal; backpack; plate at mealtime; tummy before/after eating. Play Bowling—fill some bottles full and leave others empty and find out which are the easiest to knock over. Water play—full/empty water gun, bucket, water balloons.
Hard/Soft	Brick/pillow; wood/blanket; bed/floor; wooden toys/stuffed toys; turtle shell/kitten fur; foods—apple/marshmallow; make bread—soft dough/hard crust; level of inflation of bike or car tire, basketball, or football. Cook noodles or spaghetti and observe change from hard to soft.
Young/Old	Things that grow—people, animals, trees—e.g., child/grandparents, baby/full grown animals, sapling/full-grown tree.
Old/New	Paired old and new real objects; e.g., clothes (shoe, hat, sock, shirt); items that are used so "old" (drinking straw, pencil, book); activities that are new compared with ones that have been done before; old /new way of doing something; e.g., new door to use to go out for recess. Pretend play (or real) shopping to buy a new/replacement item.
Long/Short	Measurement—compare lengths one against another or measure using a ruler or tape measure. Things that stretch from short to long—elastics, stretchy rubber toys. Things that grow—people's hair, arms, legs, animals' fur. Line up of people/animals; snakes; pencils; line drawn on paper; road/trip; map route—take the long/short way to get somewhere.

(Table 44 continued)

Descriptors	Opportunities
Thick/Thin	Tip of felt marker pens; paint brushes; sliced food; e.g., French fries, bread, cucumber, cheese, meat, apple, banana; books; jacket for winter or summer.
Rough/ Smooth	Surfaces; e.g., varnished/rough wood, plastic; fabric textures; animal fur; skins of fruits (apple/kiwi, banana/pineapple). Sandpaper/regular paper.
Open/Closed (shut)	Velcro fastener; door of classroom, cupboard, fridge; window; fingers; mouth; book; program on computer; box; backpack; lunchbox, desk.
Slow/Fast	Action or job (run, walk, finish page of school work); walk or run between pylons slow or fast; remote control vehicle. Grow bean seeds in good soil and poor—compare the speed of growth. Compare speed of animals/vehicles; e.g., horse/turtle; fire truck/bicycle.
High/Low	Shelves of different height; stand on tiptoe, reach up high/bend down low; things that fly (kite, bird). Notes on an instrument (keyboard, piano) or sing high/low. Swing on a swing.
Large/Small	Explain "large" and "small" are other words for "big" and "little." Avoid using same examples as for big/little. Compare—animals (elephant/mouse), size of clothing, space in classroom/work room, printing on blackboard.
Medium size	Objects of 3 sizes: big/little/medium; e.g., gloves, socks, shoes, containers from fast food restaurants; 3 stacking tubs or rings; snack/treat that can be divided into parts/pieces; choice of size paper or craft items for art work. Story of Goldilocks and the Three Bears.
Backwards/ Forwards	Walk, hop, jump backwards/forwards to the gym or between two pylons; move toy car, vehicle, or animal; swing on swing set; rock on rocking chair; guide remote control vehicle; point; wear clothes backwards; say things backwards; e.g., morning good.
Wide/Narrow	Compare one against another or measure with a ruler pieces of ribbon, tips of felt marker pens, pasta noodles, people's feet, space between desks, rivers, roads, and paths on a map.
Straight/ Crooked	Snakes; sticks; trees; pasta noodles; roads and rivers on a map or made in sandbox; draw lines; roll marbles in finger paint; write letters/words; picture hanging on the wall; stand straight.
Broken/Fixed	Any functional item that can be broken and fixed with glue, tape, or a tool or by replacing a part; e.g., toy, window pane, computer, chair. Things that can break but not be fixed; e.g., a stick, cookie, or chip. Broken bones/cast.
Spotted/ Striped	Cheetah/tiger; Dalmatian dog/zebra; fabric; drawing (butterfly—stripes/spots on wings); pattern on t-shirt, umbrella, hat, or pajamas.

(Table 44 continued)

Descriptors	Opportunities
Easy/Difficult	Have the student carry out a variety of jobs or activities that vary in degree of difficulty and decide if they are easy or difficult; e.g., remove tops of different tightness from bottles, build a tower of 3–15 blocks, do up zipper/buttons, stand on one foot, jump skipping rope, thread beads of different sizes, walk toe to heel, throw beanbags at targets of varying size, balance on a narrow beam, pour water in containers without spilling it.
Quiet/Noisy (loud)	Volume of radio/CD player, instruments; voices in classroom (indoor/outdoor voice); compare animal noises.
Missing	Hide or fail to provide a needed item; e.g., spoon at dessert time or shoe at recess. Toys, objects, or commercial pictures of items that have parts missing; e.g., bike without wheel or Mr. Potato Head with missing front teeth. Game—show 4 objects, student closes eyes while you take one object away, then student guesses what is missing. See also: Chapter 13 (Advanced Expressive Language), Goal 5, p. 272.
Other	Pairs of identical items or pictures—select one/have the student show you the other one from a group; e.g., here is a dog—show me the other dog. Play Memory using any pictures—find the other; e.g., cat.
Together/Separated	Put things together in pairs—shoes, socks; put hands/feet together; put multiple items together—all the books, blocks; snap together toys— beads, Unifix cubes; associated items such as toothbrush/toothpaste; join things together—train cars, magnets, craft items; do a joint activity together with a peer. Sing the folk song "The More We Get Together."
First/Last	Line up of animals, people, or peers waiting for something (drink, bus, to go to another classroom). Must be an obvious beginning/end to the line; e.g., line up animals to go into a barn; cars going into a garage. Marble run—order of colored marbles. Place pencils in a line (left to right) on the table—give directions to use the first or last one; e.g., draw a circle with the first pencil; draw a line with the last pencil.
Second/Third	Line up of cars, train coaches, people, animals; stacking colored rings; marble run—order of colored marbles as you send them through the run.
Front/Back	Clothing—front/back of shirt, coat; own body; entrance to building—front door/back door; animals—front leg/back leg; bike—front wheel/back wheel. Book—front/back cover. Row of seats or desks—front row/back row.
Same/Different	See Chapter 3 (Same and Different).

Table 45: TRACKING DESCRIPTORS

Descriptor	Receptive	Expressive	Established
Wet			
Dry			
Hot			
Cold			
Clean			
Dirty			
Tall			
Short			
Heavy			
Light			
Empty			
Full			
Hard			
Soft			
Young			
Old			
New			
Long			
Short			
Thick			

(Table 45 continued)

Descriptor	Receptive	Expressive	Established
Thin			
Rough			
Smooth			
Open			
Closed (shut)			
Slow			
Fast			
High			
Low			
Large			
Small			
Medium size			
Backwards			
Forwards			
Wide			
Narrow			
Straight			
Crooked			
Broken			
Fixed			

(Table 45 continued)

Descriptor	Receptive	Expressive	Established
Spotted			
Striped			
Easy			
Difficult			
Quiet			
Noisy (loud)			
Missing			
Other			
Together			
Separated			
First			
Last			
Second			
Third			
Front			
Back			

Table 46: TELL ME ABOUT....

Item	Student Response	Correct/Incorrect
1. Ball		
2. Rabbit		
3. Cookie		
4. Book		
5. Lemon		
6. Mirror		
7. Snow		
8. Cup		
9. Tree		
10. Chair		
11. Soup		
12. Lunch bag		
13. Cat		
14. Bike		
15. Spoon		
16. Clock		
17. Pencil		
18. Frog		
19. Apple		
20. Brush		

Provide support by offering choice questions; e.g., is the boy happy or sad? Support readers as needed with the target feeling or emotion written on a cue card.

Introduce a new feeling or emotion when the target name is 80–90 percent established.

7 SUGGESTIONS FOR TEACHING FEELINGS AND EMOTIONS

1. Present several pictures that illustrate the same target feeling or emotion. Name the target in each picture; e.g., happy. Have the student imitate the name.
2. Present a choice of two pictures and have the student select the one that represents the feeling or emotion that you name.
3. Lay 4 pictures of the target feeling or emotion face up on the table and add one picture that shows a different one. Have the student find and name all the pictures that show the target feeling or emotion.
4. Describe a real-life situation relevant to the target feeling or emotion and ask the student how you/the person might feel in this situation. Use sentence completion or word choices if necessary; e.g., I did not sleep well last night; I feel _____ (tired); if I lost my cat, how would I feel—happy or sad?
5. Describe what is happening in a picture and have the student name how the person feels by completing your sentence. Examples: The girl has a balloon; she feels _____ (happy); the boy is yawning; he feels _____ (tired).
6. Describe how someone feels and discuss what might have happened to make him/her feel that way; e.g., the teacher is angry—what might have happened? (students were making a noise in the classroom).
7. Discuss how a person looks when she has a specific feeling or emotion and have your student copy you as you show the appropriate facial expression (use a mirror so that she can see herself). Be selective and note that not all feelings and emotions have a specific facial expression

Use the form TRACKING FEELINGS AND EMOTIONS to track the student's progress in acquiring the name of the emotion receptively and expressively and when it is established in her spontaneous language.

Carryover

- Discuss the feelings and emotions experienced by peers in real-life or "set-up" situations. Take photos (with permission). For example, Kyle won a prize for his good work—how does he feel? (proud); Sandy lost her new backpack—how does she feel? (sad).
- Encourage the student to look at your face to interpret what you are feeling. Limit your language and smile or frown to show approval or disapproval. Ask the student how she thinks you feel.
- Prompt the student to verbalize her feelings and emotions frequently throughout the day; e.g., before lunch—"how are you feeling?" (hungry).
- Read stories, sing songs, and watch videos, and discuss the feelings and emotions involved.

Table 47: OPPORTUNITIES FOR TEACHING FEELINGS AND EMOTIONS

Note: *Work first on feelings and emotions that pertain to the student's own behavior and experiences.*

Emotion	Opportunities
Happy	Enjoying an object or event; e.g., new toy; playing on preferred play equipment or computer. Having a good time. Smiling. Happy face stickers. "Your good work makes me happy."
Sad	Having to stop an activity; missing a person or object (e.g., if peer moves to another school). Mouth turned down. Sad face stickers. "Bad behavior makes me sad."
Angry/mad	Frustrated with an activity, person, or thing. Student not allowed to have her own way. Frowning. Tantrum.
Sleepy/tired	Yawning; bedtime; naptime; after heavy exercise (e.g., running in phys ed or during recess); at the end of class time or school day; storybooks such as *Good Night Moon* by Margaret Wise Brown.
Hungry	Before a meal or snack; pictures of people/animals eating— how did they feel before they ate? Storybooks such as *The Very Hungry Caterpillar* by Eric Carle.
Thirsty	After exercise or recess; peers waiting in line at water fountain or drinking from a water bottle. Pictures of people/animals drinking—how did they feel before they drank?
Friendly	Peers showing friendly behavior toward student; student being friendly to a peer (e.g., sharing; allowing a turn on play equipment, with a toy, or other shared item); saying "hello." Puppies or other baby animals playing together.
Afraid/frightened/scary	New situation, person, or thing. Loud noise. Scary part of a movie. Storybooks about Halloween and Halloween costumes.
Sick	Physically ill; absent from school; hospital; doctor. Specific diseases; e.g., cold, flu, chickenpox, sick to your stomach.
Kind	Do a considerate or helpful act for someone; e.g., pick up something that they dropped, open the door for them. Give a toy or book that you are playing with to a peer who wants it.
Gentle	Pet or touch an animal kindly, soothingly, softly. Use gentle hands. Be quiet, calm, and polite.
Busy	A person is "tied up" doing something. "Don't interrupt when the teacher is busy." Lots of activities in a timeframe; e.g., a busy morning. Animal scurrying around; e.g., squirrel busy gathering food.
Proud	Special accomplishment, good behavior, new skill, new item; e.g., new jacket, bike, or toy.

(Table 47 continued)

Emotion	Opportunities
"Cool"	Fashionable and attractive; e.g., a cool T-shirt, jacket, backpack.
"Cute"	Really attractive due to being pretty, charming, and/or quaint. Appropriate for girls or something small such as a baby animal; e.g., a cute hairstyle, cute dress, cute little feet, cute box.

Table 48: TRACKING FEELINGS AND EMOTIONS

Emotion	Receptive	Expressive	Established
Happy			
Sad			
Angry/mad			
Sleepy/tired			
Hungry			
Thirsty			
Friendly			
Afraid/frightened			
Sick			
Kind			
Gentle			
Busy			
Proud			
"Cool"			
"Cute"			

Goal 6: The student will understand and use descriptors that are opposites (antonyms); e.g., hard/soft (with 80–90 percent accuracy).

Materials

1. Real-life situations and commercial picture cards that illustrate descriptors that are opposites; e.g., happy/sad, fast/slow (as suggested in list below).
2. List TRACKING OPPOSITE DESCRIPTORS, Table 50, below.
3. Activity OPPOSITE DESCRIPTORS, Table 49, below.

Introduction

Tell the student that she has learned many descriptive words and give her some examples; e.g., wet, soft, long. Explain that you are now going to work on "opposite" descriptors—"opposite" means "very different from something"; e.g., wet/dry, soft/hard, long/short.

Select target opposites from the list TRACKING OPPOSITE DESCRIPTORS and activities from OPPORTUNITIES FOR TEACHING DESCRIPTORS, Goal 4, p. 131.

Activity **Receptive**

Use real-life situations: Model the use of opposite descriptors in set-up or naturally occurring situations. Examples: We <u>open</u> the door, then we <u>close</u> the door. Your lunch bag was <u>full</u> and now it is <u>empty</u>. This towel is <u>dirty;</u> let's find a <u>clean</u> one.

Have the student point to the item that meets your description; e.g., show me the <u>dirty</u> towel/show me the <u>clean</u> towel; show me a lunchbox that is <u>closed</u>/show me a lunchbox that is <u>open</u>.

Use commercial pictures: Have the student identify the picture described; e.g., show me <u>hard</u>/show me <u>soft</u>; show me <u>fast</u>/show me <u>slow</u>. Keep your language simple so that the descriptor is emphasized.

Have the student match a given picture with its opposite; e.g., hard/soft (brick/pillow).

Activity **Expressive**

Have the student:
1. Fill in the blank at the end of a sentence with the appropriate word; e.g., a tree is tall and a mushroom is _____ (short). Present the sentence again at a later time but reverse the descriptors; e.g., a mushroom is short and a tree is _____ (tall). Model and prompt as needed.
2. Label the descriptor and generate its opposite in response to your question in real-life situations and in pictures. Example—Instructor: "Tell me about this girl." Student: "This girl is happy." Instructor: "What is the opposite of happy?" (sad).
3. Change a sentence to mean the opposite. Example—Instructor: "This airplane is going up." Student: "This airplane is going down." Instructor: "This shoe is old." Student: "This shoe is new."

4. Give the opposite response automatically (by rote) when presented with a single descriptor and no context. Use the activity OPPOSITE DESCRIPTORS. Read the words one at a time and have the student say the opposite (provide word choices if necessary).

For the reader: *print the list on cardstock and cut into individual words. Have the student find the matching word pairs (provide written word choices as needed).*

Note: *the list includes some descriptors not included in previous structured activities.*

Carryover

- Play Memory or Go Fish. Make pairs by matching opposites; e.g., big/little; hot/cold.
- Have an "Opposites Day"—say the opposite to what you would usually say and have the student correct you; e.g., Bad night! (good morning); Kate is going up (down) the slide.

Table 49: OPPOSITE DESCRIPTORS

Wet	Dry	Hot	Cold
Clean	Dirty	Tall	Short
Heavy	Light	Empty	Full
Hard	Soft	Young	Old
Thick	Thin	Rough	Smooth
Open	Closed	Slow	Fast
Large	Small	Backwards	Forwards
Wide	Narrow	Straight	Crooked
Broken	Fixed	Spotted	Striped
Easy	Difficult	Quiet	Loud
Big	Little	Happy	Sad
Tight	Loose	Cheap	Expensive
Good	Bad	Beautiful	Ugly
Black	White	Fat	Skinny

Table 50: TRACKING OPPOSITE DESCRIPTORS

Opposite	Receptive	Expressive	Established
Wet/Dry			
Hot/Cold			
Clean/Dirty			
Tall/Short			
Heavy/Light			
Empty/Full			
Hard/Soft			
Young/Old			
Thick/Thin			
Rough/Smooth			
Open/Closed			
Slow/Fast			
Large/Small			
Backwards/Forwards			
Wide/Narrow			
Straight/Crooked			

(Table 50 continued)

Opposite	Receptive	Expressive	Established
Broken/Fixed			
Spotted/Striped			
Easy/Difficult			
Quiet/Loud			
Big/Little			
Happy/Sad			
Tight/Loose			
Cheap/Expensive			
Good/Bad			
Beautiful/Ugly			
Black/White			
Fat/Skinny			

9.
Concepts

These goals are appropriate for students with one or more of the following characteristics:

- has difficulty understanding concepts of position, time, quantity, and inclusion/exclusion resulting in limited ability to follow directions and weak understanding of spoken or written information; e.g., before you take some of the books out of the bag, put both of the pencils inside your desk

- presents an unclear message due to omission or confusion of concepts

Concepts Goals

The student will understand and use concepts of:

    Goal 1: position (prepositions); e.g., out of, down, across.

    Goal 2: quantity; e.g., some dogs, both cats.

    Goal 3: inclusion/exclusion; e.g., or, either one, but not.

    Goal 4: time; e.g., same time, while, beginning/end.

    Goal 5: before/after (time); e.g., point to the cup before you point to the pen.

For each goal see: *General Suggestions for Teaching Concept Understanding and Use, below.*

General Suggestions for Teaching Concept Understanding and Use

1. Use real-life situations and whole body experiences; e.g., student gets <u>in/out</u> of a box, student goes to the <u>top/bottom</u> of slide (see OPPORTUNITIES FOR TEACHING CONCEPTS listed in each goal). Also look for teachable moments unique to the student's situation and interests.
2. Select target concepts that are relevant to the student's communication needs from the lists in each goal. Concepts can be worked on in any order.
3. Start with concepts that "follow on" from those that the student already knows; e.g., if the student understands and uses "under," then work on "over."
4. Work on one or more concept(s) at a time depending on the student's ability level. Select these concepts from different groups (do not work all through one type of concept before progressing to another type). For example, you may work on "in" (concept of position) while also working on "more" (concept of quantity) at separate times during the student's work period or day.
5. Present a choice of objects, pictures, or situations and have the student identify the one that shows the concept that you name; e.g., show me the one that is <u>up</u> (kite in sky). Have him imitate as you model the concept name. Encourage independent naming of the concept through word choices and/or sentence completion; e.g., is the kite <u>up</u> or <u>under</u>? (up); the kite is _____ (up).
6. During initial teaching, use different objects, toys, or situations to teach each concept in order to avoid having the student associate the concept being taught with the materials being used.
7. Once a concept is established, use the same materials to teach opposite or contrasted concepts; e.g., under/over, some/one. The student then learns to process the concept accurately without contextual clues. Example: Give me <u>some</u> blocks (established concept); give me <u>one</u> block (new concept).
8. Give single-step directions that include the target concept. Begin the direction with: point to, show me, give me, put. Examples: point to <u>some</u> of the blocks; show me the car <u>at the beginning</u> of the line; put your hand <u>on the corner</u> of the table.
9. Use the *Listen, Repeat, Do* strategy from Chapter 1 (Following Directions), Goal 1, p. 14. Have the student repeat the direction verbatim before carrying it out. When he has completed the direction, have him tell you what he did; e.g., I pointed to <u>some</u> of the blocks.
10. Build to 2-step directions by first using the same concept; e.g., give me <u>some</u> of the flowers and <u>some</u> of the frogs—and then using contrasted concepts; e.g., give me <u>some</u> of the flowers and <u>one</u> of the frogs.
11. Support the reader as needed with the target concept written on a cue card.
12. Use the tracking forms provided to record the student's progress as he learns to understand (receptive), use (expressive), and establish (generalize) the concept.

Goal 1: The student will understand and use concepts of position (prepositions); e.g., out of, down, across (with 80–90 percent accuracy).

Prerequisite: *Understanding and use of prepositions "in," "on top of," "under," "beside," "between," "next to," "in front of," and "behind," from Chapter 1 (Following Directions), Goal 2, p. 18.*

Materials

1. List GENERAL SUGGESTIONS FOR TEACHING CONCEPT UNDERSTANDING AND USE, above.
2. List and materials as suggested in OPPORTUNITIES FOR TEACHING CONCEPTS OF POSITION, Table 51, below.
3. Activity OPPOSITE CONCEPTS, Table 52, below.
4. List TRACKING CONCEPTS OF POSITION, Table 53, below.

Introduction

Tell the student that he is going to learn words that tell us where something is.

Model the target concept by making statements about toys, objects, and real-life situations; e.g., the man is <u>outside</u> his truck; the monkey is <u>on top of</u> the house. Emphasize the target concept and use minimal wording so that the student hears the concept clearly.

Activities **Receptive** and **Expressive**

Select a target concept from OPPORTUNITIES FOR TEACHING CONCEPTS OF POSITION. Follow the General Suggestions for Teaching Concept Understanding and Use and the specific suggestions for that concept.

To teach the rote recall of opposite concepts (antonyms) use the activity OPPOSITE CONCEPTS:

For the nonreader: *Present a concept and ask the student to name the opposite; e.g., under/over; up/down. Prompt with word choices as needed.*

For the reader: *Print the list on cardstock and cut it into individual words. Present a word and have the student tell you the opposite spontaneously or through written word choices. Play Memory. Turn the words face down and take turns to pick up two words. Keep the pair if they match as opposites.*

Use TRACKING CONCEPTS OF POSITION to track concepts learned (receptive, expressive, and established).

Carryover

- Include concepts of position in statements and directions on a daily basis; e.g., put the chair in the middle of the circle; stand beside your desk.
- Play Simon Says using concepts of position; e.g., put your hands on your head; put your hands behind your head.
- Give directions that involve the target concept using a pencil and paper; e.g., draw a circle around the flower; write the letter A 3 times in a row.
- Play Hide and Find. Hide an object (within sight in the early stages of playing the game) and have the student ask/answer concept questions in order to find it. Examples: Is it in the classroom? Is it on the shelf? Is it behind a book?
- Play Blow Football. Arrange small objects, animals, or toys on the table. Use straws to blow a small ball of tissue paper across the table. Describe where the ball stops in relation to one or more of the objects; e.g., beside the cup; near the car; between the horse and the chicken.
- Make an obstacle course. Give the student directions on how to get around the course; e.g., climb over the chair; go around the pylon; crawl under the parachute.
- Take photos (with permission) of the student's peers in real-life situations that illustrate concepts; e.g., Kyle going down a slide; Amanda climbing over a chair. Play Go Fish with paired photos.
- Play commercial concept games, computer programs, and apps.
- Inform the family and caregivers of the position concepts that the student is working on and suggest they carry out the same or related activities outside of school hours.

Table 51: OPPORTUNITIES FOR TEACHING CONCEPTS OF POSITION

Concept	Activities
Above/below	Fish/animals swimming above/below surface of the water (pond, lake, ocean); bubbles floating; animals above/below soil/earth; monkey above/below branch. Write/draw above/below line on paper.
Across	Vehicles, animals, and people going across bridge, carpet, rug, field, water; roll ball, run, or hop across line painted on ground; pass something across the table or desk. Play "Blow football"—blow a cotton ball across the table to the goal on the other side.
After/Before	Line-up of toys or people (X is standing in line before/after Y); cars at a drive-through, driving on highway (blue car before red car); checkout line at grocery store; Noah's ark line-up of animals. Patterning—write out a visual sequence of letters/numbers or colors; e.g. red/blue/yellow— what color is before/after the blue one? T, M, B—what letter came before "M"?
Against	Stand a ladder against a wall; stand with your back against a wall; sit back to back with someone on the floor—lean against each other.
Apart/together	Pull Play-Doh or modeling clay apart; plastic Easter egg (comes apart in middle); Lego—take model or tower of blocks apart; do a jigsaw, then take it apart. Pop beads. Train tracks.
Around	Walk, run, or jump around a circle. Put something around your wrist (bracelet) or finger (ring); turn around to face the other way; collar around dog's neck; run around a tree or pylon; duck swims around pond; play game "Follow My Leader"—walk around things. Play ring toss—make the ring go around the post. Sing "Ring around the Rosie." Play with a spinning top or merry-go-round—make/watch it go around.
At the beginning/end	Line up items, letters/numbers, or students (direct each one where to stand in the line); path, maze, ball of yarn, piece of rope/string, river, train.
At the side of *	*See also "beside"; Chapter 1 (Following Directions), Goal 3, p. 21.* Dog on leash at person's side; child walking at adult's side; tree at the side of a lake or house; stand at the side of a chair, wall, or another student.

(Table 51 continued)

Concept	Activities
At (or "on") the top/bottom	Anything standing vertically—stairs, ladder attached to slide, tree, rocket, hill, mountain, pole/flag; floors inside a building/apartment block or skyscraper; elevator going to top/bottom floors. Play a matching game—cut pictures of single objects into 2 parts (top and bottom); e.g., tree, apple, shirt. Mix up the pieces and place them face down on the table. Take turns to pick up a piece—winner is the player with the most complete objects.
At (or "in") the corner	Corner of table, window, room, square; draw in the corner of chalkboard or whiteboard; fold corner of a piece of paper (art project). Street map—drive toy car and turn at the corner.
Down/up	Go down/up stairs; ladder attached to slide; cat climb tree; pick up/put down; up in sky/down on ground (airplane, balloon, kite); hang up/take down coat (hook); hold up hand; sit up/lie down. Bowling ball and pins—stand up/fall down; helium balloon; parachute; Songs: "London Bridge Is Falling Down," "Jack and Jill Went up the Hill." Play Snakes (Chutes) and Ladders with any theme. Put thermometer in hot/cold liquids.
In/out of *	*See also "in," Chapter 1 (Following Directions), Goal 3.* In/out of a box, pocket, lunch bag, backpack, door, jug (pour liquid), bed, dog/doghouse, oven (baking cookies), dryer (drying clothes). Place a hula hoop on the ground—jump in/out.
Inside/outside	Inside/outside box, bag, house, school, pocket, drawn circle/square; tongue/mouth; foot/sock; wash or clean inside/outside of a car. Read *Inside, Outside, Upside Down* by Stan and Jan Berenstain.
In the middle/center of	Middle of shape (circle, square); middle of horizontal line-up of objects; middle of your hand; middle of page in workbook or reader; identify the letter in the middle of a word; e.g., water—"t" is in middle. Center of cookie, pizza, cake, drawn circle, room; circle of students. Cut pictures of items into 3 parts—see "Top/bottom," above.
In a row	Students, birds—stand/sit in a row; arrange items—colors, chairs, toy cars, beads, blocks in a row; plants in vegetable garden; write letters/numbers/words in a row.
Near to/far from	Visually compare or measure actual distance—item put at a distance from or close to others; distance to another classroom, peer sitting at same table; drive to school, store (refer to a map).

(Table 51 continued)

Concept	Activities
Left/right ("on" or "to" the left/right)	Teach distinction between left/right hands, feet, eyes, ears. Student can wear bracelet on right hand as a reminder. Stand on left or right of an object or person; turn left or right to find a treasure; follow a map—turn on streets; guide remote control vehicle; follow a maze. Marble run. Pin the Tail on the Donkey—use a large picture of a donkey (or other animal). Blindfold the student and have him pin the tail onto the correct place on the picture. Assist him by giving him left/right and up/down directions. Then wear the blindfold and have him direct you.
On/off *	** See also "on top of," Chapter 1 (Following Directions), Goal 3.* Turn on/off light, flashlight, fan, music, TV, radio, other appliance; put item on/take off table; take off/put on mitts, hat, coat. Beanbag toss—throw the beanbag—did it land on or off a square of a specific number or color? Mr Potato Head—body parts on/off. Arrange parts on/off a magnetic scene; fridge magnets on/off fridge.
Over/under*	** See also "under," Chapter 1 (Following Directions), Goal 3.* Over/under a gate, fence, chair, skipping rope; weave place mat using strips of construction paper; parachute game in phys ed; lie on floor—roll over; do a somersault (make your feet go over your head); bridge over a river or railway line.
Through	Train through tunnel; climb though a hoop in an obstacle course or wiggle through long cardboard box open at each end on floor; pass thread through beads to make necklace; lacing craft—yarn though hole; look through hole in wall, piece of paper, cardboard tube, binoculars/telescope; flour though sieve (baking); water or sand through water wheel (water play); arm through sleeve; basketball through hoop;
To/from	Give something to someone/get something from; e.g., birthday present, letter; go to a destination/come back from; e.g., to/from the gym or another classroom. Stand or put something close to/far from something.

Table 52: OPPOSITE CONCEPTS

In	Out	On	Off
Up	Down	Before	After
Through	Around	Under	Over
Above	Below	To	From
Inside	Outside	Beginning	End
Top	Bottom	Near	Far
Left	Right	Behind	In front

Table 53: TRACKING CONCEPTS OF POSITION

Concept	Receptive	Expressive	Established
Above			
Across			
After			
Against			
Apart			
Around			
At (in) in corner			
At the beginning			
At the bottom of			
At the end			
At the side of			
At the top of			
Before			
Below			
Down			
Far from			
From			

(Table 53 continued)

Concept	Receptive	Expressive	Established
In a row			
In center of			
In middle of			
Inside			
Left ("on" or "to")			
Near to			
Off			
On			
Out of			
Outside			
Over			
Right ("on" or "to")			
Through			
To			
Together			
Under			
Up			

Goal 2: The student will understand and use concepts of quantity; e.g., some dogs, both cats (with 80–90 percent accuracy).

Prerequisite: *Understanding of "no" and "not"—Chapter 2 (Negative "No/not"), Goal 2, p. 25.*

Materials

1. General Suggestions for Teaching Concept Understanding and Use, above, p. 148.
2. List OPPORTUNITIES FOR TEACHING CONCEPTS OF QUANTITY, Table 54, below.
3. Familiar toys and objects including single items and groups of both identical and non-identical items; e.g., 4 blocks, 6 decorative erasers, 4 straws, 10 buttons, 5 toy cars, 10 stickers, 1 teddy bear. Non-identical items should vary by color, size, shape, or name within a category; e.g., 5 cars but of different colors; 10 cardstock circles—6 blue and 4 yellow; 6 animals (2 cats, 1 cow, 3 horses).
4. List TRACKING CONCEPTS OF QUANTITY, Table 55, below.

Introduction

Tell the student that he is going to learn words that tell us how much there is or how many there are of something.

Model the target concept by making statements about toys, objects, and real-life situations; e.g., here is a dog and here is <u>another</u> dog; this water bottle is <u>full</u> and this water bottle is <u>empty</u>.

Activities **Receptive** and **Expressive**

Select a target concept from OPPORTUNITIES FOR TEACHING CONCEPTS OF QUANTITY and follow the General Suggestions for Teaching Concept Understanding and Use, above, and the specific suggestions for that concept.

Model the concepts; e.g., this is <u>an</u> egg; these are <u>some</u> eggs.

Track concepts learned (receptive, expressive, or established) using TRACKING CONCEPTS OF QUANTITY.

Carryover

- Include quantity concepts in statements and directions on a daily basis. Examples: put one of your pencils in your desk; give a book to every student.
- Inform the family and caregivers of the quantity concepts that the student is working on and suggest they carry out the same or related activities outside of school hours.
- Play commercial concept games, computer programs, and apps.

Table 54: OPPORTUNITIES FOR TEACHING CONCEPTS OF QUANTITY

Concept	Activities
A/an *	*See also Chapter 11 (Word and Sentence Structure), Goal 2, p. 212.* Use objects and toys (or pictures), some of which are identical—a book, pen, shoe; an egg, apple, elephant, airplane, owl. Say, e.g., give me a shoe; give me an apple. Contrast with "some" or "all"; e.g., show me a frog; show me all of the frogs. Contrast with "the," using singles and multiples of identical and non-identical toys and objects. Say, e.g., "give me the…" if there is only one of the item, and "give me a…" if there is more than one of the item; e.g., "give me a dog" (from a group of 3 dogs); "give me the car" (only 1 car in the group of toys).
All	Identical toys and objects or items in the same category—contrast with one and some; e.g., give me all of the animals. Make comments such as you ate all your lunch/yogurt; all the students are going to the gym; all coats are hung up.
Another	Identical toys and objects or items in a category. Hold up one object and ask for another; e.g., give me another cat. Offer another turn on swing or computer; give a few of a small single-food item such as grapes and have student request another.
As many as	Requires the ability to count. Arrange identical toys and objects in piles of same and different quantities. Count—which pile has as many as this pile? Discuss which has "more" and "less." Share snack items; e.g., cereal, popcorn, grapes—you have as many as I do.
Both	Pairs of identical objects and toys. Contrast with "one," "a," "an"; e.g., give me one cup; give me both cups. Comment on two people carrying out the same activity or things that are the same; e.g., both boys are painting; both of your hands are wet.
Empty/full	Use pairs of identical clear plastic containers; e.g., boxes, tubs, bags. Fill some with liquids or solids; e.g., water; sand, rice, cereal, coins and leave others empty—which one is full/empty? Play Bowling with full/empty bottles—which is easiest to knock over? Comment about lunch bag/plate/tummy full/empty before/after meal; backpack; water bottle.
Equal	As for more and less—quantities of items in groups (counting); amounts of liquid in identical containers—which has more/less/equal? Divide snack food, Play-Doh, Lego pieces into equal amounts.

(Table 54 continued)

Concept	Activities
Every	Use toys, objects, and/or stickers, some of which are identical. Place them in mixed groups; e.g., cars and trucks—show me every truck; happy and sad face stickers—show me every happy face. Contrast with one and some. Talk about activities that you do every day; e.g., circle time, lunch, recess. Picture scenes—find everyone who is wearing a hat.
Few	Identical objects and toys or items in the same category; e.g., vehicles. Contrast with one; e.g., give me a few cars; give me one car; give me a few more cars. Offer a few craft items during art— would you like a few sparkles?
Last one/ none	Divide up identical toys, objects, and/or snacks between two people or places. Ask: Where does the last one go? Who gets the last one? When they are all distributed, there are none left. Ask for some of one item and none of another; e.g., give me some of the frogs and none of the flowers. Provide a finite number of craft items at art time; e.g., pom-poms, google eyes—last one/none left.
Less	As for more,—compare quantities of items in groups (counting) and amounts of liquid in identical containers—which has more? Which has less? Divide a snack such as popcorn between you—ask for more or less.
Many	Use lots of identical items or items in the same category; e.g., blocks, animals. Contrast with one; e.g., give me one frog; give me many frogs. Make comments; e.g., many students are wearing jackets today.
More	Fill identical containers with water—which has more? Arrange quantities of identical items in groups; some groups with obviously more than others—which group has more than this group? (estimate or count). Contrast with one; e.g., give me one block; give me more blocks. Give small amount of food/drink and ask, "do you want more?" Response: "more please."
Most/Least	Place varying quantities of identical small toys and objects in piles; e.g., Unifix cubes. Ask which pile has the most or least? Count them. Play Snap or Memory—who won the most/least?
One/one of	Identical toys and objects arranged in groups and singles; e.g., group of pencils together and one pencil set apart. Contrast one with some or all; e.g., point to one cat; point to some cats; show me one of the dogs; show me all of the dogs. Make comments; e.g., one of the boys is wearing a hat.

(Table 54 continued)

Concept	Activities
Pair	Use objects that come in pairs; e.g., socks, shoes, gloves—mix them up and sort them into their pairs. Play Memory and Go Fish with any theme.
Part	Use objects that are made up of parts that can be separated; e.g., jigsaw puzzles, Mr. Potato Head. Take turns to select a part and reconstruct the puzzle or object—ask what <u>part</u> did you get/put in?
Some	Identical objects and toys; e.g., pick up <u>some</u> flowers; pick up <u>some</u> buttons. Contrast with <u>a</u>, <u>one</u>, or <u>all</u>; e.g., give me <u>some</u> dinosaurs; give me <u>a</u> dinosaur. Make comments: e.g., <u>some</u> of the students are going on the bus.
The	*(See also Chapter 11 (Word and Sentence Structure), Goal 2, p. 212.* Present a selection of single toys and/or objects and request a specific one; e.g., give me <u>the</u> horse; give me <u>the</u> fire truck.
Whole/ Half	Use objects and foods that can be divided in half; e.g., sandwich, Play-Doh. Share a treat—half each. Compare the halves to show that they are the same size. Cut pictures of objects or greeting cards in half; e.g., ball, leaf—put them back together. Play Memory—use picture cards that are cut in half and find the other half. Cut pictures of animals in half and put two non-matching halves together to create a new animal and give it a name.

Table 55: TRACKING CONCEPTS OF QUANTITY

Concept	Receptive	Expressive	Established
A/an			
All			
Another			
As many as			
Both			
Empty			
Equal			
Every			
Few			
Full			
Half			
Last one			
Least			
Less			
Many			
More			
Most			
None			
One/one of			
Pair			
Part			
Some			
The			
Whole			

Goal 3: The student will understand and use concepts of inclusion/exclusion; e.g., or, either one, but not (with 80–90 percent accuracy).

Materials

1. General Suggestions for Teaching Concept Understanding and Use, above, p. 148.
2. List OPPORTUNITIES FOR TEACHING CONCEPTS OF INCLUSION/EXCLUSION, Table 56, below.
3. As for Concepts Goal 2—familiar toys and objects, including single items and groups of both identical and non-identical items; e.g., 4 blocks, 6 decorative erasers, 4 straws, 10 buttons, 5 toy cars, 10 stickers, 1 teddy bear. Non-identical items should vary by color, size, shape, or name within a category; e.g., 5 cars but of different colors; 10 cardstock circles—6 blue and 4 yellow; 6 animals (2 cats, 1 cow, 3 horses).
4. List TRACKING CONCEPTS OF INCLUSION/EXCLUSION, Table 57, below.

Introduction

Tell the student that he is going to learn words that tell us which things we should do something with and which things we should leave alone.

Model the target concept by making statements about toys, objects, and real-life situations. For example, create a group of toys (animals, blocks, cars) and say, "These are all toys." Then pick up all of the toys but leave the cars and say, "I picked up all the toys except the cars." Present other examples as needed.

Activities **Receptive** and **Expressive**

Select a target concept from list OPPORTUNITIES FOR TEACHING CONCEPTS OF INCLUSION/EXCLUSION and follow the General Suggestions for Teaching Concept Understanding and Use, above, and the specific suggestions for that concept.

Model the target concept and give the student directions starting with "give me," "show me," "point to," or "pick up." Keep the wording the same throughout the teaching session to reduce the amount of processing required.

After the student has carried out the direction, ask him to tell you what he showed you, pointed to, gave you, or picked up; e.g., I picked up all the dinosaurs except the red ones.

Track concepts learned (receptive, expressive, or established) using TRACKING CONCEPTS OF INCLUSION/EXCLUSION.

Carryover

- Use inclusion/exclusion concepts in statements and directions on a daily basis. Examples: Put all your crayons except the red one in your backpack. Give the reading book to either Mary or Ann.
- Set up shared activities. Discuss which toys/objects/materials the student wants to keep for himself for an activity/snack and which ones he is willing that others eat/use/have. Example, during a craft activity—you can have all of the beads except the blue ones; during snack time—I want all of the chips but none of the popcorn.

Table 56: OPPORTUNITIES FOR TEACHING CONCEPTS OF INCLUSION/EXCLUSION

Concept	Activities
All	See OPPORTUNITIES FOR TEACHING CONCEPTS OF QUANTITY, Goal 2, p. 157.
All but one	Use groups of toys/objects that have the same name or category name; e.g., give me <u>all but one</u> of the blocks; give me <u>all but one</u> of the animals. Contrast with <u>one</u>; e.g., give me <u>one</u> ball; give me <u>all but one</u> of the balls. Share treats; e.g., you can have <u>all but one</u> of the cookies.
All . . . but none	Use groups of toys and objects that have the same name or category name and some of which are identical; e.g., give me <u>all</u> of the blocks <u>but none</u> of the big ones; give me <u>all</u> the vehicles <u>but none</u> of the cars. Share treats of different colors or size such as grapes or M&Ms; e.g., you can have <u>all</u> the red grapes <u>but none</u> of the green grapes; you can have <u>all</u> the big marshmallows <u>but none</u> of the little ones.
All except	Use groups of toys and objects some of which are identical or in the same category; e.g., give me <u>all</u> the cars <u>except</u> the red ones; give me <u>all</u> the animals <u>except</u> the horse. Give directions such as: you have time to eat <u>all</u> your lunch <u>except</u> the apple; put <u>all</u> your books on the desk <u>except</u> your math book.
But not	Use groups of toys/objects, some of which are identical or in the same category; e.g., pick up the blocks <u>but not</u> the yellow ones; pick up the animals <u>but not</u> the cow. Provide a choice of craft items and direct him as to which to use; e.g., use the brushes <u>but not</u> the long ones.
Either one	Use items that come in pairs, such as shoes, mitts, feet, ears, eyes, hands; e.g., put <u>either one</u> of your mitts on the table; touch <u>either one</u> of your ears; you can sit on <u>either one</u> of the chairs.
Either . . . or	Use a selection of familiar objects and toys; e.g., give me <u>either</u> a dog <u>or</u> a cat. Give choices; e.g., you can have <u>either</u> your yogurt first <u>or</u> your apple; you can sit with <u>either</u> Paul <u>or</u> Tom. Try not to use this in negative situations; e.g., <u>either</u> behave <u>or</u> go to timeout!
Neither . . . nor	Use groups of toys and objects or pictures that have the same name but some features that vary; e.g., give me a car that is <u>neither</u> red <u>nor</u> blue (yellow); give me a cup that is <u>neither</u> little <u>nor</u> yellow (large and white); show me a boy who is <u>neither</u> walking <u>nor</u> climbing (swimming); show me a shape that is <u>neither</u> a circle <u>nor</u> a triangle (square). Share treats such as crackers of different shapes; e.g., you can have the crackers that are <u>neither</u> round <u>nor</u> have seeds on them (square and plain).

(Table 56 continued)

Concept	Activities
None of	See OPPORTUNITIES FOR TEACHING CONCEPTS OF QUANTITY, Goal 2, p. 157.
Not	See Chapter 2 (Negative "No/Not"), Goals 1–3, pp. 24-27.
Or	Use a selection of objects and toys and request one; e.g., give me the dog <u>or</u> the cat. Pick up the car <u>or</u> the truck. Give choices; e.g., you can wear your red T-shirt <u>or</u> your blue T-shirt—which would you prefer? We can go this way to the gym <u>or</u> that way—which way shall we go?

Table 57: TRACKING CONCEPTS OF INCLUSION/EXCLUSION

Concept	Receptive	Expressive	Established
All but one			
All except			
All . . . but none			
But not			
Either . . . or			
Either one			
Neither . . . nor			
Or			

- Inform the family and caregivers of the inclusion/exclusion concepts that the student is working on and suggest they carry out the same or related activities outside of school hours.
- Play commercial concept games, computer programs, and apps.

Goal 4: The student will understand and use concepts of time; e.g., same time, while, beginning/end (with 80–90 percent accuracy).

Materials

1. General Suggestions for Teaching Concept Understanding and Use, p. 148.
2. List OPPORTUNITIES FOR TEACHING CONCEPTS OF TIME, Table 58, below.
3. Single familiar toys and objects and/or pictures of single toys and objects.
4. List TRACKING CONCEPTS OF TIME, Table 59, below.

Introduction

Tell the student that he is going to learn words that tell us about when something happened, is happening, or is going to happen.

Model the target concept by making statements about toys, objects, and real-life situations; e.g., I can touch my head <u>while</u> I stand on one foot; we <u>always</u> eat lunch in the lunch room.

Activities **Receptive** and **Expressive**

Select a target concept from OPPORTUNITIES FOR TEACHING CONCEPTS OF TIME and follow the General Suggestions for Teaching Concept Understanding and Use and use the specific suggestions for that concept.

Model the target concept and give the student directions, then ask him to tell you what he did. Example: I pointed to the blocks <u>at the same time</u>.

Track concepts learned (receptive, expressive, or established) using TRACKING CONCEPTS OF TIME.

Carryover

- Use concepts of time in directions and statements on a daily basis; e.g., when you have finished your lunch, we will go outside; while you are playing, we will have the music on.
- Inform the family and caregivers of the time concepts that the student is working on and suggest they carry out the same or related activities outside of school hours.
- Play commercial concept games, computer programs, and apps.

Table 58: OPPORTUNITIES FOR TEACHING CONCEPTS OF TIME

Concept	Activities
Almost	Set up small tasks including some that are slightly beyond the student's ability level; e.g., build a tower of 3 blocks (easy) and 10 blocks (too difficult)—comment after trials "you <u>almost</u> did it!" Point out upcoming events during the day; e.g., it's <u>almost</u> time for recess/bus/go home/finish the lesson/lunch/work.
Always	You must <u>always</u>….! Discuss things that you must <u>always</u> do, such as classroom rules; e.g., you must <u>always</u> hang up your coat. Ask questions— should I take my clothes off when I go in the shower? (always); do you go to sleep at night only on Mondays or always? (always).
Beginning/ end	Discuss what happened or is going to happen during time periods; e.g., recess, class time—what did you do at the <u>beginning/end</u> of recess? You are going to play on the trampoline at the <u>end</u> of gym time. Discuss what happened at the <u>beginning/end</u> of a story or movie.
Before/after	See Concepts Goal 5, p. 168.
Finish/start	Set up small tasks that have a clear start and finish; e.g., do a jigsaw puzzle, make a tower of blocks, run a race. Blow a whistle at the <u>start/finish</u>; use a clock/stopwatch. Daily tasks—<u>start/finish</u> lunch, snack time, lesson period.
First/last	Perform 2 actions with toys/objects—student is to describe what you did first/last. Example: Pick up a ball and turn over a book— what did I do <u>last</u>? Discuss the order of steps in a sequential event or story (Chapter 13, Goal 2, p. 265). Example: Arriving at the classroom in the morning—take off coat/sit at desk; baking—what did we mix in <u>first/last</u>? 3-step sequential stories—what did the boy do <u>first</u>? What did he do <u>last</u>? Have a "backwards" day—perform a sequential activity in reverse. Example (at lunch): Eat dessert <u>first</u> and sandwich <u>last</u>. Say 2 words to the student; e.g., cat/dog. Ask "what did I say <u>first</u>?" (cat); "what did I say <u>last</u>?" (dog).
Never	You must <u>never</u> do that! Discuss things that you must <u>never</u> do—both serious rules and absurdities; e.g., you must <u>never</u> run across the road; <u>never</u> get in the bath with your clothes on. Ask questions; e.g., should I walk in the snow with bare feet? (never); should I brush my teeth with soap? (never)
Same time	Use single toys/objects or pictures and give directions; e.g., point to the cat and the horse <u>at the same time</u> (student may need to be taught to use both hands for this). Pretend to be circus performers—how many things can you do <u>at the same time</u>; e.g., stand on one foot and clap <u>at the same time</u>; shut your eyes and open your mouth <u>at the same time</u>.

(Table 58 continued)

Concept	Activities
Then/and then	See Chapter 1 (Following Directions), Goal 1, Step 4, p. 15.
When	Use single toys/objects—have the student wait for a signal before performing an activity; e.g., <u>when</u> I blow the whistle, pick up the block; <u>when</u> I clap my hands, put your hands in the air. Give directions/make comments in the classroom. Examples: Go to the teacher <u>when</u> she calls you; <u>when</u> you get to the end of the story, draw a picture; we will pack your backpack <u>when</u> it is time to go home.
While	Have the student carry out an activity while you perform a different continuous action; e.g., clap your hands <u>while</u> I play the xylophone (student must stop his action when you stop yours). Make comments/give directions; e.g., wait in a line <u>while</u> the other students get ready; use quiet voices <u>while</u> you are in the hallway.

Table 59: TRACKING CONCEPTS OF TIME

Concept	Receptive	Expressive	Established
Almost			
Always			
Beginning			
End			
Finish			
First			
Last			
Never			
Same time			
Start			
Then/and then			
When			
While			

Goal 5: The student will understand and use concepts of time "before" and "after"; e.g., point to the cup before/after you point to the pen (with 80–90 percent accuracy).

Prerequisites: *Understanding of concepts before/after used as concepts of position; e.g., the blue car is <u>before</u> the red car in the line-up—Concepts Goal 1, p. 149. Ability to follow 2-step directions—Chapter 1 (Following Directions), Goals 1–3, pp. 14-22.*

Examples of Before/After

The concepts "before" and "after" can be very confusing because their position within the direction changes the meaning of the direction. See examples below. The numbers after the words show the order in which the student should give you the items.

Compare:
Give me a ball (1) <u>before</u> you give me a cup (2)   *("before" in the middle)*

<u>Before</u> you give me a book (2), give me a pen (1) *("before" at the beginning)*

Give me a ball (2) <u>after</u> you give me a cup (1)   *("after" in the middle)*

<u>After</u> you give me a book (1) give me a pen (2)   *("after" at the beginning)*

Note: *When **"before" is in the middle** of a direction or **"after" is at the beginning** of the direction, then the student should give the first item mentioned first. When **"before" is at the beginning** or **"after" is in the middle**, then the student should give the first item mentioned second.*

Many students want to give the first item they hear to the instructor first regardless of the position of the concept in the direction

Materials

1. Pictures of single familiar toys/objects, as listed at the beginning of each step.
2. List TRACKING UNDERSTANDING and USE OF BEFORE/AFTER, Table 68, below.
3. Blank copies of BEFORE/AFTER DIRECTIONS, Table 67, below.

Introduction

Introduce each step by telling the student that he is going to learn to understand the words "before" or "after" at the beginning or in the middle of a sentence (as appropriate to the step). Model as described at the beginning of each step.

Note: *Read Activity Expressive (All Steps) and Carryover **before you start Step 1.***

Activity **Receptive** (All Steps)

Follow Steps 1–7 below. Present 2-step directions that involve the target concept "before" or "after." Use the strategy "Listen, Repeat, Do" from Chapter 1 (Following Directions), Goal 1, p. 14. Say the direction over as many times as the student needs in order to be able to repeat it correctly. Have the student carry out the direction. Demonstrate it if he has difficulty carrying it out.

Use "point to," "show me," or "give me." Keep the word that you use consistent over all directions throughout each teaching session. For example, use "give me" for all directions during one session, then use "show me" throughout the next session that you work on the goal.

Follow the directions listed and for further practice, write your own directions for the teaching session on a blank copy of BEFORE/AFTER DIRECTIONS. Be sure to record the Step number that corresponds with each direction; e.g., <u>after</u> you give me a flower give me a pencil—Step 2 ("after" at the beginning).

Use the materials as suggested in each Step or substitute a variety of other pictures or familiar objects (keep to words of 1 or 2 syllables to reduce auditory memory difficulties). Whenever possible, use a different set of objects/pictures for each set of directions.

Work on each Step to 80–90 percent accuracy, then progress to the next Step. Review previous Steps periodically.

Track progress using TRACKING UNDERSTANDING and USE OF BEFORE/AFTER.

Step 1—"Before" in the Middle: When "before" is in the middle of a direction, the student will give the item that he hears named *first* to you *first* (this is the easiest direction to follow). Examples: give me the car <u>before</u> you give me the block; give me the pen <u>before</u> you give me the eraser.

Follow the directions in Table 60 and create directions for further practice on blank copies of BEFORE/AFTER DIRECTIONS.

Step 2—"After" at the Beginning: When "after" is at the beginning of a direction, the student will give you the item that he hears named *first* to you *first* (as for Step 1 "before" in the middle). Examples: <u>after</u> you give me the car, give me the block; <u>after</u> you give me the dog, give me the crayon.

Follow the directions in Table 61 and create directions for further practice on blank copies of BEFORE/AFTER DIRECTIONS.

Step 3—Mix "Before" in the Middle and "After" at the Beginning: This Step is a combination of Steps 1 and 2. The student will give you the item that he hears named *first* to you *first* for both directions.

Follow the directions in Table 62 and create directions for further practice on blank copies of BEFORE/AFTER DIRECTIONS.

Step 4—"Before" at the Beginning: When "before" is at the beginning of a direction, the student will give you the item that he hears named *first* to you *second*. Examples: <u>before</u> you give me a car, give me a block; <u>before</u> you give me a cat, give me a dinosaur.

Some students find this difficult as they want to give you the item that they heard first as in the Steps already completed. Extra teaching may be needed.

Follow the directions in Table 63 and create directions for further practice on blank copies of BEFORE/AFTER DIRECTIONS.

Step 5—"After" in the Middle: As with "before" at the beginning, when "after" is in the middle of the direction, the student will give you the item that he hears named *first* to you *second*. Example: Give me the car <u>after</u> you give me the block; give me the ball <u>after</u> you give me the apple.

Follow the directions in Table 64 and create directions for further practice on blank copies of BEFORE/AFTER DIRECTIONS.

Step 6—Mix "Before" at the Beginning and "After" in the Middle: This Step is a combination of Steps 4 and 5. The student will give you the item that he hears named *second* to you *second* for both directions. Examples: <u>before</u> you give me the book, give me the pen; give me a block <u>after</u> you give me a dog.

Follow the directions in Table 65 and create directions for further practice on blank copies of BEFORE/AFTER DIRECTIONS.

Step 7—Mix "Before" and "After" at the Beginning and in the Middle: Present directions from Steps 1, 2, 4, and 5 ("before" and "after" at the beginning and in the middle) in random order.

Follow the directions in Table 66 and create directions for further practice on blank copies of BEFORE/AFTER DIRECTIONS.

Activity **Expressive (All Steps)**

Provide opportunities for him to use the target word in the target position:
   a. At each Step, once the student is able to follow your directions to 80–90 percent accuracy, pick up 2 pictures, one after the other, and have him tell you what you did using "before" or "after" in the same position as you are working on in that Step; e.g., "you picked up the ball <u>before</u> you picked up the car" ("before" in the middle); "after you picked up the dog you picked up the horse" ("after" at the beginning).
   b. After the student has carried out each direction in a Step, have him tell you what he did.

Carryover

- Discuss actions and events that happen before or after another action; e.g., before lunch we are going to the gym; after lunch it will be recess; after school you go to the babysitter.
- Have the student (or both of you) carry out 2 familiar actions; e.g., clap your hands, then touch the table (Chapter 1, Following Directions, Goal 1). Ask questions; e.g., what did I/we do before I/we touched the table? What did I/we do after I/we clapped our hands? Have him describe the complete sequence: e.g., we touched the table after we clapped our hands.
- Use inset puzzles and magnetic and felt scenes. Give the student directions as to which pieces to put in or on; e.g., put in the tree before you put in the bird; before you put the girl on the scene put on the dog.
- Give directions during daily activities. Example: During gym class—"Before you put away the hoops, give the ball to Andrew"; "After you pick up the jump ropes, pick up the beanbags."

Table 60: Step 1—"BEFORE" IN THE MIDDLE

Materials: single-item pictures—cat, horse, cow, frog, dog.

Direction	Correct/Incorrect
1. Give me the cat before you give me the dog.	
2. Give me the cow before you give me the frog.	
3. Give me the dog before you give me the cat.	
4. Give me the horse before you give me the cow.	
5. Give me the frog before you give me the horse.	
6. Give me the cat before you give me the cow.	
7. Give me the horse before you give me the frog.	
8. Give me the cow before you give me the cat.	
9. Give me the dog before you give me the horse.	
10. Give me the frog before you give me the dog.	

Table 61: Step 2—"AFTER" AT THE BEGINNING

Materials: single-item pictures—car, bus, boat, plane, bike.

Direction	Correct/Incorrect
1. After you give me the car, give me the bike.	
2. After you give me the boat, give me the plane.	
3. After you give me the bike, give me the car.	
4. After you give me the bus, give me the plane.	
5. After you give me the bike, give me the bus.	
6. After you give me the car, give me the boat.	
7. After you give me the plane, give me the bus.	
8. After you give me the boat, give me the car.	
9. After you give me the bus, give me the bike.	
10. After you give me the plane, give me the boat.	

Table 62: Step 3—Mix "BEFORE" IN THE MIDDLE and "AFTER" AT THE BEGINNING

Materials: single-item pictures—apple, banana, carrot, orange, grapes.

Direction	Correct/Incorrect
1. Give me the apple <u>before</u> you give me the grapes.	
2. <u>After</u> you give me the carrot, give me the orange.	
3. <u>After</u> you give me the grapes, give me the apple.	
4. Give me the banana <u>before</u> you give me the carrot.	
5. <u>After</u> you give me the orange, give me the banana.	
6. Give me the apple <u>before</u> you give me the carrot.	
7. Give me the banana <u>before</u> you give me the orange.	
8. <u>After</u> you give me the carrot, give me the apple.	
9. Give me the grapes <u>before</u> you give me the banana.	
10. <u>After</u> you give me the orange, give me the grapes.	

Table 63: Step 4—"BEFORE" AT THE BEGINNING

Materials: single-item pictures—pen, crayon, eraser, scissors, book.

Direction	Correct/Incorrect
1. <u>Before</u> you give me the pen, give me the book.	
2. <u>Before</u> you give me the eraser, give me the scissors.	
3. <u>Before</u> you give me the book, give me the pen.	
4. <u>Before</u> you give me the crayon, give me the scissors.	
5. <u>Before</u> you give me the scissors, give me the crayon.	
6. <u>Before</u> you give me the pen, give me the eraser.	
7. <u>Before</u> you give me the crayon, give me the book.	
8. <u>Before</u> you give me the eraser, give me the pen.	
9. <u>Before</u> you give me the book, give me the crayon.	
10. <u>Before</u> you give me the scissors, give me the eraser.	

Table 64: Step 5—"AFTER" IN THE MIDDLE

Materials: single-item pictures—ball, bubbles, doll, (teddy) bear, swing.

Direction	Correct/Incorrect
1. Give me the ball <u>after</u> you give me the swing.	
2. Give me the doll <u>after</u> you give me the bear.	
3. Give me the swing <u>after</u> you give me the ball.	
4. Give me the bubbles <u>after</u> you give me the doll.	
5. Give me the bear <u>after</u> you give me the bubbles.	
6. Give me the ball <u>after</u> you give me the doll.	
7. Give me the bubbles <u>after</u> you give me the bear.	
8. Give me the doll <u>after</u> you give me the ball.	
9. Give me the swing <u>after</u> you give me the bubbles.	
10. Give me the bear <u>after</u> you give me the swing.	

Table 65: Step 6— MIX "BEFORE" AT THE BEGINNING and "AFTER" IN THE MIDDLE

Materials: single-item pictures—bed, chair, stove, table, TV.

Direction	Correct/Incorrect
1. Give me the bed <u>after</u> you give me the TV.	
2. <u>Before</u> you give me the stove, give me the table.	
3. Give me the TV <u>after</u> you give me the bed.	
4. <u>Before</u> you give me the chair, give me the stove.	
5. <u>Before</u> you give me the table, give me the chair.	
6. Give me the bed <u>after</u> you give me the stove.	
7. Give me the chair <u>after</u> you give me the table.	
8. <u>Before</u> you give me the stove, give me the bed.	
9. Give me the TV <u>after</u> you give me the chair.	
10. <u>Before</u> you give me the table, give me the TV.	

Table 66: Step 7—MIX "BEFORE" AND "AFTER" AT THE BEGINNING AND IN THE MIDDLE

Materials: single-item pictures—bird, tree, house, sun, moon.

Direction	Correct/Incorrect
1. Give me the bird <u>after</u> you give me the moon.	
2. Give me the house <u>before</u> you give me the sun.	
3. <u>After</u> you give me the moon, give me the bird.	
4. <u>Before</u> you give me the tree, give me the house.	
5. Give me the sun <u>before</u> you give me the tree.	
6. <u>After</u> you give me the bird, give me the house.	
7. Give me the tree <u>after</u> you give me the sun.	
8. <u>Before</u> you give me the house, give me the bird.	
9. Give me the moon <u>before</u> you give me the tree.	
10. <u>After</u> you give me the sun, give me the moon.	

Table 67: BEFORE/AFTER DIRECTIONS

Direction	Step #	Correct/ Incorrect
1.		
2.		
3.		
4.		
5.		
6.		
7.		
8.		
9.		
10.		
11.		
12.		
13.		
14.		
15.		
16.		
17.		
18.		
19.		
20.		

Table 68: TRACKING UNDERSTANDING and USE OF BEFORE/AFTER

Position of Concept	Receptive	Expressive	Established
Step 1: Before—in the middle e.g., Give me a ball <u>before</u> you give me a cup			
Step 2: After—at the beginning e.g., <u>After</u> you give me a book, give me a pen			
Step 3: Mixed Steps 1 and 2			
Step 4: Before—at the beginning e.g., <u>Before</u> you give me a book, give me a pen			
Step 5: After—in the middle e.g., Give me a ball <u>after</u> you give me a cup			
Step 6: Mixed Steps 4 and 5			
Step 7: Mixed Steps 1, 2, 4 and 5			

10.
"Wh" Questions
What? Who? Where? Which? When? Whose? Why?

These goals are appropriate for students with one or more of the following characteristics:

- has difficulty understanding and answering "wh" questions; e.g., where is the dog? What is on the table?

- confuses one "wh" question word with another; e.g., answers "Who is this?" with the name of a place not a person

- does not use "wh" question words when asking a question, but may use rising inflection; e.g., says "Mommy?" to mean "Where is Mommy?"

- has difficulty using reasoning to answer "why?" questions

"Wh" Questions Goals

The student will understand and use:

WHAT? **Goal 1:** question "what is it?"
Goal 2: a variety of "what?" questions.

WHO? **Goal 1:** question "who is it?"
Goal 2: a variety of "who?" questions.
Goal 3: contrasted "what?" and "who?" questions.

WHERE? **Goal 1:** "where" questions related to place names and position
Goal 2: contrasted "what/where?"; "who/where?"; and "what/who/where?" questions.

WHICH? **Goal:** "which?" questions related to choices.

WHEN? **Goal:** "when?" questions related to daily activities, calendar, seasons, conditions, and clock time.

MIXED QUESTION WORDS—1

Goal: "who?" "what?" "where?" "when?" related to the same subject.

WHOSE? **Goal:** "whose?" questions related to ownership (nouns and possessive pronouns "my," "your," "his," "her").

WHY? **Goal:** "why?" questions related to:
A. function; e.g., why do we need an eraser?
B. action; e.g., why is John running?
C. association; e.g., why do a dog bowl and a dog go together?
D. categorization; e.g., why are cows, horses, pigs, and chickens in the same group?
E. cause and effect; e.g., why is the peanut butter jar empty?
F. absurdity; e.g., why can't you brush your teeth with a hairbrush?

MIXED QUESTION WORDS—2

Goal: "what?" "who?" "where?" "which?" "when?" "whose?" "why?" related to the same subject.

WHAT? QUESTIONS

What? Goal 1:
The student will understand and use the question "what is it?" (with 80–90 percent accuracy).

Materials

1. 20 single toys/objects or pictures of toys/objects or animals familiar to the student; e.g., toy dog, pencil, glove, book.
2. Magic Bag.

Introduction

Introduce this goal by telling the student that she is going to learn to ask the question "what is it?" Pick up some of the toys/objects one at a time and model "what is it?" and give the answer; e.g., what is it? car; what is it? dog.

Activity **Receptive** and **Expressive**

Place some of the toys/objects or pictures in the Magic Bag and close it so that the student cannot see the items inside. Have the student reach through the opening and take out an object or picture. Ask her, "What is it?" Have the student name the item.

Then take turns taking an item/picture from the bag. When it is your turn, have the student ask you the target question. Model the question or prompt by giving the first word. Write the question on a cue card to give visual support to students who can read, as needed.

Carryover

- Play Memory, Lotto, or Tim's game. Take turns to ask and answer "what is it?" each time a new card is turned up.
- Model the question and answer when the student uses rising inflection. Example: Student: "Dog?" Instructor: "What is it? Yes, it is a dog."
- Ask "what is it?" in a variety of different situations through the day; e.g., when looking at pictures in a storybook; during a nature walk.
- Set up situations in which the student wants to know what something is. Example: Hide something behind your back and say, "I am hiding something—do you want to know what it is?" Prompt use of "what is it?"
- Provide a food unfamiliar to the student at a mealtime and encourage the student to ask "what is it?"

What? Goal 2:
The student will understand and use a variety of "what?" questions with 80–90 percent accuracy.

Materials

1. List WHAT? QUESTIONS ACTIVITIES, Table 69, below.
2. List WHAT? QUESTIONS (no visuals), Table 70, below.

Introduction

Tell the student that she is going to learn to use other "what?" questions, such as "what do you want?" or "what are you wearing?"

Activity **Receptive** and **Expressive**

Step 1: Use the list WHAT? QUESTIONS ACTIVITIES. Choose a target question and carry out the activities to elicit the question as suggested. Use a turn-taking format. Your turn will give the student a model of the target question. When it is the student's turn prompt as needed with verbal cues, or for the reader, write the question on a cue card.

Step 2: Use the list WHAT? QUESTIONS (no visuals):

For the nonreader: *Ask the questions orally.*

For the reader: *Print the questions on cardstock and cut them out. Either present each question individually and provide choice answers (if necessary) or play a turn-taking "ask and answer" game.*

Carryover

- Ask and encourage the student to ask "what?" questions in real-life situations throughout the day; e.g., what is Emma holding? What is Kyle wearing?
- Read stories and look at pictures and videos. Ask and answer "what?" questions.

TARGETING LANGUAGE DELAYS | 181

Table 69: WHAT? QUESTIONS ACTIVITIES

Question	Material	Activity
What did you get?	Lotto or Memory cards showing familiar single toys and objects A wrapped gift	Ask/answer the question each time a player turns up a card. Set up a situation in which the student or instructor is given a gift.
What is [person's name] doing? What is the boy/girl/animal/person doing? What are you doing?	Photos of family and peers (with permission) carrying out actions Lotto and Memory Picture books TV and videos Charades	Describe the action taking place in response to the question. Perform an action word; e.g., brushing teeth.
What do you want?	Go Fish game Play "restaurant"	Ask the other player the question before she asks for a card to match one that is in her hand; e.g., what do you want? Response: I want the turtle. Ask the "customer" what he wants to eat/drink.
What is/are he/she/you wearing?	Dolls/stuffed toys with clothing Department store catalog Everyday clothing Dress up clothes	Take turns describing clothing on toys, in pictures, or on peers and yourselves and ask the target question.
What did you put on?	Magnetic/felt scene	Take turns putting an item onto the scene and ask the other person, "What did you put on?"
What do you have?	Single-item pictures of familiar toys and objects	Deal out 5 pictures to each player and place them face down on the table. Take turns to turn up a picture and ask/answer, "What do you have?"

(Table 69 continued)

Question	Material	Activity
What can you see?	Look around the room or out of a window using binoculars or a telescope (paper towel roll) Play "I Spy"	Take turns to ask, "What can you see?" and name the item(s). Ask what a player can see and guess what she describes; e.g., what can you see? I can see something red. Response: Is it the mailbox?
What are you eating?	Shared meal or snack; e.g., crackers, grapes, M&Ms	Ask the other person, "What are you eating?" Response: e.g., a grape; a red M&M.
What is his/her name? What is your name?	Peers in the classroom or photos (with permission) of people familiar to the student and instructor; e.g., family, teachers	Name the person in the photo or circle of peers and ask what is the name of the next person; e.g., This is ____ (name). What is his/her name [pointing to next person]?
What is in there?	Box and collection of 5 toys, each small enough to fit into the box one at a time	Look at and memorize the collection of toys. Have the student close her eyes. Place one of the toys in the box. Ask, "What is in there?" Student looks at the remaining toys and guesses which toy is in the box. Have the student put one of the toys in the box while you close your eyes and then ask you the question.
What color is it?	Memory game using pairs of cards of primary colors Play I Spy (as above)	Ask "what color is it?" when opposing player turns up a card.

Table 70: WHAT? QUESTIONS (no visuals)

Question	Answer
1. What shines up in the sky?	Sun, moon, stars
2. What do we use to clean our teeth?	Toothbrush, toothpaste
3. What do we need to eat soup?	Spoon
4. What animal says "quack?"	Duck
5. What do we give someone on his birthday?	Gift
6. What is a lawnmower for?	Cut grass
7. What do we wear when it is cold out?	Coat, jacket
8. What do we use to cut up our food?	Knife
9. What does a zipper do?	Zip up a coat
10. What grows on trees?	Leaves
11. What feels cold?	Ice, snow
12. What animal likes to eat cheese?	Mouse
13. What do we use to dig a hole?	Shovel
14. What could you play on at the playground?	Swing, slide, climber
15. What keeps us warm in bed?	Blanket
16. What is a band-aid for?	Put on a cut (sore)
17. What do we eat for breakfast?	Cereal
18. What might we see at the zoo?	Elephant, tiger, lion, monkey
19. What do we turn on when it gets dark?	Light
20. What does fire do?	Burn

WHO? QUESTIONS

Who? Goal 1:

The student will understand and use question "who is it?" (with 80–90 percent accuracy).

Materials

1. 10 close-up photos of individual members of the student's family or individual friends of the student (with permission); e.g. Sarah, Kyle, Mommy.
2. 10 photos or pictures of people unknown to the student; e.g., boy/girl, man/lady.
3. 10 photos or pictures of people in familiar occupations/community helpers; e.g., fireman, doctor.

Introduction

Tell the student that she is going to learn to ask the question "who is it?" Use some of the pictures and photos from materials #1–3 and present them to the student one at a time. Model "who is it?" and give the answer. Examples: "Who is it?" "It is Mom." "Who is it?" "It is a doctor."

Activity **Receptive** and **Expressive**

Step 1: Present the photos of familiar people (materials #1) one at a time or place 2–6 face *up* on the table and spread them out. Name each person. Then point to one at a time and ask, "Who is it?" Have the student give the name. Repeat the activity and have the student use the target question to ask you the name of each one.

Step 2: Place 2 photos of familiar people (materials #1) face *down* on the table. Pick up one photo and hold it so that the student cannot see it. Have the student ask you, "Who is it?" and give the answer. Provide verbal prompts or, for the reader, the target sentence written on a cue card as needed.

Step 3: Repeat Steps 1 and 2 using the photos/pictures of people unknown to the student (materials #2) and those of community helpers (materials #3); e.g., boy/girl; fireman, teacher. Tell the student which group of pictures you are now working on; e.g., "Now we are going to play with the community helpers." Ask and answer "who is it?"

Carryover

- Ask "who is it?" in a variety of situations throughout the day; e.g., while looking at picture books, TV, and videos.
- Hide photos of familiar people between the pages of a storybook. As you turn the pages when reading the story, a photo will fall out, prompting the question "who is it?"

- Set up a situation where you and the student are in a room together with the door closed. Arrange for a third person to knock on the door. Encourage the student to ask "who is it?"
- Play commercial games that require a player to describe a person and the other players to guess who it is.

Who? Goal 2:

The student will understand and use a variety of "who?" questions (with 80–90 percent accuracy).

Materials

1. List WHO? QUESTIONS ACTIVITIES, Table 71, below.
2. List of WHO? QUESTIONS—OCCUPATIONS, Table 72, below.

Introduction

Explain to the student that she is going to learn to use other "who?" questions such as "who did you get?" or "who needs this?"

Activity **Receptive** and **Expressive**

Step 1: Use the list WHO? QUESTIONS ACTIVITIES. Choose a target question and carry out the activities to elicit the question as suggested. Use a turn-taking format. Model the target question. When it is the student's turn to use the question, prompt as needed with verbal cues, or for the reader, write the question on a cue card.

Step 2: Use the list WHO? QUESTIONS—OCCUPATIONS:

For the nonreader: *ask the questions orally.*

For the reader: *print the questions on cardstock and cut them out. Either present each question individually and provide choice answers (if needed) or play a turn-taking "ask and answer" game.*

Carryover

- Ask "who?" questions in many situations throughout the day. Examples: Who is your teacher? Who is helping you with your shoes? Who is coming home?
- Play Hide the Sticker. Place a sticker under one of several pictures of people spread out face down on the table. Take turns turning up a picture to find the sticker. Ask "who was that?" as you turn up people and "who was it under?" when the sticker is found.
- Play with toys that have miniature people; e.g., house, farm, garage. Ask questions about "who" is doing "what"; e.g., who is driving the tractor? Who is fixing the car?
- Make a collage of pictures of people cut from catalogs and magazines. Ask "who?" questions about them: Who is this? Who is wearing a red dress? Who is playing on the swing?

Table 71: WHO? QUESTIONS ACTIVITIES

Question	Material	Activity
Who did you get?	Pictures and photos of familiar people (with permission).	Take turns to take a picture out of the bag and ask, "Who did you get?"
	Lotto or Memory games using family members, boys and girls, or people in occupations (if the student knows the required vocabulary; e.g., fireman, doctor).	Ask, "Who did you get?" when the other player turns up a card.
Who is ____ ing? e.g., who is walking?	20 pictures or photos of individual people carrying out an action.	Take turns to pick up a card and ask; e.g., who is running? Response: a boy is running (or "a boy").
	TV, videos, picture books, magnetic scenes.	Discuss who is doing what.
Who did you put on?	Magnetic/felt scenes, scene-building computer games.	Take turns adding a person to the scene and asking the question.
Who needs this?	Commercial association cards; e.g., paintbrush/painter; dog bowl/dog.	Take turns to select the picture of an object and ask the other person the target question, then match it with the user.
Who has it?	Ball, circle of students, and music.	One student is in the middle of the circle. The students in the circle pass a ball from one to the next behind their backs. When the music stops, the students ask, "Who has it?" and the student in the middle guesses who has the ball. That person is then in the middle.

Table 72: WHO? QUESTIONS—OCCUPATIONS

Question	Answer
1. Who likes to play with toys?	Children
2. Who helps people when they are sick?	Doctor
3. Who teaches children at school?	Teacher
4. Who delivers the mail?	Mailman
5. Who takes care of children when their parents go out?	Babysitter
6. Who picks up the garbage?	Garbage man
7. Who drives a car?	Grown-up
8. Who is in charge of the school? .	Principal
9. Who cuts your hair?	Hairdresser
10. Who checks our teeth?	Dentist
11. Who cleans the school?	Janitor
12. Who drives the school bus?	Bus driver
13. Who looks after animals on the farm?	Farmer
14. Who looks after children at home?	Moms and Dads
15. Who rides in a stroller?	Baby
16. Who wears a dress?	Girl
17. Who goes in a rocket to the moon?	Astronaut
18. Who looks after us in the swimming pool?	Lifeguard
19. Who plays with us at recess?	Friend
20. Who helps a doctor?	Nurse

Who? Goal 3:

The student will understand and use contrasted "what?" and "who?" questions; e.g., what is the girl holding? Who is holding the ball? (with 80–90 percent accuracy).

Materials

1. Action picture scenes or magnetic/felt scenes with familiar people, animals, and objects arranged in an appropriate design.
2. 20 pictures of single people or single animals carrying out an action that is familiar to the student; e.g., a man eating; a baby sleeping; a dog running.

Introduction

Tell the student that you are going to ask her "what?" and "who?" questions. She will need to listen hard so that she does not get mixed up!

Show a picture scene or a magnetic/felt scene with items and people already arranged. Ask "what?" and "who?" questions and model the answer; e.g., what is the girl doing? (sliding); who is sliding? (the girl])

Emphasize the question word to draw the student's attention to it. Examples: *Who* is this? *What* is she doing? Provide visual support to the reader as needed by showing her "what?" or "who?" written on separate cue cards

Activity **Receptive** and **Expressive**

Step 1: Use the picture scenes or magnetic/felt scenes (material #1). Ask the student a variety of randomly mixed "who?" and "what?" questions. Examples: What is this? Who is this? What is on the grass? Who is on the swing?

Step 2: Use the materials as in Step 1. Have the student be the teacher and ask you questions. Prompt by pointing to the thing, person, or activity that you want her to ask you about.

Step 3: Use the action pictures. Ask who is carrying out the action and what action the person is carrying out; e.g., *who* is walking? (the boy); *what* is the boy doing? (walking).

Step 4: Use the action pictures as in Step 3. Have the student take turns to ask you questions.

Carryover

- Ask a variety of "who?" and "what?" questions through the day that refer to things and people in sight. Point out things that are novel to the student and encourage her to ask a question about them; e.g., an unfamiliar person, a strange object.

- During circle time or class assemblies ask "who?" and "what?" questions about students; e.g., who is missing today? Who has a blue shirt on? What is Kyle wearing? Who has a cat at home?

WHERE? QUESTIONS

Where? Goal 1:

The student will understand and use "where?" questions related to place names and positions; e.g., in the classroom, under the chair (with 80–90 percent accuracy).

Prerequisite: *Understanding of prepositions "in," "on top of," "under," "beside," "between," "next to," "in front," and "behind"—Chapter 1 (Following Directions), Goal 2, p. 18.*

Materials

1. 10 familiar toys, objects, or animals; e.g., ball, toy car, pencil, glove, cup, toy dog.
2. Large hand-drawn picture map of a town. (See below for directions.)
3. 5 toy people.
4. List WHERE? QUESTIONS, Table 73, below.

Map of a town: *On a white file folder, draw a layout of roads leading to a house, a school, a store, a park/pond/lake, or any other feature (e.g., arena) that would be significant to the student. Draw the buildings and write the name on each one. Simple outlines and squares or rectangles for the buildings are fine—this does not have to be a work of art! Involve the student in the design so that it is more meaningful to her.*

Introduction

Tell the student that she is going to learn to ask and answer "where?" questions. These tell us where we are or where someone or something is.

Model some examples: "Where are we?" (in the work room); "Where is my pencil?" (on the table).

Activity **Receptive** and **Expressive**

Step 1: Walk with the student from one room to another within the school. Each time you are in a new area, ask, "Where are we?" Have the student respond with the name of the room; e.g., library, gym, lunchroom. Then ask, "Where are we going?" as you plan to leave for a different room.

Have the student be the teacher and ask you, "Where are we?" Give verbal prompts or written support to the reader as needed.

Step 2: Use the familiar objects (materials #1). Place an object such as a ball in a specific location within the school or in relation to another object so that the student can see it easily. Ask the student, for example, "Where is the ball?" (in the library; beside the cup).

Alternate turns and have the student place an object and ask you where it is.

Encourage the student to include prepositions that she is familiar with, particularly those already learned in Chapter 1, Goal 2 ("in," "on top of," "under," "beside," "between," "next to," "in front," and "behind").

Step 3: Use the hand-drawn map. Take turns placing one of the people on the map and asking "where is the _____ (e.g., boy)?" Response: e.g., at the park, in the school. Make a person walk from one location to another on the map and ask, "Where is the _____ going?"(e.g., to the park).

Step 4: Present WHERE? QUESTIONS:

For the nonreader: *Ask the questions orally.*

For the reader: *Print the questions on cardstock and cut them out. Either present each question individually or play a turn-taking "ask and answer" game. Provide choice answers, if necessary.*

Carryover

- Ask "where are we going?" and "where are we?" frequently throughout the day. Sometimes act as though you are going to leave the room or guide the student on an unfamiliar route to the gym or playground, prompting the student to ask "where are you/we going?"
- Set up an activity for the student to do but omit or remove a critical item, so the student is prompted to ask where it is. Examples: Give the student her soup for lunch but don't give her a spoon (where is my spoon?); hide the student's boots when she is getting ready to go out at recess (where are my boots?); hide a puzzle piece (where is the piece?).
- Play Hide and Go Seek. One player is to hide and the "seeker" calls out "where are you?" The "hider" replies "here." The seeker calls the question frequently until she can locate the "hider" by listening to where her voice is coming from.
- Play verbal Hide and Find. One player hides an item such as a ball, and the other player tries to find the item by asking where it is; e.g., where is the ball? Is it on the shelf? The player who hid the item replies "yes" or "no." Questions and answers continue until the item is located. Each new question must begin with "where is the _____?" followed by a specific location.
- Play a cooperative Memory game. Use paired cards of any theme. Take turns to turn up one card and together find the matching pair by asking "where is the _____?" Time your game and see if you can find all of the cards in fewer minutes the next time that you play.
- Draw a picture of the interior of a house showing the different rooms. Cut out pictures of furniture and appliances from catalogs and arrange them in their correct rooms by asking the student, "Where do we put/glue the _____ (e.g., bed)?" (in the bedroom).
- Read stories and play commercial games that involve describing the position of a person, animal, or object.

Table 73: WHERE? QUESTIONS

Question	Answer
1. Where do we see the sun?	in the sky
2. Where is a bathtub?	in the bathroom
3. Where do some people keep their car?	in a garage
4. Where does a whale swim?	in the ocean
5. Where would you find a bird's egg?	in a nest
6. Where would you see a fridge?	in the kitchen
7. Where does a leaf grow?	on a tree
8. Where would you see your teacher?	in school
9. Where do we put gloves?	on our hands
10. Where do we have a pillow?	in bed
11. Where do we keep our clothes?	in a closet or dresser
12. Where do you see lots of books?	in the library
13. Where do you play at recess?	in the playground
14. Where do you keep your lunch?	in a lunchbox
15. Where do you change your shoes?	in the hallway
16. Where would you find a worm?	under the ground
17. Where is our hair?	on our head
18. Where do people live?	in a house
19. Where do you hang up your jacket?	on a hook
20. Where do you sit?	on a chair

Where? Goal 2:

The student will understand and use contrasted "what/where?"; "who/where?"; and "what/who/where?" questions related to visual items (with 80–90 percent accuracy).

Materials

1. Action picture scenes and magnetic/felt scenes with people and items arranged in an appropriate design.
2. Large hand-drawn map of a town and miniature people (as for where? Goal 1, above).

Introduction

Tell the student that now that she has learned to understand and use "what/who/where?" questions separately, you are going to work on them all together. She will need to listen carefully to the question word so that she can give the correct answer.

Show an action picture scene and model questions and answers. Examples: *Who* is at the playground? (a boy); *What* is the boy doing? (playing ball); *Where* is the boy? (at the playground).

Emphasize the question word to draw the student's attention to it.

Activity **Receptive** and **Expressive**

Use the action picture scenes, magnetic/felt scenes, and/or toy figures placed on the map. Ask the student a variety of "what/who/where?" questions about:

1. Different topics; e.g., where is the girl? What is the dog doing? Who is sitting on the bench?
2. The same topic; e.g., what is this? (swing set); Who is playing on the swing set? (boy); Where is the boy? (on the swing set).

Have the student take turns at being the teacher and ask you questions. If necessary, point to the item that you want her to ask you about. Provide verbal prompts for the non-reader and written prompts for the reader as needed.

Carryover

- Ask a variety of "what/who/where?" questions referring to the same people and things in real life, on TV, in videos, and in storybooks.
- Take photos of the student or you and the student together in different places and ask questions such as "who are you/we talking to?"; "where are you/we?"; what are you/we doing?"
- Going on an Adventure—create an imaginary adventure together and discuss who might go with you, where you might go, and what you might do there. Or take the student on a real adventure around the school; e.g., to find a treat at the office. Prompt her to ask "what/who/where?" questions to find out where you are taking her, what she will find there, who she will meet, etc.

WHICH? QUESTIONS

Which? Goal:

The student will understand and use "which?" questions related to choices; e.g., which book do you need for math class? (with 80–90 percent accuracy).

Materials

1. 20 single toys, objects, and animals or pictures of people, toys, objects, and animals that/who are familiar to the student.
2. Identical paired picture cards for Go Fish game.
3. List WHICH? CHOICE QUESTIONS, Table 74, below.

Introduction

Introduce this goal by telling the student that she is going to learn to ask and answer questions that begin with "which?"

Place 2 objects or object pictures face up on the table and model asking and answering. Example: Which one is the cow? This one is the cow. Provide several examples.

Activity **Receptive**

Use the real objects and/or single-item pictures:

Step 1: Place 2 objects or pictures face up on the table. Ask the student to point to the one that you name; e.g., which one is the car? Which one is the flower?

Step 2: Gradually increase the level of difficulty by:
   a. Increasing the number of objects/picture choices
   b. Raising the complexity of the question; e.g., which one has four feet? Which one has leaves? Which one is yellow? Which one can we eat?

Activity **Expressive**

Step 1: Play Go Fish (materials #2) and have each player ask "which one do you want?" before the other player requests a card to make up a pair. Provide verbal or written prompts as needed.

Step 2: Present WHICH? CHOICE QUESTIONS:

For the nonreader: *Ask the questions orally.*

For the reader: *Print the questions on cardstock and cut them out. Either present each question individually and provide choice answers (if needed) or play a turn-taking "ask and answer" game.*

Table 74: WHICH? CHOICE QUESTIONS

Question	Position of Answer	Correct Response	Correct/ Incorrect
1. Which do you use to tell the time? A *clock* or a necklace.	First		
2. Which would you ride on? A *bike* or a turtle.	First		
3. Which do you put on your cereal? Ketchup or *milk*.	Last		
4. Which do we pet? A *puppy* or a tiger.	First		
5. Which do you find at the beach? books or *sand*.	Last		
6. Which do we drink from? A pretzel or a *straw*.	Last		
7. Which do we find in a library? A *book* or a hammer.	First		
8. Which do we buy from the grocery store? Tires for the car or *food*.	Last		
9. Which one would a child play with? A *ball* or a saw.	First		
10. Which one is food? A rock or a *carrot*.	Last		
11. Which color means "stop"? Green or *red*.	Last		
12. Which do we walk on? *Feet* or hands.	First		
13. Which would you see in the classroom? A *desk* or a tree.	First		
14. Which animal lives on a farm? An elephant or a *cow*.	Last		
15. Which do we drink? *Water* or paint.	First		
16. Which animal makes a nest? A horse or a *bird*.	Last		
17. Which would you turn on to watch a movie? A *TV* or a fan.	First		
18. Which one do we use for cooking? A *stove* or a lawnmower.	First		
19. Which one smells nice? A dirty sock or a *flower*.	Last		
20. Which would we use to take a bath? A sink or a *bathtub*.	Last		
Total Correct: First		Last	

Note: *Be aware of the position of the answer in the choices that you present (first or last). Difficulty answering questions in which the answer occurs first of the two choices may suggest processing or auditory memory difficulties.*

Carryover

- Ask the student choice questions throughout the day. Examples: Which do you want to eat—the apple or the banana? Which T-shirt do you want to wear—the green one or the blue one?
- Set up situations in which the student is to offer choices to peers such as during art class. Have her ask, for example, "Paul, which color paper do you want?" Provide verbal prompts as needed.
- Play the Shell Game: Use 4 different-colored cups and a small treat or toy. Hide the toy under one of the upturned cups and shuffle them around. Have the student guess which cup the treat is under in response to "which one is it under?" Once the student understands the game, teach her to play it with peers and adults. Make sure that she asks the question correctly.

WHEN? QUESTIONS

When? Goal:

The student will understand and use "when?" questions (with 80–90 percent accuracy) related to:

- **daily activities; e.g., before supper, after recess.**
- **calendar; e.g., months of the year, days of the week, today/tomorrow/ yesterday.**
- **seasons; e.g., summer/winter/spring/fall, Christmas, Halloween.**
- **conditions; e.g., when it's hot, when you are tired.**
- **clock time.**

Prerequisite: *Understanding of concepts of time such as "before/after"—Chapter 9 (Concepts), Goal 4, p. 165 and Goal 5, p. 168.*

Materials

1. Calendar of student's activities and important events.
2. List of WHEN? QUESTIONS, Table 75, below.

Introduction

Tell the student that she is going to learn to ask and answer questions starting with "when?" to find out about time.

Model the use of "when" in statements during calendar time and other activities throughout the day. Examples: "We will eat lunch <u>when</u> we have finished art." "<u>When</u> you go to the library, you can get a new book." "It is cold today. You will need your coat on <u>when</u> you go outside."

Model how to ask and answer "when?" questions. Examples: "When do we come to school?" (in the morning). "When do we go to the playground?" (at recess). Support the reader with key words written on cue cards; e.g., attach "today," "tomorrow," "yesterday" to a calendar.

Activity **Receptive** and **Expressive**

Step 1—Daily Activities: Ask the student "when?" questions related to her daily activities. Have her fill in a daily schedule; e.g., "when are we going to the gym?" "When do we have lunch?" Use "before" and "after" or concepts of quantity; e.g., after recess; before lunch; every day.

Step 2—Calendar: Have the student complete a weekly or monthly calendar. Use key words "today," "tomorrow," and "yesterday." For example, "The field trip is tomorrow."

Step 3—Seasons: Discuss seasons. Examples: "When will it start to feel hot outside?" (summer). "When will the flowers begin to grow?" (spring).

Step 4—Conditions: Have the student complete your sentence. Examples: "Take off your jacket when… (you get to the classroom). "You should go to bed when…" (you feel tired).

Step 5—Clock Time: Ask questions related to clock time. Examples: "What do you do when it is 12 o'clock?" (have lunch). "When do we go home?" (3 o'clock).

Note: *Present Step 5 only if the student is already able to tell time. Teaching clock time is not included in this manual.*

General "When?" Questions—present WHEN? QUESTIONS:

For the nonreader: *Ask the questions orally.*

For the reader: *Print the questions on cardstock and cut them out. Either present each question individually and provide choice answers (if needed) or play a turn-taking "ask and answer" game. Encourage the student to use "when?" and concepts of time in her answer.*

Carryover

- Read isolated sentences that involve time from stories and ask "when?" questions; e.g., "the children went to the store after school." Question: "When did the children go to the store?" (after school).
- Look at pictures and discuss when the events are taking place; e.g., "there are leaves on the trees and the children are wearing shorts—when is this?" (summer).
- Sort seasonal pictures. Place a picture of each season face up on the table and have a stack of pictures of seasonal activities and holidays; e.g., swimming, skating, planting

Table 75: WHEN? QUESTIONS

Question	Answer
1. When do you get out of bed?	in the morning
2. When do we eat cereal?	at breakfast
3. When do we use a lawnmower?	when the grass is long
4. When do we take a bath?	when we are dirty
5. When do we get in the car?	when we want to go somewhere
6. When do we turn on the lights?	when it is dark
7. When do we close our eyes?	when we are sleepy
8. When do the stars and moon come out?	at night
9. When do we see new leaves on the trees?	in the spring
10. When do we brush our teeth?	before we go to bed
11. When do we answer the phone?	when it rings
12. When do children ride a bus?	when they go to school
13. When do we wear pajamas?	at night time
14. When do we use a toothbrush?	when we clean our teeth
15. When do we look at a clock?	when we want to know the time
16. When do we need a pencil sharpener?	when we have to sharpen a pencil
17. When do we drink water?	when we are thirsty
18. When do we call a fireman?	when there is a fire
19. When do we go to the mailbox?	when the mailman has delivered the mail
20. When do we use a spoon?	when we eat soup

flowers, jack-o'-lantern. When the student takes a card from the stack, ask her when she would do that particular activity. Examples: "When do we go swimming?" (summer). "When do we send someone a Valentine card?" (Valentine's day).

- Sort clothing pictures. Discuss when you or someone else would wear each piece of clothing; e.g., swimsuit (when it is hot); thick jacket (when it is cold); bike helmet (when riding a bike).
- Make a collage of seasonal activities and/or clothing using pictures from catalogs.
- Hide the student's visual schedule for part of the day and encourage her to ask when she is to go to her various activities.
- Discuss TV and sports schedules. Examples: "When are the Blue Jays playing next?" "When is the movie *Cinderella* on TV?"

Mixed Question Words—1 Goal:

The student will answer questions beginning with mixed question words relating to the same subject (who? what? where? when?); e.g., where do we sleep? When do we sleep? Who sleeps? What do we sleep on? (with 80–90 percent accuracy).

Materials

1. 20 pictures of single people or single animals carrying out an action that is familiar to the student; e.g., a man eating; a baby sleeping; a dog running.
2. 20 pictures of single familiar household items; e.g., toothbrush, chair, saucepan.

Introduction

Tell the student that you are going to ask different questions about the same thing, and you will use lots of different question words. She will need to listen carefully to the question word that you use.

Choose a single person or animal picture and/or a picture of a familiar household item and model questions/answers related to it. Example—action picture of "dog running": "What is running?" "Where is it running?" "Who can run?" "When do we run?" Object picture of "toothbrush": "What do we do with a toothbrush?" "Where do we keep a toothbrush?" "Who uses a toothbrush?" "When do we use a toothbrush?"

Activity **Receptive** and **Expressive**

Present mixed "who/what/where/when?" questions related to single people or animals carrying out actions and/or familiar household items (materials #1 and #2). Example—stove: "Who uses the stove?" "What is a stove?" "Where is the stove?" "When does someone use the stove?"

Use the same materials and have the student ask you questions.

Add variety by placing the pictures in a Magic Bag and taking turns to take one out, or use Tim's Game.

Carryover

- Read a story to the student and ask questions about a specific sentence; e.g., Jane is going to the park after school. Questions: "Where is Jane going?" "Who is going to the park?" "What is Jane doing?" "When is she going to the park?"
- Encourage the student to ask and answer a variety of questions on many subjects within her general knowledge throughout the day; e.g., "What do we do with a bicycle?" "Where do you ride your bicycle?" "When do we ride a bicycle?" "Who rides a bicycle?"

WHOSE? QUESTIONS

Whose? Goal:

The student will understand and use "whose?" questions related to ownership (nouns and possessive pronouns "my," "your," "his," "her") with 80–90 percent accuracy.

Prerequisite: *Use of possessive "s" marker; e.g., Tom's, and possessive pronouns "my," "your," "his," "her"—Chapter 11 (Word and Sentence Structure), Goal 7, p. 230 and Chapter 12 (Pronouns), Goal 4, p. 254 and Goal 5, p. 257.*

Materials

1. 20 objects that belong to specific people familiar to the student including you and the student; e.g., your coat, Mom's shoe, Isobel's crayon, student's hat.
2. 20 pictures of people and animals with an object that they own; e.g., dog with its bone; man with his coat; girl with her bike.

Introduction

Tell the student that when we find something and want to know to whom it belongs, we ask a "whose?" question. For instance, if the teacher finds a coat on the floor, she might ask, "Whose coat is this?" and a student might answer, "It is my coat" or "It is Kyle's coat." She is going to learn to understand and use questions that start with "whose?"

Activity **Receptive** and **Expressive**

Step 1: Use the collection of objects (materials #1). Take turns to pick up an object and ask "Whose is it?" The other person will reply; e.g., my coat; your shoe; Mom's glove.
Provide verbal prompts, or prompt students who can read with the written word "whose?" as needed.

Step 2: Use the pictures of people and animals with an object that they own. Take turns to point to the object in the picture and ask/answer a "whose?" question; e.g., whose cat is this? (the girl's cat).

Carryover

- Sort laundry at home and the "Lost and Found" at school. Example: "Whose shoes are these?" Response: A boy's shoes.
- Set up situations in which objects are in the wrong place; e.g., clothing on the floor; a workbook on the wrong table. Have the student ask her peers questions such as "whose backpack is on the floor?" "Whose workbook is this?"

WHY? QUESTIONS

Why? Goals A-F:

The student will understand and use "why?" questions (with 80–90 percent accuracy) related to:

    A. function; e.g., why do we need an eraser?
    B. action; e.g., why is John running?
    C. association; e.g., why do a dog bowl and a dog go together?
    D. categorization; e.g., why are cows, horses, pigs, and chickens in the same group?
    E. cause and effect; e.g., why is the peanut butter jar empty?
    F. absurdity; e.g., why can't you brush your teeth with a hairbrush?

General Suggestions for Developing Reasoning Skills Required to Understand & Answer "Why?" Questions

Prior to and during work on "why?" questions:

1. Make statements about everyday events, objects, or actions that include a reason; e.g., we are going to the playground *because it is recess time;* you need a coat *so you can keep warm.*
2. Make reasoning statements and follow them immediately with a "why?" question about the information. Example: "We need scissors to cut paper. Why do we need scissors?" To cut paper (answer the question yourself or have the student answer it).
3. Start statements and have the student finish them. Examples: "I am putting on my coat because _____" (it's cold outside); "we wash our hands because _____" (they are dirty).

Encourage the student to use conjunctions "because," "to," "so," and "so that."

If the student is unable to answer a "why?" question, try either or both of these strategies:

a. Supply the statement and question again and model the answer; e.g., "I am putting on my coat because it's cold outside. Why am I putting on my coat? Because it's cold outside."
b. Supply the statement and question and provide a choice answer; e.g., "I am putting my coat on because it is supper time or because it is cold outside?"

Note: *The student may give a reason that is not the one you are expecting. Example: "Why do we need a spoon?" Student: "Because I like ice cream." Acknowledge her answer, since she did use reasoning and "because," and then model the answer you were expecting; e.g., we need a spoon because we are going to eat some ice cream.*

Goal A: The student will understand and use "why?" questions related to *function*; e.g., why do we need an eraser? (with 80–90 percent accuracy).

Prerequisite: *Ability to describe object function—Chapter 5 (Nouns), Goal 2, p. 58.*

Materials

1. 20 familiar single objects or pictures of single objects that have a function; e.g. pen, cup, car, T-shirt.
2. List WHY? QUESTIONS RELATED TO FUNCTION, Table 76, below.

Introduction

Introduce this goal by saying that you are going to talk about why we have or why we need certain things. Point to an object in the room, ask a question about it, and model the answer. Example: "Why do we need a chair? Because we sit on it (or so we have something to sit on)." Model other examples.

Activity **Receptive** and **Expressive**

Step 1: Use the collection of familiar objects. Take turns to ask and answer "why?" questions related to object function, such as "why do we need _____?"; "why do we use _____?"; or "why do we have _____?" Examples: "Why do we need gloves?" "Why do we use a toothbrush?" "Why do we have erasers?"

Provide verbal prompts, or for students who can read, write the question word "why?" on a cue card and use as needed.

Step 2: Present WHY? QUESTIONS RELATED TO FUNCTION:

For the nonreader: *Ask the questions orally.*

For the reader: *Print the questions on cardstock and cut them out. Either present each question individually and provide choice answers (if needed) or play a turn-taking "ask and answer" game.*

Note: *There is more than one possible answer to some of the questions.*

Carryover

- Ask "why?" questions related to the function of objects in everyday life within the student's general knowledge; e.g. why do you need a backpack?

Table 76: WHY? QUESTIONS RELATED TO FUNCTION

Question	Answer
1. Why do we have chairs?	To sit on
2. Why do we need a school bus?	To take children to school
3. Why do we need a bed?	To sleep in
4. Why do we need a house?	To live in
5. Why do we use a telephone?	To talk to someone
6. Why do we need water?	To drink
7. Why do we need teeth?	To bite things
8. Why do we use a table?	To put things on
9. Why do we have ears?	To hear
10. Why do we need a clock?	To tell time
11. Why do we have a nose?	To smell
12. Why do we use a lawnmower?	To cut grass
13. Why do birds have wings?	To fly
14. Why do people have dogs?	To pet
15. Why do we need doors?	To stop someone coming in
16. Why do we need a shovel?	To dig
17. Why do we need a bell?	To ring
18. Why do we have chickens?	To lay eggs
19. Why do we use a hammer?	To hit nails
20. Why do we use a toothbrush?	To clean our teeth

Goal B: The student will understand and use "why?" questions related to *action;* e.g., why do we climb a ladder? (with 80–90 percent accuracy).

Review: *Chapter 7 (Verbs), Goal 6, p. 114. Emphasize "why?" questions.*

Goal C: The student will understand and use "why?" questions related to *associated items;* e.g., why does the dog bowl go with the dog? (with 80–90 percent accuracy).

Review: *Chapter 5 (Nouns), Goal 3 Association 1–5, pp. 61-71. Emphasize "why?" questions.*

Goal D: The student will understand and use "why?" questions related to *categories;* e.g., why do the cow, the pig, and the horse go together? (because they are all animals) (with 80–90 percent accuracy).

Prerequisite: *Ability to generate the name of the category, given a list of items, and to generate a list of items in a given category or classification—Chapter 6 (Classification and Categorization), Goal 3, p. 81 and Goal 4, p. 89.*

Materials

- Toys, objects, and animals and/or pictures of toys, objects, and animals (at least 3 of each) that belong in the same category (minimum 10 categories).

Introduction

Tell the student that you are going to talk about why we put things in the same group. Use the pictures of objects, items, and animals. Lay 3 pictures from the same category face up on the table; e.g., cow, horse, pig. Ask a "why?" question about the relationship between the pictures and model the answer; e.g., "why do the cow, horse, and pig go together?" (because they are all animals). Present several examples from different categories.

Activity **Receptive** and **Expressive**

Step 1: Use the pictures of objects, items, and animals in a variety of categories. Have the student sort the pictures into their category or classification and ask her why they belong together; e.g., "why do the car, the truck, and the bus go together?" (because they are all vehicles).

Step 2—Exclusion: As for Chapter 6, Goal 4, p. 89—arrange 3 pictures that belong in the same category face up on the table along with one picture that does *not* belong; e.g., horse, pig, <u>bus</u>, sheep. Ask, "Why does this one *not* belong in the category?" e.g., "why does the bus *not* belong with the farm animals?" (because it is *not* an animal).

Carryover

- Ask "why?" questions about categorized items in real life; e.g., "why has the teacher put pictures of a pumpkin and a witch on the wall?" (because they are for Halloween).
- Play Lotto, Go Fish, and Memory using pictures in the same categories.
- Play commercial category games, computer games, and apps and discuss why the items go together.

Goal E: The student will understand and use "why?" questions related to *cause and effect*; e.g., why is Julie wearing a Band-Aid? (with 80–90 percent accuracy).

Materials

- Commercial picture card sets for cause and effect.

Introduction

Tell the student that you are going to talk about why things happen. Show her one of the commercial pictures that shows something that has happened and discuss what caused it to happen; e.g., a piece of cheese with a big piece missing from it (caused by a mouse eating it); children cheering at a soccer game (caused by one of their team scoring a goal).

Table 77: CAUSE AND EFFECT SAMPLE QUESTIONS

Why is the car dirty?	Why is the dog food bowl empty?
Why is the sidewalk wet?	Why is Anna laughing?
Why is the dog barking?	Why is the window closed?
Why is the ice cream melting?	Why is Jane's hair messy?
Why is the flower wilting?	Why are there crumbs on the table?
Why is Kyle crying?	Why is there paint on Paul's shirt?
Why is the grass short?	Why are the toys all over the floor?
Why is the toothpaste tube empty?	Why is there no picture on the TV?

Activity **Receptive** and **Expressive**

Step 1: Use the commercial pictures and ask a "why" question about the cause of the event or happening. Provide choice answers if necessary. Example: "Why is the grass short?" ("Because someone cut it with a lawnmower or because someone cut it with scissors?")

See sample questions in Table 77 on page 204.

Step 2: Ask "why?" questions about cause and effect in stories: e.g., "why are the boys going to the park?" "Why is the boat on the beach?"

Step 3: Ask "why?" questions related to cause and effect in real-life situations: e.g., "why is Sandy sharpening her pencil?" "Why is it dark in the classroom?"

Reverse roles and encourage the student to ask you questions about pictures and real-life events.

Carryover

- Set up situations and discuss why things happen or happened. Examples: Put ice cubes in a bowl in the sun (why did the ice melt?); leave a bowl under a dripping tap (why is the bowl full of water?).
- Read storybooks or watch TV or movies and ask why the characters did/are going to do something. Examples: "Why is she crying?" "Why is he yelling?"
- Play games or play with toys and discuss cause and effect. Examples: "Why did the block tower fall down?" "Why is she 'out'?" "Why did he move 3 spaces?"

Goal F: The student will understand negative "why?" questions involving *absurdity*; e.g. why can't you brush your teeth with a hairbrush? (with 80–90 percent accuracy).

Prerequisite: *Ability to recognize what is wrong (absurd) in situations, pictures, or spoken sentences—Chapter 4 (Yes/No), Goals 1–4 pp. 40-45 and Chapter 13 (Advanced Expressive Language), Goal 4, p. 269.*

Materials

- List of NEGATIVE "WHY?" QUESTIONS RELATED TO ABSURDITY, Table 78, below.

Introduction

Introduce this goal by saying to the student that sometimes we ask questions that are silly! For instance, you might ask, "Why can't we put ice cream in the oven?" "That is silly! We can't put ice cream in the oven because it would melt."

Activity **Receptive** and **Expressive**

Present NEGATIVE "WHY?" QUESTIONS RELATED TO ABSURDITY:

For the nonreader: *Ask the questions orally.*

For the reader: *Print the questions on cardstock and cut them out. Either present each question individually and provide choice answers (if needed) or play as a turn-taking "ask and answer" game.*

Note: *There is more than one possible answer for some of the questions.*

Carryover

- Discuss absurdities in real-life situations. Examples: "Why can't the bus have square wheels?" "Why can't we eat lunch as soon as we get to school in the morning?"
- Look at books and pictures with absurdities and discuss; e.g., *Cloudy with a Chance of Meatballs* by Judi Barrett.
- Look at hidden picture scenes and ask questions such as why you would not really find a fish in a tree.

Mixed Question Words—2 Goal:

The student will answer questions beginning with mixed question words relating to the same subject without visual support ("who?" "what?" "where?" "which?" "when?" "whose?" "why?"); e.g., who sleeps? What do we sleep on? Where do we sleep? Which one is sleeping? When do we sleep? Whose dog is sleeping? Why do we sleep?

Note: *This is a review of Mixed Questions—1 with the addition of "which?," "whose?," and "why" questions.*

Materials

- 10 picture scenes (paper, magnetic, or felt) in which a variety of people and animals are carrying out familiar activities; e.g., a girl flying a kite; a man feeding ducks; a boy riding his bike.

Introduction

Tell the student that you are going to ask questions about the same picture using lots of different question words. She will need to listen carefully to the question word that you use.

Select one of the picture scenes. Model questions and answers related to it. Example (picture scene of a park): "What is the dog doing?" "Where is the dog running?" "Who is running with the dog?" "There are two dogs—which dog is running?" "When does a dog run?" "Whose dog is running?" "Why is the dog running?"

Table 78: NEGATIVE "WHY?" QUESTIONS RELATED TO ABSURDITY

Question	Student Response	Correct/ Incorrect
1. Why wouldn't you have a tiger as a pet?		
2. Why don't you carry water in a sock?		
3. Why can't you comb your hair with a spoon?		
4. Why don't we keep a car in the kitchen?		
5. Why can't you take a bath in the sink?		
6. Why don't we keep ice cream in the oven?		
7. Why can't we build a snowman in the summer?		
8. Why can't you take your socks off before your shoes?		
9. Why can't you eat a sandwich under water?		
10. Why can't a sheep go to school?		
11. Why can't you have bare feet outside in winter?		
12. Why isn't a window made out of bricks?		
13. Why can't you put your pen in the pencil sharpener?		
14. Why can't you eat soup with a fork?		
15. Why can't you ride an airplane to school?		
16. Why can't you use a balloon to play baseball?		
17. Why wouldn't you pour juice on your cereal?		
18. Why wouldn't you eat a potato for dessert?		
19. Why wouldn't you wear eyeglasses on the back of your head?		
20. Why wouldn't you cut up your food with a pencil?		

Activity **Receptive** and **Expressive**

Present mixed questions beginning with "who/what/where/which/when/whose/why?" related to people, animals, and activities in the picture scenes.

Encourage the student to ask you questions. If necessary, point to a particular person, animal, or activity that you want her to ask you about.

Carryover

- Read a story to the student and use multiple question words to ask her about specific sentences. Example: "Jane is going to the park after school." Questions: "Where is Jane going?" "Who is going to the park?" "What is Jane doing?" "When is she going to the park?" "Why is she going to the park?" "Which park is she going to?"
- Encourage the student to ask and answer a variety of questions on many subjects within her general knowledge throughout the day. Examples: "What do we do with a bicycle?" "Where do you ride your bicycle?" "When do we ride a bicycle?" "Who rides a bicycle?" "Whose bicycle is John riding?" "Why do you ride a bicycle?" "Which bicycle do you like to ride best—your new one or your old one?"
- Plan together a field trip, party, or other special event (real or imaginary) and discuss: "Who will go with you?" "Where will you go?" "When will you go?" "What will you take?"

Note: *Additional "Wh" questions can be found in:*
- Chapter 16 (Listening Skills: Auditory Processing), Goals 1–7, pp. 309-26
- Chapter 7 (Verbs), Goal 5, p. 110, Goal 6, p. 114, and Goal 7, p. 116
- Chapter 5 (Nouns), Goal 2, p. 58 and Goal 5, p. 71

11.
Word and Sentence Structure

These goals are appropriate for students with one or more of the following characteristics:

- has difficulty understanding oral or written language due to limited knowledge of the rules of word and sentence structure; e.g., personal pronouns, irregular plurals, past tense verbs

- expresses himself in single words, phrases, or incomplete sentence structures

- delivers an unclear message due to grammatical errors; e.g., me wented tomorrow

Word and Sentence Structure Goals

The student will increase length and complexity of utterance by the use of:

Goal 1: subject + is/are + "ing" verb; e.g., Dad is running; horses are eating.

Goal 2: article (the, a/an) + is/are + "ing" verb; e.g. the dog is running.

Goal 3: article + is/are + "ing" verb + article + object or place; e.g., the cat is climbing a tree; the dogs are running in the field.

Goal 4: subjective and possessive personal pronouns; e.g., he, she, they, his, my (see Chapter 12, Pronouns, p. 247).

Goal 5: present, past, and future verb tenses (regular and irregular); e.g., is walking/walked/will walk; is catching/caught/will catch.

Goal 6: noun plurals (regular and irregular); e.g., dogs, mice.

Goal 7: possessive "s" marker; e.g., Ann's hat, the dog's collar.

Goal 8: descriptors (adjectives and adverbs); e.g., the big dog; running fast (see Chapter 8, Descriptors, p. 119-45).

Goal 9: conjunction "and" to connect two nouns or two related sentences; e.g., dog and cat; the sun is shining and the sky is blue.

Goal 10: comparative "er" and superlative "est" forms of descriptors:

    a. big, bigger, biggest.
    b. small, smaller, smallest.
    c. a variety of common descriptors.
    d. good, better, best

Goal 1: The student will develop use of subject + is/are + "ing" verb (present progressive verb tense, singular and plural); e.g., Dad is running; cats are playing (with 80–90 percent accuracy).

Prerequisite: *Understanding and use of at least 20 verbs and familiarity with present progressive "ing" verb ending—Chapter 7 (Verbs), Goals 1–3 p. 100-108.*

Materials

1. 20 photos (with permission) of single people known to the student by name and/or single animals carrying out a familiar action; e.g., Mom is eating; cat is sleeping; Ella is walking.
2. 20 photos (with permission) or pictures of groups of people or animals all carrying out the same action; e.g., dogs are running; horses are eating; girls are clapping.
3. 10 pairs of pictures of single and multiple people/animals carrying out the same action; e.g., cat is sleeping/cats are sleeping; girl is climbing/girls are climbing.

Introduction

Introduce this goal by saying that you are going to talk about who is doing what in a picture. Select some of the photos/pictures of people or animals carrying out an action and model subject + is/are + "ing" verb; e.g., Mom is clapping; Kyle is jumping; cats are sleeping.

Activity **Receptive**

Step 1—"Is": Place a choice of two (or more depending on the student's ability) of the photos of single people known to the student by name and/or a single animal carrying out a familiar action (materials #1) face up on the table. Describe a picture using subject + <u>is</u> + "ing" verb (avoid including an article). Have the student point to or give you the picture that you describe; e.g., point to "Dad is sitting"; "Andy is jumping"; "bird is flying."

Confirm the student's correct use of the structure. Example: "Good, you pointed to 'Dad is sitting.'"

When the student has demonstrated the understanding of "is" to 80–90 percent accuracy, progress to Step 2.

Step 2—"Are": Present a choice of two or more pictures of more than one person or animal carrying out the same action (materials #2) and have the student point to the one that you describe using subject + <u>are</u> + "ing" verb; e.g., give me "frogs are swimming"; give me "boys are playing."

When the student has demonstrated understanding of "are" to 80–90 percent accuracy, progress to Step 3.

Step 3—"is" and "are": Present pairs of mixed pictures of single people/animals and groups of people/animals carrying out the same action (materials #3). Have the student discriminate "is" and "are" in your description. Examples: Find "dogs <u>are</u> playing" (paired with "dog <u>is</u> playing"); Find "boy <u>is</u> eating" (paired with "boys <u>are</u> eating").

Activity **Expressive**

Step 1: Present materials #1 and #2 and have the student imitate as you model first singular and later, plural structures; e.g., Mom <u>is</u> walking; dogs <u>are</u> playing.

Step 2: Have the student describe the pictures using "is" and "are" independently. Support the non-reader with verbal prompts and the reader with written "is" and "are" cue cards as needed.. Use a Magic Bag or Tim's Game to add interest.

Note: *It is not necessary for the student to use articles in this activity.*

Carryover

- Describe everyday actions being carried out by people and animals familiar to the student; e.g., Laurie is standing; Jess is sitting; birds are singing.
- Play Memory, Go Fish, and Snakes/Chutes and Ladders using action pictures.

Goal 2: The student will develop use of articles (the, a/an) + "is/are" + "ing" verb (present progressive verb tense singular and plural); e.g., a dog is running; the stars are shining (with 80–90 percent accuracy).

Prerequisite: *Understanding of "the," "a," and "an"—Chapter 9 (Concepts), Goal 2, Teaching Concepts of Quantity, p. 157.*

Materials

- 20 pictures of single and groups of people and/or animals carrying out familiar actions; e.g., dogs are running; horse is eating; girls are clapping; ducks are swimming. Include animals whose name begins with a vowel; e.g., elephant is eating; owl is flying.

Introduction

Tell the student that he is going to learn to make his sentences a little longer by adding "the," "a," or "an."

Select some of photos/pictures of people or animals carrying out an action and model the use of "the." Emphasize the article to make it more obvious; e.g., <u>the</u> dog is eating; <u>the</u> girls are running.

When the student has completed Step 1 below and has established the use of "the," introduce Step 2 by modeling the use of "a" and "an"; e.g., <u>an</u> elephant is eating; <u>a</u> dog is barking. Provide modeling and verbal prompts as needed. Prompt the reader with the written words.

Activity **Receptive**

Step 1—"The": Use 10 of the photos of single people and/or animals carrying out an action (*exclude* those names that start with a vowel). Place a choice of two (or more depending on the student's ability) face up on the table. Have the student point to or give you the picture that you describe using "the"; e.g., show me "<u>the</u> boy is standing"; show me "<u>the</u> girls are sitting."

Step 2—"A" and "An": Use the remaining 10 pictures of single people and/or animals carrying out an action (*include* those names that start with a vowel). Present a choice of two or more. Have the student point to or give you pictures that you describe using "a" or "an"; e.g., point to "<u>a</u> dog running"; point to "<u>an</u> owl flying."

Activity **Expressive**

Step 1: Use the same pictures as in Step 1 and 2 Activity *Receptive* above. Have the student imitate you as you model use of articles; e.g., <u>the</u> dogs are playing; <u>a</u> dog is jumping.

Step 2: Have the student describe the pictures independently using "the," "a," and "an."

Carryover

- Play Snap using a 2-word response (article and noun) when 2 black cards or 2 red cards come together. Instead of saying "snap," players say a prearranged article + noun; e.g., "the dog" or "a cookie," or "an elephant." Players must say both words to win the stack of cards.
- Play Lotto and Memory games. Use verb cards and encourage the use of the full sentence structure; e.g. an elephant is eating; the horse is jumping.
- Set up situations in which there are groups of items, some of which are single and others multiple; e.g., craft/art items (crayons, pom-poms, paper of different colors); snack foods (chips, crackers, M&Ms); toys (vehicles, animals). Have the student request the item(s) that he wants. Examples: "I want the red crayon" (when there is only 1 red available); "I want a blue crayon" (when there are lots of blue crayons); "I want the cookies"; "I want a big cookie."
- Model and encourage correct use of articles and present progressive verb tense throughout the day; e.g., I am using a blue crayon; you are eating the big cookie.

Goal 3: The student will develop use of article + is/are + "ing" verb + article + object or place; e.g., the cat is climbing a tree; the dogs are running in the field (with 80–90 percent accuracy).

Prerequisite: *Understanding and use of prepositions—Chapter 1 (Following Directions), Goal 2, p. 18; understanding of "what? who? and where?" questions—Chapter 10 ("Wh" Questions, What? Who? Where?), pp. 179-92.*

Materials

1. 20 pictures of people and animals (single and in groups) carrying out a familiar action with a familiar object; e.g., girls riding bikes; a dog chasing a ball.

2. 20 pictures of single people and animals carrying out a familiar action, each in a different but familiar place; e.g., a girl sitting on a chair; a dog running in the park.
3. Written sentences cut into word chunks that describe the action pictures;
e.g., the cat | is climbing | a tree.

Introduction

Tell the student that he is going to learn to make sentences that tell us "who is doing what with what" and "who is doing what where." For instance, if I say "the girl is eating an apple," you would know who is doing something (the girl), what she is doing (eating), and what she is eating (an apple). If I say "the boy is working in the classroom," you know who is doing something (the boy), what he is doing (working), and where he is doing it (in the classroom). Model several examples.

Activity **Receptive**

Step 1: Present a choice of action pictures showing people or animals performing a familiar action with a familiar object (materials #1). Have the student point to the picture that you describe using article + is/are + "ing" verb + article + object; e.g., point to "the dog is eating *a bone*"; point to "the boys are climbing *a tree.*"

Step 2: Present a choice of pictures of people and/or animals performing an action in a variety of familiar places (materials #2). Have the student show you the picture that you describe using article + is/are + "ing" verb + article + place; e.g., show me "the dogs are playing *in the park;* show me "the boy is standing *beside the chair.*"

Activity **Expressive**

Step 1: Have the student imitate you as you model the target sentence structures using materials #1 and then materials #2; e.g., the boys are eating *hot dogs*; the girls are swimming *in the pool.*

Step 2: Start a sentence and have the student complete it by adding the object (materials #1) or the place (materials #2). Examples: The girl is holding _____ (a ball); the dog is lying _____ (on the grass).

Step 3: Have the student describe the pictures independently. Provide verbal prompts as needed. Use a Magic Bag or Tim's Game to add interest.

Step 4—For the Reader: Use the written sentences that have been cut into word chunks (materials #4). Present the target picture and the word chunks of the matching sentence. Mix up the order of the chunks and have the student arrange them correctly:
e.g., in the park | the dogs | are walking
is arranged to: the dogs | are walking | in the park

Carryover

- Play Lotto and Memory using verb cards and encourage the use of full sentence structures.
- Describe pictures, photos, movie scenes, and real-life situations.

Goal 4: The student will understand and use subjective and possessive personal pronouns (with 80–90 percent accuracy).

Due to the many steps involved in the learning of personal and possessive pronouns, this goal has been placed in a chapter of its own—Chapter 12 (Pronouns), p. 245.

Goal 5: The student will understand and use present, past, and future verb tenses (regular and irregular); e.g., the boy is walking/walked/will walk; the cat is catching/caught/will catch a mouse (with 80–90 percent accuracy).

Prerequisite: *Knowledge of concepts of time—Chapter 9 (Concepts), Goals 4 and 5 pp. 165, 168; understanding of sequential events—Chapter 13 (Advanced Expressive Language), Goal 2, p. 265.*

Materials

1. Photos or pictures of a single person or animal carrying out the same *regular verb* (action) in the same setting. 1 photo/picture of each person/animal in each tense—present progressive, regular past, and future; e.g., the boy <u>is jumping</u> the fence; the boy <u>jumped</u> the fence; the boy <u>will jump</u> the fence. Show 6 regular verbs; e.g., walk, cry, clap, mail, paint, pour.
2. Photos or pictures of a single person or animal carrying out the same *irregular verb* (action) in the same setting. 1 photo/picture in each tense—present progressive, irregular past, and future; e.g., the boy <u>is eating</u> an apple; the boy <u>ate</u> an apple; the boy <u>will eat</u> an apple. Show 6 irregular verbs; e.g., blow, catch, make, read, sit, throw.
3. Large hand-drawn picture map of a town (see below for instructions).
4. 5 toy people.
5. 10 picture scenes (paper, magnetic, vinyl, or felt) in which a variety of people and animals are carrying out familiar activities; e.g., a girl flying a kite; a man feeding ducks; a boy riding his bike.
6. Sequence story cards showing a variety of people and animals carrying out familiar activities.
7. List TRACKING VERB TENSE—REGULAR PAST and FUTURE, Table 79, p. 221 and TRACKING VERB TENSE—IRREGULAR PAST and FUTURE, Table 80, p. 223.
8. Activity IRREGULAR PAST TENSE VERBS FOR MATCHING, Table 81, p. 224.

Map of a town: *On a white file folder or large piece of white cardstock, draw a layout of roads leading to a house, a school, a store, a park/pond/lake, or any other feature that would be significant to the student; e.g., arena. Draw the buildings and write the name on each one. Simple outlines and squares or rectangles for the buildings are fine—this does not have to be a work of art! Involve the student in the design so that it is more meaningful to him.*

Introduction

Tell the student that when we talk about things that are happening now, have happened in the past, or are going to happen sometime in the future we change the ending of the "doing" (action) word. Give an example relevant to the student. Example: "We are <u>working</u> in the work room now"; "we <u>worked</u> in the classroom this morning"; "we <u>will work</u> in the library this afternoon."

Model each Step below before having the student carry it out. Provide verbal prompts or written support for students who can read as needed.

Use TRACKING VERB TENSE—REGULAR PAST and FUTURE and TRACKING VERB TENSE—IRREGULAR PAST and FUTURE to track the student's progress as he learns to understand and use the correct tense.

Step 1: Present Progressive "ing" and Regular Past Tense

Activity **Receptive**

Tell the student to listen for "is" and "ing" in verbs that are happening now and for "ed" at the end of verbs that have already happened; e.g., walking/walked.

a. Use materials #1. Select a verb and place the present progressive "ing" and regular "ed" past tense picture cards of the same verb face up on the table. Model a short sentence in the appropriate tense when pointing to each card; e.g., "the girl <u>is kicking</u> the ball"; "the girl <u>kicked</u> the ball."

b. Use materials #1. Have the student show you the picture that goes with the sentence that you say; e.g., show me "the girl <u>is kicking</u> the ball"; show me "the girl <u>kicked</u> the ball."

Increase the level of difficulty by presenting more than one pair of pictures at a time.

Activity **Expressive**

a. Use materials #1. Point to one of the pictures and have the student describe it using the correct tense; e.g., "what is the frog doing?" (the frog <u>is hopping</u>); what did the frog do?' (the frog <u>hopped</u> on the lily pad." Some students may need extra practice with one of the tenses, so present many questions in that tense before presenting questions in either tense at random.

b. Use sequence story cards from materials #5. Make up stories in a specific tense (present or past). Examples (present): "She <u>is climbing</u> on the play structure"; "she <u>is walking</u> to the swing"; "she <u>is playing</u> on the swing." Examples (past): Yesterday she <u>climbed</u> on the play structure"; "she <u>walked</u> to the swing"; "she <u>played</u> on the swing."

Work up to having the student point to or create a sentence for any picture at random when pictures of all 6 verbs are presented at the same time.

Record progress on TRACKING VERB TENSE—REGULAR PAST and FUTURE.

Carryover

- Play Lotto using pictures of verbs in both the present and regular past tense.
- Give the student a direction, then ask him what he did. Example: "Pick up your shoes"

(student picks up shoes). "What did you do?" Response: "I picked up my shoes."

- Play with a dollhouse or toy farm. Make people and animals carry out different actions. Make the action complete (do it and then ask the question—past tense) or continuous (continue doing it while you ask the question—present tense). Ask, for example, "What is she doing?" (jumping on the bed); "what did he do?" (jumped over the fence). Have the student take turns performing actions with the toys and asking you the questions.
- Describe events that are happening or happened during the school day; e.g., we are getting ready for gym; you played with Jordan at recess.

When the student is able to understand and use present progressive "ing" and regular past tense verb forms with 80–90 percent accuracy, progress to Step 2.

Step 2: Present Progressive "ing" and Future Tense

Activity **Receptive**

Tell the student that he is to listen for "is" and "ing" in verbs that are happening now and for "will" in verbs that are going to happen.

    a. Use materials #1 and 2. Select a verb and place the present progressive "ing" and the future tense picture cards of the same verb face up on the table. Model a short sentence in the appropriate tense when pointing to each picture; e.g., this is "the girl is walking to school"; this is "the girl will walk to school."

    b. Use materials #1 and 2. Have the student show you the picture that goes with the sentence that you say; e.g., find "the horse is jumping the fence"; find "the horse will jump the fence."

Increase the level of difficulty by presenting more than one pair of pictures at a time.

Activity **Expressive**

    a. Use materials #1 and 2. Present a pair of pictures and point to one. Have the student describe the action using the same tense as your question; e.g., "what will the cat do?" (the cat will drink the milk); "what is the cat doing?" (the cat is drinking the milk) . If necessary present only questions in one verb tense at first until the student uses that tense competently. Then introduce questions in the other tense, and eventually present the different tenses at random. Gradually present more than one pair of pictures at a time.

    b. Use the sequence story cards from materials #5. Have the student tell the story in the present progressive or future tense. Examples (future): "Tomorrow the girl will get on the bus"; "the girl will sit with her friend"; "the girl will get off the bus at school."

Record progress on TRACKING VERB TENSE—REGULAR PAST and FUTURE.

Carryover

- Play Lotto using pictures of verbs in the present and future tense.
- Describe events that are happening and going to happen during the school day; e.g., "we <u>are eating</u> lunch"; "we <u>will go</u> to the gym after lunch."
- Read storybooks and/or watch videos. Pause periodically and ask about the action; e.g., "what will she do?"; "what is the boy doing?"

When the student is able to understand and use present progressive "ing" and future tense verb forms with 80–90 percent accuracy, progress to Step 3.

Step 3: Present Progressive "ing," Future Tense, and Regular Past

Activity **Receptive** and **Expressive**

Tell the student that now he is to listen for "ing" in verbs that are happening, for "will" in verbs that are going to happen, and for "ed" at the end of verbs that have happened; e.g., "walking," "walked," "will walk."

    a. Use materials #1. Present pictures of the same verb in all three tenses, and, as for Steps 1 and 2, have the student find the picture that matches your spoken sentence, and then have him describe the picture using the correct verb tense.

    b. Use sequence story cards and have the student tell the complete story in a given tense— today/yesterday/tomorrow.

    c. Use action picture scenes from materials #4. Ask questions in random mixed tenses. Examples: "What <u>will</u> the boy ride on?" "What <u>did</u> the cat climb?" "What <u>is</u> the girl doing?" Model the correct response when the student makes an error.

Carryover

- Carry out an action or use props to show that you are going to carry out an action. Ask the student mixed tense questions; e.g., "what did I do?" (picked up a pencil); holding an apple—"what am I going to do?" (you are going to eat the apple); "what am I doing?" (coloring with a crayon).
- Bowl using pins of different colors. Each player at the beginning of his turn must predict which pin(s) he is going to knock down; e.g., "I will knock down two red pins." After his turn, he will describe what actually happened; e.g., "I knocked down a blue pin and a purple pin."
- During activities, discuss what the student will do, what he did, and what he is doing now. Example during art class: "I will paint a house and a tree"; "now I am painting the house"; "I painted a brown house and a tree." Baking: "I will stir the batter"; "I am stirring the batter"; "I stirred the batter."

When the student is able to understand and use present progressive "ing," future tense, and regular past tense verb forms with 80–90 percent accuracy, progress to Step 4.

Step 4: Present Progressive "ing," Future Tense, and Irregular Past Verb Tense

Activity **Receptive** and **Expressive**

Tell the student that some verbs do not follow the "ed" rule when we are talking about an activity that has happened. Instead, they change completely. For instance, "catch" becomes "caught," and "fall" becomes "fell." Give other examples as needed.

a. Use materials #2. Present a picture of the same verb in the present progressive and irregular past tense. Have the student match the picture that you describe to your spoken sentence. Then have him describe the picture using the correct verb tense; e.g., the dog <u>is digging</u> a hole; the dog <u>dug</u> a hole. **Note:** *The irregular past tense form is sometimes difficult for a student to learn. He may persist in adding "ed" to the end of the verb as for the regular past tense; e.g., catched. Provide extra modeling, have him say the word with you, use sentence completion, prompt with the first syllable, or write the target word on a cue card to support the reader.*

b. Present pictures of the same verb in the present progressive and irregular past tense and have him tell you about the action using the correct verb tense in response to your questions ("what is the ___ doing?" "What did the ___ do?"). Examples: "The boy <u>is holding</u> a ball"; "the boy <u>held</u> the ball."

c. Present IRREGULAR PAST TENSE VERBS FOR MATCHING (Table 81) to develop rote responses for irregular past tense verbs.

   For the nonreader: *Present a verb orally and have the student respond with the irregular past tense (e.g., "sit" becomes "sat"). Provide verbal choices as needed (e.g., does "catch" become "catched" or "caught"?).*
   For the reader: *Print the verbs on cardstock and cut them out. Play a turn-taking matching game—find the past tense that goes with the verb. Provide choices as needed.*

d. Present activities (receptive and expressive) in all 3 verb tenses as for Step 3 above (single pictures, story sequences, and action picture scenes).

Record progress on TRACKING VERB TENSE —IRREGULAR PAST and FUTURE.

Carryover

- Set up activities that require the student to use irregular past tense verbs when he tells about them. Ask, "What did you do?" in situations such as art class (I drew a picture); sand play (I dug a hole); playing ball (I threw the ball); playing Hide and Go Seek (I hid behind the chair).
- Play Beanbag Toss with a group of peers. Take turns tossing the beanbag to another player and say to whom you are going to throw it. Then, after throwing it, say who you threw it to. Example: "I will throw it to Jason"; "I threw it to Jason."

- Do craft activities and talk about what you will make, how you will make it, what you are doing now, and what you made. Examples: "I will make a caterpillar"; "I am putting on the eyes"; "I made a caterpillar out of an egg carton."
- Have the student help you to prepare a snack and serve it to his peers. Have him tell you what he did. Examples: "I cut up the apple"; "I put it on the plate"; "I gave it to Ann and Ryan."

Step 5: "Go/Went" Irregular Past Verb Tense
Activity **Receptive** and **Expressive**

Tell the student that the verb "go" is special. It changes completely when we use it to talk about what happened. Use the present progressive "is going" and the irregular past "went." Model sentences relevant to the student and emphasize "went" when it occurs. Examples: "Today we <u>are going</u> to the gym"; "yesterday we <u>went</u> to the gym." Ask: "Did you hear how 'go' changed to 'went'?" Provide further examples; e.g., going/went on the bus; going/went to the mall/a movie/a hockey game/birthday party.

Use a large hand-drawn picture map of a town (materials #3) and toy people. Move one of the people from one place to another as though he were walking—e.g., from the house to the school. Describe what the person is doing; e.g., "the boy is <u>going</u> to the school." Then when he gets to the location, describe what he did; e.g., "he <u>went</u> from the house to the school." Take turns to act out and describe different trips that the toy people make using "is/are going" and "went."

Provide verbal prompts and the target word "went" written on a cue card for readers as needed. A common error is for students to add "ed" to the end of "went" ("wented"). If this happens, provide extra modeling or have the student correct your deliberate errors. Example: "The man wented to the store." "Was I right or wrong?" (wrong). "The dog went to the park" (right).

Carryover

- Take photos of where the student goes on a typical school day and have him tell you about where he went and what he did at each specific time and place. Examples: "I went to the classroom." "I did math." "I went to the gym." "I played with the balls." "I went to the library." "I took out a library book."
- Play with toy people and vehicles. Take turns making up stories about where they are going and where they went.

Table 79: TRACKING VERB TENSE—*REGULAR* PAST and FUTURE

Verb	Reg. Past Receptive	Reg. Past Expressive	Reg. Past Generalized	Future Receptive	Future Expressive	Future Generalized
Bounce						
Brush						
Carry						
Chase						
Clap						
Clean						
Climb						
Color						
Comb						
Cook						
Count						
Crawl						
Cry						
Dance						
Drop						
Dry						
Help						
Hop						
Hug						
Jump						
Kick						
Kiss						
Knock						
Laugh						
Lick						
Like						
Listen						
Love						

(Table 79 continued)

Verb	Reg. Past Receptive	Reg. Past Expressive	Reg. Past Generalized	Future Receptive	Future Expressive	Future Generalized
Mail						
Mix						
Nod						
Open						
Paint						
Pick						
Pick up						
Play						
Pour						
Pull						
Push						
Race						
Roll						
Scratch						
Shout						
Skip						
Smile						
Spill						
Stop						
Talk						
Thank						
Tickle						
Turn						
Wait						
Walk						
Want						
Wash						
Watch						
Wave						

Table 80: TRACKING VERB TENSE—*IRREGULAR* PAST and FUTURE

Verb	Irreg. Past Receptive	Irreg. Past Expressive	Irreg. Past Generalized	Future Receptive	Future Expressive	Future Generalized
Bite						
Blow						
Break						
Buy						
Catch						
Cut						
Dig						
Draw						
Drink						
Eat						
Fall						
Feed						
Find						
Fly						
Get						
Give						
Go						
Have						
Hide						
Hit						
Hold						
Lose						
Make						
Read						
Ride						
Run						
Sing						
Sit						
Sleep						
Shut						
Stand						
Sweep						
Swing						
Throw						
Wear						
Write						

Table 81: IRREGULAR PAST TENSE VERBS FOR MATCHING

Bite	Bit	Blow	Blew
Break	Broke	Buy	Bought
Catch	Caught	Cut	Cut
Dig	Dug	Draw	Drew
Drink	Drank	Eat	Ate
Fall	Fell	Feed	Fed
Find	Found	Fly	Flew
Get	Got	Give	Gave
Go	Went	Have	Had
Hide	Hid	Hit	Hit
Hold	Held	Lose	Lost
Make	Made	Put	Put
Read	Read	Ride	Rode
Run	Ran	Sing	Sang
Sit	Sat	Sleep	Slept
Shut	Shut	Stand	Stood
Sweep	Swept	Swing	Swung
Throw	Threw	Wear	Wore
Write	Wrote		

Goal 6: The student will understand and use regular and irregular noun plurals; e.g., dogs, mice (with 80–90 percent accuracy).

Materials

1. Identical toys and objects and/or pictures of single identical toys/objects and animals (4 or more of each) for *regular* plurals; e.g., 4 identical cups; 4 pictures of the same tree; 5 dogs.
2. Identical toys and objects and/or pictures of single and groups of identical toys/objects and animals (3 or more of each) for *irregular* plurals; e.g. 1 mouse/3 mice; 1 man/4 men; 1 sheep/3 sheep.
3. Cardboard barrier for Barrier game (p. 7).
4. List IRREGULAR PLURALS FOR MATCHING, Table 83, below.
5. List TRACKING IRREGULAR PLURALS, Table 82, below.

Introduction

Introduce this goal by telling the student that he is going to learn to add the "s" sound to the end of words when he talks about more than one of a thing. Present one object and a group of the same object and say, for example, "This is one ca<u>t</u>, but these are two *cat<u>s</u>*" (emphasize or elongate the "s" sound as you say it). Ask, "Did you hear the 's' at the end of 'cat<u>s</u>'?" Model more examples.

Note: *When "s" plural follows a voiced consonant ("b," "g," "m," "n," "v," "th," "z," "ge"), it sounds like "z" (compare the "s" on the end of "cats" with the sound on the end of "dog<u>s</u>."). The student may use the "z" sound automatically following your model, or you may need to explain this change to him.*

Step 1—Regular Plurals
Activity **Receptive**

Use materials #1. Select 3 identical items (or pictures) and arrange them on the table so that there is a group of 2 items and 1 item set slightly apart from the group; e.g., 2 cups together and 1 cup a slight distance away.

Be careful *not to use an article or concept of quantity* before the noun in the following activities, as this would indicate singular or plural.

a. Model the singular and plural form as you point to the single item and the group of 2 items; e.g., "cup" (pointing to the single cup); "cup<u>s</u>" (pointing to the group of cups). Emphasize the final "s" or "z" sound so that the student can hear it clearly. Provide the reader with the target word written on a cue card and draw his attention to the word ending (as needed).

b. Arrange the items in groups of 2 and 1 and have the student show you the one that you name; e.g., show me "pen<u>s</u>"; show me "pen" (be careful to vary the position of the group and single item so that one is on the left and the other on the right at random and vary the order in which you request the singular and plural).

  c. Play a Barrier game. Place several groups of identical items on either side of the barrier so that each of you has the same choice of items; e.g., 2 identical balls, 2 pencils, 2 blocks. Without the student being able to see what you are doing, pick up either one or more than one of your identical items. Tell the student to do the same, then lift the barrier to compare what the student has picked up with what you are holding; e.g. "pick up balls"; "pick up cup."

As the student becomes more comfortable with these tasks, increase the number of each item to more than 2 in order to avoid him associating the plural form only with "2."

Activity **Expressive**

Use materials #1.

  a. Point to and label singular and plural forms. Have the student imitate your model; e.g., glove/gloves, hat/hats.

  b. Have the student complete your sentence; e.g., "here is one shoe"; "here are two _____" [shoes]; "here are some _____" [shoes]. **Note:** Use numbers and quantity concepts in this activity; e.g. some, a (Chapter 9, Goal 2, concepts of quantity, p. 157).

  c. Point to a single item and groups and have the student label it/them without a model. Include items that he has not heard modeled so that you know that he has generalized the rule of pluralization. It is not necessary for him to use a full sentence at this time; just the name of the item(s) is sufficient.

  d. Play the Barrier game and have the student direct you to pick up one or more of the items.

Step 2—Irregular Plurals

Note: *Select target words from TRACKING IRREGULAR PLURALS, but be careful to target only those that the student is likely to use in real life.*

Tell the student that we do not put "s" on *all* words to tell us there is more than one. There are some words that we change completely. Model examples; e.g., "mouse" changes to "mice"; "man" changes to "men." The strangest words of all are the ones that do not change at all even though there is more than one of them; e.g., "sheep" stays as "sheep"; "fish" stays as "fish."

Track progress using TRACKING IRREGULAR PLURALS.

Activity **Receptive**

Use materials #2. Model and teach *irregular* plurals as for *regular* plurals in Step 1 of Activity *Receptive* for Regular Plurals. When you play the Barrier game, use materials #2, but only those words that change when they become plural (omit "sheep," "fish," "deer," "moose").

Activity **Expressive**

Use materials #2 and Step 1 a–d for *regular* plurals, above.

Present IRREGULAR PLURALS FOR MATCHING to develop rote memory for irregular plurals.

For the nonreader: *Present a word orally in the singular and have the student respond with the irregular plural, or present the plural and have the student respond with the singular. Example: "Mouse becomes _____" (mice); "mice becomes _____" (mouse). Provide word choices as needed; e.g., "leaf" becomes "leafs" or "leaves"?*

For the reader: *Print the singular and irregular plurals on cardstock and cut them out. Play a turn-taking matching game—find the singular and plural that go together. Provide choices as needed.*

Carryover

- Play singular/plural Lotto, Snakes/Chutes and Ladders, Magic Bag, and Memory. Describe the cards that you pick up/land on/take out; e.g., "I found 2 trucks"; "I found 2 mice"; "I found 1 dog and 1 sheep"; "I landed on a sheep."
- Read stories and sing songs/nursery rhymes with themes that involve regular and irregular plural nouns. Examples: *Three Blind Mice*; *Sheep in a Jeep* by Nancy E. Shaw and Margot Apple.
- Look at pictures in story books, magazines, and catalogs. Have the student complete your sentences; e.g., "this girl has one flower"; " this girl has two _____" (flowers).
- Use pictures from catalogs and magazines to make a collage of plural items.
- Play Snap. Choose an irregular plural to say instead of "snap"; e.g., mice.

Table 82: TRACKING IRREGULAR PLURALS

Singular/Plural	Receptive	Expressive	Established
Tooth/Teeth			
Foot/Feet			
Mouse/Mice			
Fish/Fish			
Goose/Geese			
Sheep/Sheep			
Child/Children			
Man/Men			
Woman/Women			
Elf/Elves			
Shelf/Shelves			
Deer/Deer			
Calf/Calves			
Wolf/Wolves			
Hoof/Hooves			
Leaf/Leaves			
Moose/Moose			
Scarf/Scarves			
Knife/Knives			
Thief/Thieves			

Table 83: IRREGULAR PLURALS FOR MATCHING

Tooth	Teeth	Shelf	Shelves
Foot	Feet	Deer	Deer
Mouse	Mice	Calf	Calves
Fish	Fish	Wolf	Wolves
Goose	Geese	Hoof	Hooves
Sheep	Sheep	Leaf	Leaves
Child	Children	Moose	Moose
Man	Men	Scarf	Scarves
Woman	Women	Knife	Knives
Elf	Elves	Thief	Thieves

Goal 7: The student will use possessive "s" marker; e.g., Ann's hat, the dog's collar (with 80–90 percent accuracy).

See also: *Chapter 10 ("Wh" Questions), "Whose?," p. 199.*

Materials

1. 20 objects that belong to specific people familiar to the student, including several similar objects that they each own; e.g., Jack's coat, Mom's coat, Dave's coat; Isobel's crayon, Kate's crayon, Dad's hat, Susie's hat.
2. 20 pictures of people and animals with an object that they own or with identifiable parts; e.g., man with his coat; girl with her bike; dog with its ears.

Introduction

Introduce this goal by saying that when something belongs to someone or something we put a special "s" on the end of the name of the person, animal, or thing to whom it belongs. Example: "This is (use student's name)'s book"; "this is (use your name)'s pen."

Model examples from materials #1 and #2; e.g., "this is Jane's backpack"; "this is the horse's tail."

Prompt by emphasizing the "s" when you say it, modeling it during expressive activities, or by showing the reader an apostrophe "s" written on a cue card.

Activity **Receptive**

Step 1: Use the collection of objects that belong to specific people familiar to the student. Have the student point to the one that you describe; e.g., "show me Mandy's lunch pail"; "show me Jane's backpack."

Step 2: Use the pictures (materials #2). Have the student point to the item or part that you name; e.g., "show me the boy's hat"; "show me the dog's ear/the cup's handle/the tree's leaves."

Activity **Expressive**

Step 1: Take turns to pick up an object (materials #1) and say to whom it belongs; e.g., "Marie's hat"; "Tom's pencil."

Step 2: Use the pictures of people or animals with objects or parts that belong to them (materials #2). Point to an item or part in a picture and have the student tell you to whom or what it belongs; e.g., "the girl's ball"; "the cat's toy."

Carryover

- At circle time, have the children each place an item into the center of the circle. Pick up each item in turn and ask to whom it belongs; e.g., "whose shirt is this?" Response: "Andy's shirt."

- Sort laundry or "Lost and Found" items; e.g., "this is a boy's shirt"; "this is a girl's shoe."
- On the playground, have the student tell you whose turn it is to play on the play equipment; e.g. "it is Evan's turn to go down the slide"; "it is Drew's turn on the swing."
- Play with a boy and a girl doll or play figures such as Playmobile or Star Wars characters. Use doll clothes or items associated with the figures/characters such as a helmet or spaceship. Discuss to whom each piece of clothing or item belongs; e.g., this is the boy's jacket; this is Luke Skywalker's light saber.

Goal 8: The student will use descriptors (adjectives and adverbs) to describe nouns and verbs; e.g., the big dog; Kate is running fast (with 80–90 percent accuracy).

See Chapter 8 (Descriptors), p. 119. Repeat the expressive activities for all goals and encourage the use of full sentence structures.

Goal 9: The student will use the conjunction "and" to connect two nouns or two related sentences; e.g., dog and cat; the sun is shining and the sky is blue (with 80–90 percent accuracy).

Prerequisite: *Understanding of "and" in directions—Chapter 1 (Following Directions), Goal 1, p. 14.*

Materials

1. 20 toys/objects and/or pictures of toys/objects, people, or animals familiar to the student.
2. 20 pictures of single people or single animals carrying out an action that is familiar to the student; e.g., a man eating; a baby sleeping; a dog running.
3. 10 picture scenes (paper, magnetic, or felt) in which a variety of people and animals are carrying out familiar activities; e.g., a girl flying a kite; a man feeding ducks; a boy riding his bike.

Introduction

Tell the student that he is going to learn to join words and sentences together using the word "and."

Present two objects or toys and model the use of "and"; e.g., here is a ball <u>and </u>a pen. Present 2 pictures of single people/animals carrying out an action (materials #2) and model; e.g., the girl is playing <u>and</u> the boy is digging. Provide additional examples.

Emphasize the target word and prompt the reader with "and" written on a cue card as needed.

Activity **Receptive**

Step 1: Place 3–8 objects, toys, or single-item pictures on the table and have the student give you the 2 that you request; e.g., "give me the car <u>and</u> the ball."

Step 2: Place 4 of the action picture cards side by side face up on the table and have the student point to the 2 that you name; e.g., "point to the girl is running <u>and</u> the boy is climbing."

Activity **Expressive**

Step 1: Place 3–8 objects, toys, or single-item pictures on the table. Take turns to pick up (or take out) 2 of them and say what you picked up/got; e.g., "I picked up the box <u>and</u> the eraser"; "I got the star <u>and</u> the horse." Encourage the student to use the full sentence structure. Use Tim's Game or Magic Bag to add interest.

Step 2: Spread out 3–8 action pictures face down on the table. Take turns turning over 2 of them and describing what is happening in both of them by joining your sentences with "and"; e.g., "the horse is eating and the dog is sleeping."

Step 3: Use the action pictures or magnetic/felt scenes (materials #3). Take turns to describe 2 things that are happening in the picture; e.g., "the girl is playing on the swing and the mom is waving." If necessary, prompt by pointing to 2 actions that you want the student to tell you about.

Carryover

- When the student uses a short utterance, prompt him to add more by saying "and" with rising inflection; e.g., Student: "I've got a hockey stick." You: "And?" Student: "I've got a hockey stick and a puck."
- List items that you need to take to another classroom or will need for an activity; e.g., "I need to take my pencil and notebook"; "we will need paint and paintbrushes for art class."
- Play "I went to the store and bought…." Take turns to list items. Example: "I bought an apple and a banana" (add "and' before the last item in the list—Chapter 15, (Auditory Memory), Goal 2, p. 295.)
- Play with a magnetic, vinyl, or felt scene. Take turns to place two items on the scene and say what you put on; e.g., "I put on the farmer and the cat."
- Describe activities in the classroom or on the yard at recess; e.g., "Kyle is cutting paper and Josh is using the glue."
- Describe items of two colors; e.g., "my shirt is red and blue"; "the dog is black and white."

Other Conjunctions: *teach the use of "because," "so," and "so that" using Chapter 10 ("Wh" Questions), Why? Goals A-E, p. 200. Repeat the activities and encourage the use of a full sentence that includes the conjunction to express the reason; e.g., "the sidewalk is wet because it is raining"; "Mom took her umbrella so she won't get wet."*

Goal 10: The student will understand and use comparative "er" and superlative "est" forms of descriptors (with 80–90 percent accuracy):
  A. big/bigger/biggest.
  B. small, smaller, smallest.
  C. a variety of common descriptors.
  D. good, better, best.

Prerequisite: *Ability to perceive size differences; e.g., sort nesting tubs and/or rings into their size-related order (not included in this manual). Understanding of descriptors—Chapter 8 (Descriptors), Goals 2 and 4, pp. 125 and 128. Understanding of negative "no" and "not"— Chapter 2 (Negative No/Not), Goals 1–3, pp. 24-27.*

A: Big, Bigger, Biggest
Materials

1. Objects such as nesting tubs and rings of identical color (toddler toys); sets of measuring cups/spoons that are identical except for size; and/or pictures of the same object or animal in 3 or more different sizes (a separate picture for each size).

Note: *The activities are described using objects, but pictures can be substituted. Be aware that similar but separate materials will be needed for Goal B—"Small, smaller, smallest"—so do not use all of the materials #1 and 2 suggested for Goal A; keep some for Goal B.*

2. Some of the items from the list ITEMS FOR COMPARATIVE/SUPERLATIVE SIZE ACTIVITIES, Table 84, below (again, keep some for Goal B).
3. List TRACKING COMPARATIVE/SUPERLATIVE, Table 86, p. 242.

Introduction

Tell the student that he is going to learn words that help us to tell how one thing is different from another. Today's words are "big," "bigger," and "biggest." Either introduce and model "big" and "bigger" first and wait to introduce "biggest" until they are learned. Or introduce all 3 words together, depending on the student's ability.

Use a selection of items from materials #1 and from the list EVERYDAY ITEMS FOR COMPARATIVE/SUPERLATIVE SIZE ACTIVITIES. Describe how one item is different from another/the others; e.g., "this one is <u>big</u> but this one is <u>bigger</u>"; "this one is <u>bigger</u> than that one." Present several examples.

Note: Do not *use the antonyms "small," "smaller," "smallest" during this activity. If you need to correct the student, use the negative "not bigger" or "not the biggest."*

Prompt as needed by giving choices; e.g., "is this one bigger or that one bigger?"; "bigger?" or "biggest?" For the reader, write the target words on cue cards.

Use TRACKING COMPARATIVE/SUPERLATIVE to track the student's progress as he learns to understand and use "big, bigger, and biggest."

Step 1—Comparative "Big/Bigger"
Activity **Receptive**

Use some items from materials #1 and 2 and directions "give me," "point to," or "show me."

    a. Present 2 different sizes of the same item. Point to the appropriate item and say, "This one is <u>big</u> and this one is <u>bigger</u>"; "this one is <u>bigger</u> than that one." Present many different examples and vary the order that the items are arranged in.

    b. Present 2 different sizes of the same item. Point to the big one and say, "Give me <u>bigger</u>" or "give me the ___ (name the item) that is <u>bigger</u> than this ___." Increase the level of difficulty by presenting more than 2 different sizes of the item.

Activity **Expressive**

    a. Present 2 different sizes of the same item. Point to the "big" one and use sentence completion to elicit "bigger." Example: "This one is <u>big</u>—this one is _____ (<u>bigger</u>)."

    b. Ask the student to tell you which one is "bigger" by giving a "yes/no" answer. Present 2 items; point to them one at a time as you ask; e.g., is this one <u>bigger</u> than that one? (yes/no).

    c. Present 2 items and ask; "which one is <u>bigger</u>?" Have the student point and answer using a full sentence; e.g., "this one is bigger."

Step 2—Comparative and Superlative "Big/Bigger/Biggest"
Activity **Receptive**

Use some items from materials #1 and 2 and directions "give me," "point to," or "show me."

    a. Place 3 different sizes of the item on the table arranged in size order from left to right. Point to each one in turn and describe it; e.g., "this one is <u>big</u>, this one is <u>bigger</u>, and this one is the <u>biggest</u>." Point to the biggest one again and say, "This is the "biggest." Present many different examples.

    b. Place 3 different sizes of the item on the table (at first in size order from left to right but later in mixed order). Have the student give you the one that is the "biggest"; e.g., "find the <u>biggest truck.</u>"

    c. Increase the level of difficulty by presenting the same item in *more than 3* different sizes and have the student find the "biggest" in different combinations of sizes and the overall biggest.

Activity **Expressive**

a. Present 3 different sizes of the same item. Label the first 2 "big" and "bigger" and use sentence completion to elicit "biggest"; e.g., "this one is <u>big</u>, this one is <u>bigger</u>, and this one is the _____ (<u>biggest</u>)."

b. Ask the student to decide which is the "biggest" by giving a "yes/no" answer. Present 3 items; point to them one at a time as you ask, "Is this one the <u>biggest</u>?" (yes/no).

c. Present 3 different sizes of the item and ask, "Which one is the <u>biggest</u>?" Have him point and answer using a full sentence; e.g., "this one is the <u>biggest</u>."

d. Place 3 different sizes of the same item on the table in random order. Have the student arrange them in size order from left to right and tell you about them. Example: "Tell me about the gloves" (this one is <u>big</u>, this one is <u>bigger</u>, and this one is the <u>biggest</u>." Increase the level of difficulty by presenting more than 3 different sizes.

Provide verbal prompts and support the reader with the written target word as needed. When the student is able to use "big, bigger, and biggest" with 80–90 percent accuracy, progress to Goal B—"small, smaller, smallest."

Carryover

- Point out gradations in size in everyday situations; e.g., "that boy is <u>bigger</u> than you"; "your cookie is <u>bigger</u> than mine. You have the <u>biggest</u> cookie."
- Play I Am Bigger. Have the student compare himself to items in the room or in a picture and say whether he is bigger than the item or the item is bigger than he is. Encourage use of the complete sentence structure; e.g., "I am <u>bigger</u> than the garbage can"; "the tree is <u>bigger</u> than me." Also, ask him questions; e.g., "are you <u>bigger</u> than an elephant?" Response: "I am not <u>bigger</u>."
- Play the Bigger Chain:
  - Version 1: The first player will name an item in the room that is big (but on the small side!) and the second player will name something bigger; the third player (or the first player again) will name something even bigger, and so on until no one can think of anything bigger (physically compare the size of the objects as needed).
  - Version 2: Play as for version 1 but name items and animals shown in a picture scene or catalog.
  - Version 3: Play as for version 1, but without objects or picture clues. This is more abstract and will appeal to students who are able to visualize well. Example: A spider is big; a mouse is bigger than a spider; a rabbit is bigger than a mouse; a sheep is bigger than a rabbit, etc.

Table 84 ITEMS FOR COMPARATIVE/SUPERLATIVE SIZE ACTIVITIES

Choose items most appropriate for the student from the list of suggestions below. You will need at least 3 different sizes of each item.

- Clothing—socks, shoes, mittens, hats, t-shirts, jackets.
- Kitchen items—knives (plastic), forks, spoons; measuring cups and spoons; bowls, plates, plastic juice bottles; cups and containers from fast food restaurants.
- Foods—canned or boxed, chips, crackers, portions of cheese, slices of fruit/vegetables.
- Pieces of identical fabric, paper, or cardstock cut into varying shapes of different sizes.
- Foot- or handprints—painted or drawn around on paper; in sand/mud/snow outside.
- Toys—stacking rings/boxes/Russian nesting dolls, cars, trucks, animals, balls, blocks, dolls, stuffed toys.
- Common objects—tubes of toothpaste, flowers and leaves (real, plastic or silk), chairs in room, pencils, crayons, erasers, coins, buttons, paintbrushes, books.

B: Small, Smaller, Smallest

Materials

1. Use a selection of items or item pictures from materials #1 and 2 listed for Goal A: big, bigger, biggest but *not* those already used.
2. List TRACKING COMPARATIVE/SUPERLATIVE, Table 86, p. 242.

Introduction

Tell the student that now that he can tell you how things are different using the words "big," "bigger," and "biggest," he is going to talk about things that are "small," "smaller," and "smallest."

Introduce "small," "smaller," and "smallest" in the same way that you introduced and modeled "big," "bigger," and "biggest" in Goal A. Use materials that you have not already used.

Do not use the antonyms "big," "bigger," "biggest" during this activity. Use the negative "not smaller" or "not the smallest" instead.

Provide verbal prompts and support the reader with the written target word as needed.

Use TRACKING COMPARATIVE/SUPERLATIVE to track the student's progress as he learns to understand and use "small, smaller, smallest."

Step 1—Comparative "Small/Smaller"

Activity **Receptive**

Follow Goal A for Comparative Big/Bigger, Step 1, a and b. Substitute the words "small/smaller."

Activity **Expressive**

Follow Goal A for Comparative Big/Bigger, Step 1, a, b, and c. Elicit the words "small/smaller" in place of "big/bigger."

Step 2—Comparative and Superlative "Small/Smaller/Smallest"

Activity **Receptive**

Follow Goal A for Comparative and Superlative "Big/Bigger/Biggest," Step 2, a, b, and c. Substitute the words "small/smaller/smallest."

Activity **Expressive**

Follow Goal A for Comparative and Superlative "Big/Bigger/Biggest," Step 2, a, b, c, and d. Elicit the words "small/smaller/smallest" instead of "big/bigger/biggest."

When the student is able to use "small," "smaller," and "smallest" with 80–90 percent accuracy, progress to Goal C: A Variety of Common Descriptors.

Carryover

- Point out different sizes in everyday situations. Examples: That girl is smaller than you; your backpack is smaller than Kyle's; you are holding the smallest piece of Lego; I chose the smallest pompoms.
- Play games and do activities and crafts that involve groups of things and/or animals that are both big and small. Discuss the relative size of the items; which size would you use for a specific function; which size you would prefer. Examples: "Are your shoes bigger or smaller than mine?"; "would you like a bigger or a smaller slice of pizza than the one that I cut?"; "did you eat the biggest or the smallest cookie?"

For additional practice see the carryover suggestions in Chapter 8 (Descriptors), Goal 2, p. 125.

C: A Variety of Common Descriptors

Prerequisite: *Understanding and use of descriptors—Chapter 8 (Descriptors), Goal 4, p. 128.*

Materials

1. List OPPORTUNITIES FOR TEACHING DESCRIPTORS (Chapter 8, Goal 4, p. 128). Items and objects as suggested in the list, but in 3 different sizes or gradations; e.g., water in bottle—"hot/hotter/hottest"; paintbrushes—"thick/thicker/thickest."
    Be aware that some descriptors on this list (empty/full, open/shut) cannot be used in the comparative or superlative forms, and therefore should be omitted from this activity.
2. List TRACKING COMPARATIVE/SUPERLATIVE, Table 86, p. 242.
3. Commercial comparative/superlative picture cards.

Introduction

Tell the student that now he is going to talk about things in other ways and add "er" and "est" on the end of these words. Give examples such as "I am <u>taller</u> than you." (Ask, "Did you hear the "er" on the end of taller?"). Then, "your teacher is <u>taller</u> than me, so she is the <u>tallest</u>." (Ask, "Did you hear 'est' on the end of <u>tallest</u>?"). Model other examples using objects or pictures such as pencils (long/longer/longest) and pictures of pigs (fat/fatter/fattest).

Use TRACKING COMPARATIVE/SUPERLATIVE to help you choose target words and track progress.

Provide verbal prompts and support the reader with the target word written on a cue card as needed. Use descriptors that are already familiar to the student.

Activity **Receptive** and **Expressive**

Refer to activities suggested for the target words in OPPORTUNITIES FOR TEACHING DESCRIPTORS and present 3 examples of the target descriptor that vary in gradation; e.g., <u>wet</u> paper towel, <u>wetter</u> paper towel, <u>wettest</u> paper towel; <u>long</u> piece of yarn, <u>longer</u> piece of yarn, <u>longest</u> piece of yarn.

Step 1: Have the student arrange familiar items in their comparative order from left to right; e.g., <u>heavy</u> rock, <u>heavier</u> rock, <u>heaviest</u> rock.

Step 2: Have the student arrange commercial comparative/superlative picture cards (materials #3) in their comparative order from left to right; e.g., <u>short</u> tree, <u>shorter</u> tree, <u>shortest</u> tree.

Step 3: Present groups of 2 or 3 objects or object pictures and have the student select the comparative or superlative form as you request; e.g., show me the <u>thickest</u> book; show me a tree that is <u>taller</u> than this one.

Step 4: Present 2 or 3 objects or pictures of objects or animals that differ from each other in some way, and have the student describe the one that you point to. Examples: 3 toy snakes—"tell me about this one." ("It is the <u>longest</u> snake"); pictures of mountains—"tell me about this one" ("It is <u>higher</u> than the other mountain.")

Step 5: present objects and pictures and ask questions that require the use of opposite descriptors. Examples: "Is this pencil <u>longer</u> than that pencil?" Response: "No, this pencil is <u>shorter</u>"; is this pig <u>fatter</u> than that pig? Response: "No, this pig is <u>thinner</u>."

Carryover

- Make comparisons between everyday items, events, and situations. Examples: "Is this pencil longer than that one?" "Who ran the fastest, Paul or Scott?" Progress to more abstract comparisons, which may be more subjective; e.g., "do you think it is hotter today than yesterday?" *Be aware that there may be times when the student's opinion differs from yours.*
- Carry out activities that have specific requirements. Examples: craft—this necklace needs to be longer; the glue gun needs to be hotter. Baking—the butter needs to be softer; the milk should be warmer.
- Read stories that include comparatives and superlatives such as Goldilocks and the Three Bears; e.g. the beds were soft/softer/softest; the porridge was hot/hotter/hottest; the chairs were high/higher/highest. Have the student tell the story to a peer, younger student, or another adult.

D: Good, Better, Best

Materials

1. Objects and real-life activities that increase in desirability as they increase in number, frequency, size, or other quality; e.g., number of chips or pieces of candy, turns on the computer, small to large slices of pizza, bounces on the trampoline.
2. List OPPORTUNITIES FOR TEACHING GOOD/BETTER/BEST, Table 85, below.
3. List TRACKING COMPARATIVE/SUPERLATIVE, Table 86, below.

Introduction

Tell the student that there is one word that changes completely when we use it to compare things, and this word is "good." Present examples relevant to the student; e.g., having phys ed today would be <u>good</u>; having phys ed and art today would be <u>better</u>; having phys ed, art, and computer today would be the <u>best</u>. Then ask: "Did you hear how <u>good</u> changed to <u>better</u> and then to <u>best</u>?"

There is a little jingle to help us remember "good," "better," and "best." It goes like this:
Good, better, best,
Never let it rest
'Til the good is better
And the better is best.

Explain the jingle and have the student memorize it, if possible.

Provide verbal prompts and support the reader with the target word written on a cue card as needed.

Activity **Receptive** and **Expressive**

Step 1: Discuss which choice of desirable activities and treats that are relevant to the student is "good," "better," or "best." Example: Earning 1 M&M is good; earning 2 M&Ms is better; earning 3 M&Ms is best (the level of desirability for food items will be from the student's perspective and not necessarily from a nutritional one!).

Step 2: Use the list OPPORTUNITIES FOR TEACHING GOOD/BETTER/BEST. Create concrete situations in which to discuss what would be good/better/best. Example: Put a quantity of uncooked rice in a plastic bag. Provide 3 bowls of different sizes and colors (one too big, one too small, and one that is exactly the right size to take all of the rice). Pour the rice into each bowl in turn (starting with the smallest) and discuss which bowl is the most suitable for it. Ask, for example, "Which bowl is better?" "Which bowl is the best?" "Is the blue bowl better than the red bowl?"

Step 3: Repeat some of the activities suggested in OPPORTUNITIES FOR TEACHING DESCRIPTORS from Chapter 8 (Descriptors), Goal 4, p. 128). Discuss which items would be the most desirable for a task; e.g., lightweight bottles would be better for playing Bowling (because they fall over more easily); the driest towel would be best for drying your hands.

Use TRACKING COMPARATIVE/SUPERLATIVE to track the student's progress as he learns to understand and use "good," "better," and "best."

Carryover

● Provide opportunities for the student to make decisions based on comparisons in real-life events. Examples: "What kind of cookies should we bake?" "We should bake chocolate chip cookies because they taste better than oatmeal cookies." "Which would be better—to go outside for recess or play on the computer?" "Which would be best—to wear a jacket outside today or your swimsuit?" "Which is best—the drawing of the crooked house or the drawing of the straight house?"

Follow commercial programs to teach more advanced word and sentence structures such as:

Indirect object; e.g., the man showed the dog the cat.

Passive; e.g., the boy was followed by the dog.

Relative clause; e.g., the man who is sitting under the tree is wearing a hat.

Subordinate clause; e.g., the boy is crying because his toy is broken.

Table 85: OPPORTUNITIES FOR TEACHING GOOD/BETTER/BEST

Choice of:	Which would be good/better/best to:
Amounts of uncooked rice or pasta	Fit into bowl of a certain size
Lego pieces	Build a specific model
Building blocks (round, square, etc.)	Build a tower
Spoons of a variety of sizes	Eat cereal
Towels varying in dampness	Dry up a spill
Gloves of varying thickness	Keep hands warm in winter
Hats of varying types	Keep the sun out of your eyes
Pencils with/without erasers and pens	Do your math homework
Targets of different size	Throw a bean bag at/onto
Pillows of different softness	Lay head on
Pieces of string or ribbon of different lengths	Tie up a gift
Slices of cheese, meat, or vegetables of different thickness	Put in a sandwich
Clothes or pictures of clothes	Wear in a particular season such as summer
Marker pens of different thickness	Write with
Pieces of string or rope of different thickness	Thread beads onto
Whistles or other noise makers	Hear across the playground
Ways to throw a ball	Make the ball go the farthest
Competitive teams or players; e.g., baseball teams	Win the game
3 or more pictures of item of the same name but each with different characteristics	e.g., best ladder to reach to the top of a house; best car to go the fastest; best pet to keep in a cage.

Table 86: TRACKING COMPARATIVE/SUPERLATIVE

Descriptor		Receptive	Expressive	Established
Big	bigger biggest			
Small	smaller smallest			
Wet	wetter wettest			
Dry	drier driest			
Hot	hotter hottest			
Cold	colder coldest			
Clean	cleaner cleanest			
Dirty	dirtier dirtiest			
Tall	taller tallest			
Short	shorter shortest			
Heavy	heavier heaviest			
Light	lighter lightest			
Hard	harder hardest			
Soft	softer softest			
Young	younger youngest			

(Table 86 continued)

Descriptor		Receptive	Expressive	Established
Old	older oldest			
New	newer newest			
Long	longer longest			
Short	shorter shortest			
Thick	thicker thickest			
Thin	thinner thinnest			
Rough	rougher roughest			
Smooth	smoother smoothest			
Slow	slower slowest			
Fast	faster fastest			
High	higher highest			
Low	lower lowest			
Large	larger largest			
Wide	wider widest			
Narrow	narrower narrowest			
Good	better best			

12. Pronouns

These goals are appropriate for students with one or more of the following characteristics:

- has difficulty understanding spoken and written language when pronouns are involved; e.g., is unsure if "he" refers to a boy or a girl

- expresses herself in phrases and incomplete sentences

- omits or uses incorrect pronouns; e.g., him is running

- refers to herself by name and/or uses "me" for "I"; e.g., Kyle is [I am] happy

- does not distinguish between male/female gender-specific features (boy/girl, man/woman)

Pronoun Goals

The student will use in isolation and simple sentences:

Goal 1: gender (boy/girl).

Goal 2: personal "he," "she," "it," and "they"; e.g., she is running, he is eating, it is standing, they are jumping.

Goal 3: personal "I," "we," and "you"; e.g., I am clapping, you are clapping, we are clapping.

Goal 4: possessive "his," "her," "its," and "their"; e.g., this is his hat/her bag/its tail; these are their bikes.

Goal 5: possessive "my," "your," and "our"; e.g., my shoes, your hat, our backpacks.

Goal 6: personal "me" and "you" and possessive "mine" and "yours"; e.g., give it to me—it is mine. This hat is yours—I will give it to you.

Teach more advanced pronouns

e.g., him/her, himself/herself, them, us, ours, theirs— by using the steps described for other pronouns or using commercial programs.

Goal 1: The student will correctly identify a child in real life or in a picture as a boy or a girl (with 80–90 percent accuracy).

Note: *Students who are easily able to identify boy/girl may omit this goal.*

Materials

1. A group of children familiar to the student; e.g., circle time in classroom; children at the student's worktable.
2. Large clear photos (with permission) or pictures of boys and girls (10 of each). Each picture showing one individual sufficiently close up that facial features, hair length, and/or color or style of clothing are easily recognizable as gender specific.

Introduction

Introduce this goal by telling the student that in her grade, there are both boys and girls. She is going to learn which ones are the boys and which ones are the girls. Talk about the student's friends; e.g., Kyle is a boy; Angie is a girl. Show photos of boys and girls and name them appropriately as "girl" or "boy" (limit your language to the essential noun). Support the reader with the key word written on a cue card.

Activity **Receptive**

Step 1—Real People: At a time when the children are stationary, such as during circle time, take the student from one child to another and describe some salient features that distinguishes the child as a boy or girl; e.g., John is a <u>boy</u>—he has a brown shirt and short hair—he is a <u>boy</u>; Cindy is a <u>girl</u>—she has long hair and flowers on her shirt—she is a <u>girl</u>.

Go around the circle again and label each child <u>boy</u> or <u>girl</u>.

Step 2—Pictures: Use the 20 photos or pictures of boys and girls (materials #2):

a. Spread out some or all (depending on the student's ability) of the photos/pictures face up on the table and have the student sort them into "boy" and "girl" piles. Discuss the various features that show that the child is a boy or girl.

b. Have the student give you a boy or girl picture from the piles as you request at random, "Give me girl" or "Give me boy."

Activity **Expressive**

Step 1—Real People:

a. Have the student imitate your model as you label each child in the circle as "boy" or "girl."

b. Have the student label the child "boy" or "girl" without a model. Provide verbal prompts such as the first sound of the word and, for the reader, the target word written on a cue card as needed.

Step 2—Pictures:
a. Have the student label the photos/pictures "boy" or "girl" as she sorts them.
b. Have the student label the photos/pictures "boy" or "girl" as you present them in random order. Use Hide the Sticker, Magic Bag, or Tim's Game to add interest.

Support with verbal or written prompts as needed.

Carryover

- Play Lotto, Memory, Snap, and Go Fish using boy/girl picture cards. Use picture pairs that are identical at first; then, as the student becomes more competent, use non-matching pictures of children of the same gender so any girl will match with any other girl.
- Identify boys/girls in pictures, on TV, and videos and in everyday situations at school and at home; e.g., around the family dinner table.
- Make a collage of pictures of boys or girls cut from magazines or catalogs.

Note: *Teach "man/woman/lady" using appropriate photos/pictures and the Steps as described above.*

Goal 2: The student will use pronouns "he," "she," "it," and "they" in isolation and simple sentences; e.g., she is running, he is eating, it is standing, they are jumping (with 80–90 percent accuracy).

Prerequisite: *Ability to sort into "people" and "thing" categories—Chapter 6 (Classification and Categorization), Goal 3, p. 81. Knowledge and use of subject + is/are + "ing" verb— Chapter 11 (Word and Sentence Structure), Goal 1, p. 211.*

Materials

1. Group of children familiar to the student; e.g., circle time in classroom; children at the student's work table (as for Goal 1).
2. 20 photos (with permission) or pictures of single and groups of boys and girls—5 single girls, 5 single boys, and 10 groups (some of boys together, some of girls together, and some of both boys and girls together).
3. 20 pictures showing a single boy, girl, or animal each carrying out the same action; e.g., boy/girl/dog walking, boy/girl/dog sleeping, boy/girl/dog jumping.
4. 20 pictures of boys, girls, and animals carrying out the same action alone and in groups; e.g., 1 boy walking/a group of boys walking; 1 horse jumping/3 horses jumping.
5. 10 pictures of single, familiar toys/objects; e.g., toy car, dinosaur, fork, apple.
6. List TRACKING EARLY DEVELOPING PRONOUNS, Table 87, below.

Introduction

Explain to the student that when we talk about people we do not always call them by name. Instead, we call a boy "he" and a girl "she." Show several photos of boys and girls and label them appropriately; e.g., this is a girl—we call a girl "she"; this is a boy—we call a boy "he." Then label some using only "he" or "she."

When the student uses "he" and "she" with 80–90 percent accuracy following Steps 1 and 2 below, introduce "it" by saying that when we talk about an object or animal we use the word "it."

Introduce "they" prior to Step 4 by telling the student that when we talk about more than one person, object, or animal we call the group "they." Show pictures of groups of people, objects, and animals. Model the use of "they"; e.g., they are painting; they are in the classroom.

Emphasize the target word and support all Steps with verbal prompts or, for the reader, the target words written on cue cards as needed.

Use list TRACKING EARLY DEVELOPING PRONOUNS, Table 87, to record when "he," "she," "it," and "they" are each understood, used, and established.

Activity **Receptive**

Step 1—"He/She" Real People:
  a. As for Goal 1, Step 1, when the children are stationary (e.g., during circle time), take the student from one child to another, but this time label them "boy—he" or "girl—she."
  b. Go from one child to another again and model only "he" and "she."

Step 2—"He/She" Pictures:
  a. Spread out the photos/pictures of the 5 single boys and 5 single girls from materials #2 face up on the table (omit the groups). Have the student sort them into a "he" and a "she" pile.
  b. Have the student give you a "he" or a "she" picture as you request at random: "Give me she" or "Give me he."
  c. Use the boy and girl action pictures from materials #3. Present pairs of pictures that show the same verb; e.g., boy sleeping and girl sleeping. Present a short sentence beginning with "he" or "she" and have the student show you the corresponding picture; e.g., show me "she is sleeping"; show me "he is sleeping."

Progress to Step 3 when the understanding of "he" and "she" is 90 percent established.

Step 3—"He," "She," and "It" Pictures:
  a. Use the photos/pictures of single boys and girls (materials #2) together with the pictures of toys/objects (materials #5). Place all or some of them (depending on the student's ability) face up on the table in random order. Have the student sort them into a pile each of "he," "she," and "it."
  b. Have the student give you a "he," "she," or "it" photo/picture as you request them at random; e.g., "give me she"; "give me it."
  c. Use the action pictures showing a single boy, girl, or animal carrying out the same action (materials #3). Have the student give you the picture that cor-

responds to your sentence; e.g., give me "<u>she</u> is walking"; give me "<u>it</u> is walking"; give me "<u>he</u> is walking."

Step 4—"They":
a. Spread out the photos/pictures (materials #2) face up on the table and have the student sort them into piles of single boys, single girls, and groups of both boys and/or girls under the labels "he," "she," and "they."
b. Have the student give you the picture that you request; e.g., "give me <u>she</u>"; "give me <u>they</u>."
c. Use the single and group boy/girl and animal pictures (materials #4). Present pairs of pictures that show the same action; e.g., boy sleeping/boys sleeping. Present a short sentence beginning with "he," "she," or "they," and have the student show you the corresponding picture; e.g., show me "<u>they</u> are sleeping."

Activity **Expressive**

Step 1—"He/She" Real People:
a. Have the student imitate your model as you label "boy—he" and "girl—she" and as you label "he" and "she" without "boy" and "girl."
b. Have her label each child "he" or "she" without a model but with prompts as needed.

Step 2—"He/She" Pictures:
a. Have the student label the photos/pictures (materials #2) "he" or "she" as she sorts them.
b. Have the student label the photos/pictures (materials #2) "he" or "she" as you present them at random. To add variety, use a Magic Bag or Tim's Game.
c. Use the boy and girl pictures from materials #3. Have the student create a short sentence using "he" or "she"; e.g., <u>she</u> is eating; <u>he</u> is eating. To add variety, play Hide the Sticker.

Step 3—"He," "She," and "It" Pictures:
a. Use the photos/pictures of boys and girls (materials #2) together with the pictures of objects (materials #5). Take turns to pick up a picture and label it using "he," "she," or "it."
b. Use the boy, girl, and animal pictures (materials #3) and have the student create a short sentence using "he," "she," or "it"; e.g., <u>it</u> is jumping.

Step 4–"They":
a. Use materials #2. Have the student label the photos/pictures "he," "she," or "they" as she sorts them.
b. Use materials #2. Have the student label the photos/pictures "he," "she," or "they" as you present them in random order. To add interest, use a Magic Bag, Hide the Sticker, or Tim's Game.
c. Use the pictures of boys and girls carrying out actions alone and in groups (materials #4). Have the student create a short sentence using "he," "she," or "they"; e.g., <u>she</u> is eating; <u>they</u> are eating.

Carryover

- Label boys and girls as "he" and "she" in real life, pictures, books, magazines, store catalogs, movies, and other visual materials.
- Play Lotto, Memory, and Go Fish using pictures of boys and girls and label them "he" and "she" when you pick them up.
- Play Lotto and Memory using pictures of boys, girls, and animals carrying out activities alone and in groups. Each player makes up a sentence using the correct pronoun when he picks up a card; e.g., she is eating; they are standing.
- Play Memory with object pictures. Use the sentence "It is a _____ (e.g., dog)" each time a card is turned up.
- Play Snap with pictures of boys and girls. If two pictures of boys or two pictures of girls come together, players must say "he" or "she" appropriately to win them.
- Tell about real-life events, retell stories from books, and create sequence stories from pictures—Chapter 13, (Advanced Expressive Language), Goal 2, p. 265. Give reminders to use the correct pronouns "he," "she," "they," and "it" as appropriate; e.g., they are going to the classroom; he is eating lunch.

Teach "he" and "she" with reference to men and women

Use pictures of familiar adults such as the student's teacher and/or babysitter, as well as people in the community who are not familiar to the student such as a nurse, fireman, police officer.
Follow Step 2 Activity Receptive and Expressive.

Table 87: TRACKING EARLY DEVELOPING PRONOUNS

Pronoun	Receptive	Expressive	Established
Personal			
I			
Me			
He			
She			
It			
They			
You			
We			
Possessive			
My			
Mine			
His			
Her			
Its			
Their			
Your			
Yours			
Our			

Goal 3: The student will use pronouns "I," "we," and "you" in simple sentences; e.g., I am clapping; you are clapping; we are clapping (with 80–90 percent accuracy).

Prerequisite: *Understanding of "what?" questions—Chapter 10, ("Wh" Questions), Goals 1 and 2, pp. 179-80.*

Materials

1. Photos of the student carrying out a variety of day-to-day activities; e.g., swinging on the swing set; running; painting; eating.
2. Photos of the student and you together carrying out the same activity; e.g., both of you eating a snack; both of you wearing hats.
3. List of EASILY PERFORMED VERBS, Table 88, below, printed on cardstock and cut into individual verbs.
4. Collection of "dress-up" clothes (optional); e.g., hats, jackets, shirts.

Introduction

Tell the student that when we talk about ourselves, we use the word "I." Model sentences using "I"; e.g., I am sitting down; I am wearing a shirt; I have a blue pen.

Explain that you will give the student a visual reminder to help her remember to use "I"; e.g., you will raise your index finger or point your finger at her. Students who can read may also wear an "I" cue card to encourage them to self-correct.

Following Step 1, tell the student that when she and you (you and I) are doing the same thing, we can say "we." Give some appropriate examples: we are sitting down; we are working,

Following Step 2, introduce "you" by saying that when we talk to someone, we sometimes use "you" instead of the person's name. Provide models; e.g., I am a wearing a blue shirt; you are wearing a red shirt.

Emphasize the target word and support all Steps with verbal prompts, or for the reader, the target words written on cue cards as needed.

Use list TRACKING EARLY DEVELOPING PRONOUNS, Table 87, above, to record when "I," "we," and "you" are understood, used, and established.

Activity **Receptive** and **Expressive**

Step 1—"I":
   a. Place the individual verbs from EASILY PERFORMED VERBS face down on the table. Take turns to pick up a verb, perform the action (read the verb to the non-reader), and tell the other person what you are doing; e.g., I am walking; I am clapping.
   b. Take turns to describe an item that you are wearing (your regular clothes or dress-up clothes); e.g., I am wearing a red shirt; I am wearing blue socks; I am wearing the clown hat. Tell other things about yourself e.g., I have _____ (a cat/dog/teddy bear); I go to _____ school/swimming/dance class); I want _____ (a doll/toy car/swing set).

  c. Use the photos of the student carrying out a variety of activities (materials #1). Have her describe what she is doing in each one. Use Tim's Game to add interest.

  d. Have the student use "I" in response to "what?" questions throughout the day. Examples: What are you eating? <u>I</u> am eating an apple. What are you playing with? <u>I</u> am playing with a car. What can you see? <u>I</u> can see _____ (list items in the room or that you can see through the window).

When use of "I" is 80–90 percent established, work on Step 2, "we."

Step 2—"We":

  a. Take turns telling about things that you have in common; e.g., <u>we</u> are working in Ms. Langley's room; <u>we</u> are sitting down.

  b. Compare what you are wearing or both have; e.g., <u>we</u> are both wearing socks; <u>we</u> are wearing pants; <u>we</u> have books.

  c. Use the photos of the student and you carrying out the same activity (materials #2). Take turns to describe what you are both doing; e.g., <u>we</u> are sitting on the floor; <u>we</u> are baking cookies.

  d. Describe the activities that you are doing together throughout the day; e.g., <u>we</u> are going to the gym; <u>we</u> are eating lunch.

When use of "we" is 80–90 percent established, work on Step 3, "you."

Step 3—"You":

To provide support for the reader: place an "I" cue card in front of the student, facing her, and a "you" cue card on the table in front of you, but facing the student. Switch the cards around when it is your turn. Point to the appropriate card as needed.

  a. Take turns to describe an item that you are wearing followed by something that the other person is wearing; e.g., <u>I</u> am wearing a blue shirt; <u>you</u> are wearing a red shirt.

  b. Take turns to tell what you are wearing, then ask the other person what he/she is wearing; e.g., <u>I</u> am wearing red shoes. What are <u>you</u> wearing?

  c. Use the EASILY PERFORMED VERBS for an "ask and answer" game. Take turns to pick up a verb (read the verb to the non-reader), perform the action, and ask/answer as in a conversation; e.g., <u>I</u> am clapping. What are <u>you</u> doing?

  d. Take turns to talk about what you can do; e.g., <u>I</u> can swim at the pool. What can <u>you</u> do?

Carryover

- Have the student tell you what she is doing frequently throughout the day. For fun, have her perform actions in front of a mirror and tell you what she is doing; e.g., I am jumping.
- Instead of asking "do" questions such as "Do you want to go outside?" or "Do you have your shoes?" ask questions that require the use of "I" or "we" in the answer. Examples: "Who wants to go outside? (we do)." "Who has her shoes on? (I do)."
- During free play time in the classroom, call for a "freeze" (blow a whistle) and have individual students or groups of students tell what they are doing; e.g., I am playing blocks; we are playing in the sandbox.

Table 88: EASILY PERFORMED VERBS

WALKING	RUNNING
CLAPPING	SMILING
WAVING	JUMPING
HOPPING	POINTING
BLOWING	CRYING
SINGING	PEEKING
SITTING	SLEEPING

Goal 4: The student will use possessive pronouns "his," "her," "its," and "their" in simple sentences (with 80–90 percent accuracy); e.g., this is his hat; her bag; its tail; these are their bikes.

Materials

1. A boy and a girl figure (or picture of each) and 10 toys and objects that are not gender-specific; e.g., eraser, pencil, toy dog.
2. 2 identical sets of felt or magnetic boy and girl figures with clothing for each that is obviously gender specific; e.g., pink girl's hat/brown boy's hat; flowered girl's pants/ plain boy's pants.
3. Toys/objects and/or pictures of toys, objects, or animals that have parts that the student is familiar with; e.g., toy car (wheels, door, steering wheel); horse (eyes, ears, tail, legs).
4. 20 pictures of single and groups of boys, girls, and animals who/that are carrying out the same action alone and in groups with the same object that belongs to them; e.g., 1 boy riding <u>his</u> bike/ 3 boys riding <u>their</u> bikes; 1 rabbit eating <u>its</u> carrot/ 4 rabbits eating <u>their</u> carrots; 1 girl playing with her ball/ 2 girls playing with <u>their</u> balls.
5. Cardboard barrier for Barrier game (p. 7).

Introduction

Tell the student that when a thing belongs to someone, we use the words "his" and "her." Show pictures of single boys and girls from materials #4 and model: e.g., this is <u>her</u> ball; this is <u>his</u> dog.

When the student uses "his" and "her" with 80–90 percent accuracy following Step 1, use materials #3 and introduce "its" by telling the student that we use "its" to show that something belongs to an object or animal; e.g., these are <u>its</u> wheels; this is <u>its</u> ear.

Introduce "their" before Step 4 by telling the student that when a thing belongs to more than one person, object, or animal we use the word "their." Use some of the pictures from materials #4 to model; e.g., the boys are riding <u>their</u> bikes; the kittens are playing with <u>their</u> toys.

Emphasize the target word and support all Steps with verbal prompts or, for the reader, the target words written on cue cards as needed.

Use list TRACKING EARLY DEVELOPING PRONOUNS, p. 251 to record when "his," "her," "its," and "their" are understood, used, and established.

Activity **Receptive**

Step 1—"His" and "Her":
a. Place the boy and girl figures or pictures (materials #1) on the table with a space between them. Together with the student, lay each of the toys and objects beside the boy and the girl as though you are giving the item to them. As you give each one, say to whom it now belongs; e.g., "this is <u>his</u> car"; "this is <u>her</u> brush."

   Leave the objects in place and have the student point to the one that you name; e.g., say, "point to <u>his</u> pen"; "point to <u>her</u> cat."
b. Use the 2 identical sets of boy and girl figures with clothing (materials #2) and play a barrier game. Place a boy and girl with his/her clothing on either side of the barrier. Dress your boy or girl in one piece of clothing on your side of the barrier without the student being able to see what you are doing. Tell the student to follow your directions to dress his boy or girl the same as yours; e.g., "put on <u>her</u> hat." Lift the barrier after each direction to check that the student understood the pronoun (she might have put on <u>his</u> hat by mistake).

When "his" and "her" are understood with 80–90 percent accuracy, introduce "its."

Step 2—"Its":
a. Show the student one of the toys/objects and/or pictures of toys, objects, and animals that have parts (materials #3). Have her point to the part that you name; e.g., "point to <u>its</u> nose"; "point to <u>its</u> wheels."

Step 3—"Their":
a. Use the pictures of people or animals carrying out actions alone and in groups (materials #4). Present a pair of pictures of the same action and have the student point to the objects that you name; e.g., 1 girl wearing a hat/3 girls wearing hats—"point to <u>their</u> hats"; 1 boy riding a bike/2 boys riding bikes—"point to <u>their</u> bikes."
b. Present pairs of pictures from materials #4 again and contrast "his," "her," "its," and "their"; e.g., say, "point to <u>her</u> bike"; "point to <u>their</u> crayons"; "point to <u>its</u> carrot."

   Increase the level of difficulty by adding a personal pronoun "he," "she," "it," or "they" to the beginning of the sentence; e.g., show me "they are wearing <u>their</u> hats"; show me "she is clapping <u>her</u> hands"; show me "it is eating <u>its</u> carrot."

Activity **Expressive**

Step 1—"His" and "Her":

a. During Activity *Receptive* Step 1a, when the toys and objects have been "given" to the boy and girl, point to an object at random and ask, "Whose ___ is this?" Have the student respond with "his' or "her" and the noun; e.g., <u>his</u> pen, <u>her</u> cat.

b. Using materials #2, dress the boy and/or girl and have the student describe what he/she is wearing; e.g., the boy (or he) is wearing <u>his</u> hat; the girl (or she) is wearing <u>her</u> shoes.

    Increase the level of difficulty by dressing either the boy or girl *incorrectly* in a piece of clothing that belongs to the opposite gender. Have the student describe what he sees; e.g., the boy is wearing <u>her</u> hat; the girl is wearing <u>his</u> shoes.

c. Discuss how you can tell the difference between the boy's and the girl's clothing; e.g., <u>his</u> hat is brown; <u>her</u> hat has flowers on it.

d. Play the barrier game in the *Receptive* activity, Step 1b. Have the student be the teacher and tell you which clothing to put on the boy or girl. As the student becomes more competent at this, occasionally make an error and encourage her to correct you; e.g., put on <u>his</u> hat, when she said <u>her</u> hat.

e. Use the pictures of single people from materials #4. Encourage the use of "he" and "she" with "his/her" when describing the pictures; e.g., she is playing with <u>her</u> ball; he is riding <u>his</u> bike.

Step 2—"Its":

a. Use the toys/objects or pictures of toys, objects, and animals that have parts (materials #3). Take turns to select an object or picture and describe its parts; e.g., this is <u>its</u> nose; these are <u>its</u> wheels.

b. Use the pictures of single boys, girls, and animals from materials #4. Have the student describe the pictures using "his," "her," and "its"; e.g., she is holding <u>her</u> cat; he is wearing <u>his</u> coat; it is swimming in <u>its</u> tank.

Step 3—"Their":

a. Use the pictures of *groups* of people or animals (materials #4). Have the student label the object(s) that you point to; e.g., <u>their</u> carrots; <u>their</u> ball.

b. Use the single and groups of boys, girls, and animals (materials #4). Have the student use a full sentence to describe the pictures; e.g., the girl is riding <u>her</u> bike; the dog is chewing <u>its</u> bone; the boys are wearing <u>their</u> hats. For variety, use Tim's Game, a Magic Bag, or Find the Sticker.

c. Use the 2 identical sets of felt or magnetic boy and girl figures with clothing (materials #2). Dress them in the male and female version of the same clothes and have the student describe what they are both wearing; e.g., <u>they</u> are wearing <u>their</u> hats; <u>they</u> are wearing <u>their</u> shoes.

Carryover

- Talk about people, objects, and animals in real life, pictures, and movies that have possessions; e.g., Kate is playing with her toys; Alex is carrying his backpack; the cat hurt its paw.

- Play Lotto and Memory. Use cards that show people and animals carrying out actions that involve an object that belongs to them; e.g., a boy reading his book; a girl combing her hair; horses eating their hay; a dog playing with its ball. Create a sentence for each card when you pick it up.
- Play Go Fish. Use pairs of pictures of clothing that are obviously gender specific. Ask the other player for the piece of clothing to match the one in your hand. Make identical pairs—e.g., her hat + her hat—or opposite pairs; e.g., his hat + her hat. Take turns asking, for example: "Do you have her hat?"; "do you have his shoes?"
- Play with Mr. and Mrs. Potato Head. Use "his" and "her" to describe how you are constructing them; e.g., I am putting on his arms; I put on her hat.
- Make a creature from fruits and vegetables of assorted sizes and "accessorize" with spaghetti noodles, "google" eyes, pipe cleaners, etc. Discuss what kind of creature you are making and what you could use for its various parts. Examples: What can we use for its body? What can we use for its hair? Describe the creature when you are finished; e.g., its body is a pumpkin; its hair is made from noodles; its nose is an apple.
- Describe events in real life and in storybooks and videos using personal and possessive pronouns—he/his, she/her, it/its, they/their.

Goal 5: The student will use possessive pronouns "my," "your," and "our" in simple sentences; e.g., my shoes, your hat, our backpacks (with 80–90 percent accuracy).

Materials

1. 10 objects and/or pieces of clothing that are easily identified as belonging to you and similar ones that belong to the student; e.g., your jacket/student's jacket; your shoe/student's shoe; your t-shirt/student's t-shirt .
2. 5 individual photos of each of you and the student in a variety of places and involved in a variety of different activities; e.g., the student playing at the playground; you walking to the school bus.
3. One large individual photo of each of you and the student showing details; e.g., eyes, hair, arms.
4. Lotto, Memory, Go Fish, or any other turn-taking games on any theme.

Introduction

Tell the student that when something belongs to us, we use the words "my," "your," and "our." For instance, this is <u>my</u> chair (point to your own chair); this is <u>your</u> chair (point to the student's chair); these are <u>our</u> chairs (point to both chairs). Use materials #1 to model other examples.

Emphasize the target word and support all Steps with verbal prompts or, for the reader, the target words written on cue cards as needed. Use list TRACKING EARLY DEVELOPING PRONOUNS, p. 251 to record when "my," "your," and "our," are understood, used, and established.

Activity **Receptive** and **Expressive**

Step 1—"My" and "Your":

a. Mix up the objects and clothing (materials #1). Take turns to select one item and identify the owner; e.g., this is <u>my</u> sweater, this is <u>your</u> t-shirt.

b. Mix up the objects and clothing (materials #1). Take turns to select an item and hold it or put it on. Describe what you or the student is holding or wearing; e.g., I am wearing <u>your</u> hat; you are wearing <u>my</u> coat; I am holding <u>my</u> cup; you are wearing <u>your</u> shoes. *Note* that this is also practice for combining "I" and "you."

c. Use the large individual photos of each of you (materials #3). Take turns to describe what body parts can do (your own or the other person's); e.g., <u>my</u> eyes can see; <u>your</u> hands can clap; <u>my</u> teeth can bite <u>my</u> food; <u>your</u> legs are for walking.

d. Compare clothing, hair, or other features or belongings that you and the student or a group of students have in common; e.g., <u>my</u> hair is long; <u>your</u> hair is short. <u>My</u> shoes are brown; <u>your</u> shoes are black.

e. Play turn-taking games of any theme; e.g., Lotto, Go Fish, Snakes/Chutes and Ladders. After each turn ask, "Whose turn is it?" and have the student answer "my turn" or "your turn," as appropriate.

To support the reader: *place a "my turn" cue card in front of the player whose turn it is and a "your turn" cue card in front of the other player. Switch these cards after each turn.*

f. Use materials #2—individual photos of you and the student each in a variety of places and involved in a variety of different activities. Mix them up and take turns picking up one and telling whose photo it is. Examples: "This is <u>your</u> photo—you are sitting on <u>your</u> chair. This is <u>my</u> photo—I am clapping <u>my</u> hands."

g. Cut the large photos of you and the student (materials #3) into small pieces and mix the pieces up. Take turns to pick up a piece, identify it, and reassemble the two photos; e.g., this is <u>my</u> arm; this is <u>your</u> hair.

When "my" and "your" are understood and used with 80–90 percent accuracy, progress to Step 2, "our."

Step 2—"Our":

a. Discuss how you and the student are the same; e.g., <u>our</u> hair is brown; <u>our</u> shoes have laces.

b. Compare clothing, hair, or other belongings within a group of students and have the students group themselves according to similarities; e.g., <u>our</u> hair is short; <u>our</u> shoes are white.

c. Talk about activities that you are doing at the same time. For example, say, "We are putting on <u>our</u> coats; we are eating <u>our</u> lunch."

d. Expand your discussion of similarities to include differences. Use "my," "your," and "our"; e.g., <u>our</u> shirts are red; <u>your</u> shoes are black and <u>my</u> shoes are brown.

Carryover

- Have the student hand out workbooks and assignments to their owners in the classroom using the real name and pronoun "your." Example: Have her say, "Joe, this is your book"; "Andrea, here is your picture."
- Encourage use of "my turn/your turn/our turn" in daily activities, games, and sports e.g., playing catch with a ball (my turn to throw; your turn to catch); sharing a toy or crayon; putting a jigsaw puzzle together; playing soccer, T-ball, or team tag; playing on play equipment such as a trampoline or slide.
- Blow bubbles using bubble fluid. Take turns to pop a bubble using a particular part of your body, then tell how you or the other person popped it. For example, say, "I popped the bubble with my arm"; "you popped the bubble with your foot."

Goal 6: The student will use personal pronouns "me" and "you" and possessive pronouns "mine" and "yours" in simple sentences; e.g., give it to me—it is mine; this hat is yours—I will give it to you (with 80–90 percent accuracy).

Materials

1. Hand-held mirror.
2. Lotto games using pictures of any theme.
3. 10 objects and/or pieces of clothing that are easily identified as belonging to you, and similar ones that belong to the student; e.g., your jacket/student's jacket; your mitt/ student's mitt; your shoe/student's shoe (as for Goal 5).

Introduction

Tell the student that she is going to learn the words "me" and "you." Hold up the mirror to reflect just you and ask, "Who do I see in the mirror?—I see me." Then hold it so you are both reflected and ask again, "Who do I see in the mirror? I see you and I see me."

Following Step 1, model the use of "mine" and "yours" to introduce Step 2. Use objects that are the same that belong to you and the student (materials #3); e.g., this pencil belongs to you—it is yours; this pencil belongs to me—it is mine.

Emphasize the target word and support all Steps with verbal prompts or, for the reader, the target words written on cue cards as needed.

Use list TRACKING EARLY DEVELOPING PRONOUNS, p. 251, to record when "me," "mine," "you," and "yours" are understood, used, and established.

Activity **Receptive** and **Expressive**

Step 1—"Me" and "You":

a. Look at your reflection in the mirror and then have the student look at hers. Talk about who you can see; e.g., say, "I see me." Hold the mirror at an angle so you can see the other person without your own reflection; e.g., "I can see you." Hold it so you are both reflected; e.g., "I can see you and me."

b. Play Lotto using pictures of any theme. When a card is turned up take turns to check whose lotto card the picture belongs on and say, "This one is for me," or "this is one for you."

To support the reader: *Place a "me" cue card in front of the student facing toward her and a "you" cue card on the table in front of you facing towards the student. Switch the cards around when it is your turn. Provide support by pointing to the appropriate card.*

c. When it is time to line up in the classroom, have the student invite peers into the line and tell them where to stand; e.g., you can stand in front of me; you can stand behind me.

d. Play Hide and Go Seek. Take turns to be the person who hides or the person who "seeks" (finds). Use "you" and "me"; e.g., I am coming to find you. You are going to find me.

When the student understands and uses "me" and "you" with 80–90 percent accuracy, introduce Step 2, "mine" and "yours."

Step 2—"Mine" and "Yours"
Note: *If the student incorrectly adds "s" to "mine" ("mines"), provide extra modeling and practice the words in isolation using Quick Deal (see Carryover).*

a. Mix up the objects and/or pieces of clothing that belong to you and the student (materials #3). Have the student find the ones that belong to her and say, "This belongs to me—it is mine" for each item. Then have her find the things that belong to you and say, "This belongs to you—it is yours."

b. Set up situations in which items are shared (e.g., pencils, crayons, erasers) and each needs to be returned to his/her owner at the end of the activity; e.g., this crayon is yours; this pen is mine.

c. Have the student identify her own possessions from similar items in the classroom; e.g., this lunch bag is mine; those shoes are yours.

d. Work on negative and positive "mine/yours." Play Lotto and comment on each card that is picked up; e.g., "this one is not mine—it is yours."

Carryover

- Play Quick Deal. Use a regular deck of cards but omit the kings, queens, and jacks. Decide which of you will collect the red cards and which will collect the black. Take turns dealing out the pack. Say "yours" for a card of the other player's color and "mine" when it is your color.
- Compare size, length, or design of articles of clothing; e.g., t-shirts, hats—mine is bigger than yours; yours has stripes and mine is plain.
- Play Beanbag Toss or Bowling. Designate some targets or bowling pins as yours and others as the student's by writing your names on specific ones with a felt marker or each choosing a specific color; e.g., squares on the floor, holes in a slanted board, plastic bottles that you use for bowling pins. Describe what happened after each person's turn; e.g., I landed on a square of yours; you knocked over one of mine.

- Share a collection of stickers or treats such as small cereal, nuts, or M&Ms. Divide them up between you; e.g., one for you and one for me.
- Share blocks, crayons, or craft supplies and divide them up before an activity; e.g., these scissors can be yours; these ones can be mine. Divide up some unevenly; e.g., one student has all of the red pom-poms and another student has all of the green ones. Have the students create a craft or pattern sequence that requires both colors. Encourage them to ask or offer; e.g., may I have one of yours; would you like one of mine?

Further Work on Pronouns

Adapt the activities already described to teach the inclusion of several pronouns in the same sentence and make combinations of different personal and possessive pronouns. See SAMPLES OF PRONOUN COMBINATIONS, Table 89, below.

Table 89: SAMPLES OF PRONOUN COMBINATIONS

Pronouns	Sample sentence
I/you + my/your	I have my hat. You have your hat.
He/she + his/her	He has his coat. She has her coat.
It/they + its/their	It has its wheels. They have their backpacks.
I/you + your/my	I have your cup. You have my cup.
He/she + his/her	He has her toys. She has his toys.
I/you + his/her	I have his/her book. You have his/her book.
It/they + his/her	It has his/her picture. They have his/her picture.
We + my/our/your	We are playing with my/our/your balloon.
We + his/her/their/its	We are playing with his/her/their/its ball.
I/we + your	I am holding your hand. We are holding your hands.
He/she/you +our/your	He/she/you found our dog. He/she/you found your dog.
I/he/she/they + yours/theirs/mine	I/he/she/they have yours/theirs/mine.
He/she/they + it + me/us/you	He/she/they will give it to me/us/you.

13.
Advanced Expressive Language

These goals are appropriate for students with one or more of the following characteristics:

- has a good understanding of vocabulary, basic concepts, and "wh" questions

- has difficulty retelling a story or describing a real-life event (omits details or focuses on unimportant ones)

- has difficulty expressing feelings and opinions

- says "I don't know" rather than persisting with efforts to explain

- assumes that the listener understands his message even though the listener does not

- has difficulty initiating social conversation/does not know what to say

Advanced Expressive Language Goals

The student will:

Goal 1: spontaneously describe activities in a picture scene.

Goal 2: tell a sequence story with and without picture support.

Goal 3: predict what will happen next in or after a series of events.

Goal 4: identify what is wrong (absurd) in a situation, picture, and/or spoken sentence.

Goal 5: identify what is missing from a picture and/or spoken list.

Goal 6: make inferences from a picture or verbal information.

Goal 7: answer "how?" questions:
- How do you _____? (perform an action).
- How are things the same/different?
- How do you know/think/can you tell?
- How does something look/move/feel/taste/sound?
- How would you/someone feel if _____? (emotions).

Goal 1: The student will spontaneously describe activities in a picture scene (with 80–90 percent accuracy).

Materials

- 10 action pictures or magnetic/felt scenes in which a variety of people and animals are carrying out familiar activities; e.g., a girl riding a bike, a boy on a swing, and a man feeding ducks.

Introduction

Introduce this goal by saying that you are going to talk about the things that are happening in a picture scene. Select a picture or magnetic/felt scene and describe three activities that are shown. Example: The girl is riding her bike. The boy is feeding the ducks. The old lady is sitting on the bench. Provide other examples as needed.

Activity **Receptive** and **Expressive**

Use a picture or magnetic/felt scene and have the student describe 2 increasing to 5 (depending on ability level) activities shown, using complete sentence structures with minimal or no assistance. Progress through the following Steps in order to reach this level of ability:

Step 1: Have the student describe the activities using any words or structures. Write down exactly what he says without interrupting or prompting him; e.g., girl on bike; ducks and boy. If necessary point to a specific activity to help him initiate a description.

Step 2: Help him expand his information by asking him "what?" questions. Examples: "What is the girl doing on her bike?" (riding); "what is the boy doing with the ducks?"(feeding them).

Step 3: Help him improve his sentence structures by using sentence completion; e.g., the girl is _____ (riding her bike); the boy is _____ (feeding the ducks). Model, prompt, or ask, "What would be a better way of saying that?"

Step 4: Finish by writing down his improved response and repeat the activity using the same scene during a subsequent therapy session with the aim of having him recall his final, improved description.

Carryover

- Watch events in real life or on TV/video and take turns describing what is happening (each add a sentence to describe one activity or each describe a different one); e.g., activities on the playground at recess; during gym class.
- Describe picture scenes in storybooks, magazines, and on jigsaw puzzles.

Goal 2: The student will tell a sequence story with and without picture support (with 80–90 percent accuracy).

Prerequisite: *Ability to make or reproduce sequence patterns (not covered in this manual). Understanding of concepts of time (beginning/end, first/last, then, before/after—Chapter 9 (Concepts), Goal 4, p. 165 and Goal 5, p. 168.*

Materials

1. Photos of the student carrying out sequential activities; e.g., arriving at school, getting ready for and eating lunch; making an art project.
2. Sequence stories in interlocking puzzle or commercial picture-card format. *You will need some sequence stories that the student has not previously worked on for Goal 3 so do not use all of your materials for this goal.*
3. List SEQUENTIAL EVENTS, Table 90, below.

Introduction

Introduce this goal by saying that today you are going to tell stories. Present one of the series of photos of the student carrying out a sequential activity or present commercial sequence story pictures. Arrange the pictures in their correct order from left to right, face up on the table. Point to each picture in turn and model an appropriate sentence for each to create a sequential story.

Activity 1 **Receptive** and **Expressive** (with visual support)

Use materials 1 and 2. Start working with sequences of 3 pictures and increase to 6 or more, depending on the student's ability.

Step 1: Arrange the pictures from a 3-step story in the correct order from left to right and tell the story to the student as you point to each picture. Have the student tell the story back to you as he points to each picture. Prompt as needed and encourage him to use full-sentence structures.

Step 2: Use the *same* story as in Step 1. Arrange the 3 pictures with one picture out of sequence. Have the student correct the order of the pictures and tell the story.

Step 3: Use the *same* story again. Mix up all of the pictures and have the student lay them out in the correct order and tell the story one more time.

Step 4: Present new stories and work through Steps 1–3 if necessary before progressing to Step 5.

Step 5: Present pictures from an *unfamiliar* 3-step story in any order. Have the student arrange the pictures in the correct order (from left to right) and tell the story. Encourage complete sentence structures in the tense requested by the instructor; e.g., what is happening? (present); what happened? (past). See Chapter 11 (Word and Sentence Structure), Verb Tense Goal 5, p. 215.

Encourage use of concepts "beginning," "middle," "end," "first…then," "last," and "before/after."

Activity 2 **Receptive** and **Expressive** (without visual support)

Use the list SEQUENTIAL EVENTS:
  a. Chose a sequential event from the list and *take turns* to describe the steps in the event. Example (having lunch): "I get my lunch bag from the shelf; I open my lunch bag. I take out my sandwich and juice and set them on the table," etc.
  b. Have the student describe the event *independently*. Write down his sentences and encourage him to expand his ideas and sentence structures when you read them back to him.
Repeat topics on subsequent occasions to encourage carryover of ideas and structures.

Carryover

- Provide a verbal commentary during the student's routine activities; e.g., when the student arrives at school—"First you take off your jacket, then you take off your shoes. Then you put on your indoor shoes. Last you put your backpack on the shelf."
- Have the student show photos of a sequential event in his life (e.g., a school trip) to a person other than you and tell at least 3 sequential steps about the event.
- Encourage the student to describe sequential steps in everyday activities; e.g., what happened during the morning at school; what happened in gym time.
- Take turns to create a story or describe an imaginary event. Each of you will add a new step or idea to the story (it can become very silly!). Examples: the day that the space rocket took off from earth; the day the fairy learned to drive a car.
- Start a story and have the student finish it. For example: the grumpy frog hopped onto a lily pad and along came… (a green lizard who said to the frog _____).
- Do simple cooking activities and describe the steps as you are carrying them out; e.g., make smoothies, hot chocolate, Jello with canned fruit.
- Repair a broken item and describe the steps as you are fixing it; e.g., the wheel on a toy car, torn page in a library book.

Table 90: SEQUENTIAL EVENTS

Topic	Date and comments
1. Wash hands.	
2. Eat an ice cream cone.	
3. Make a sandwich.	
4. Have lunch.	
5. Get up in the morning.	
6. Brush teeth.	
7. Wrap a birthday present.	
8. Clean up the classroom.	
9. Go for a drive in the car.	
10. Bake cookies.	
11. Turn on the computer.	
12. Plant a garden.	
13. Get ready to go outside for recess.	
14. Paint a picture.	
15. Deliver a note to the office.	
16. Set the table for dinner.	
17. Visit the doctor.	
18. Go to a birthday party.	
19. Decorate for a special season.	
20. Make toast.	

Goal 3: The student will predict what will happen next in or after a series of events (with 80–90 percent accuracy).

Materials

1. Sequence stories in interlocking puzzle or picture-card format *not previously seen* by the student.
2. Commercial picture card sets for prediction.
3. Age-appropriate storybooks.

Introduction

Tell the student that sometimes we have to work out what is going to happen when we do something or what happened that made something else happen. We call this "predicting."

Show a picture from a sequence story that the student has *not previously seen* and discuss what might happen or what might have happened; e.g., picture of a girl going out for a walk and big rain clouds in the sky. Model your prediction; e.g., I think that it will rain while she is out walking. Then show the next picture in the story (the girl wearing a wet raincoat) and explain how you were able to predict that she would get wet (because there were big clouds in the sky). Present other examples as needed.

Activity 1 Receptive and Expressive (with visual support)

Step 1: Present the first 2 or 3 pictures of a longer (5–8) commercial picture sequence story and have the student arrange the pictures in their correct order from left to right and tell the story to this point. Ask him to predict what will happen next or at the end of the story. Examples: "What do you think is going to happen next?" "How do you think the story will end?" Provide the next or final picture(s) after he has made his prediction.

Prompt by offering choices; e.g., "do you think the dog will catch the cat or the cat will run up a tree?"

Step 2: Present commercial pictures/card sets for prediction and discuss what will happen and how you know. Use Tim's Game or Magic Bag to add interest.

Activity 2 Receptive and Expressive (without visual support)

Read a short, age-appropriate story to the student:

a. Stop at the end of a sentence, paragraph, or page and ask the student what he thinks is going to happen next. Any reasonable prediction is acceptable and can be discussed further as the story progresses and the real events become apparent.

b. Start in the middle of the story and ask what might have already happened.

Carryover

- Carry out real-life "experiments" in order to provide concrete examples for predictions. Have the student predict what will happen if you do something and then compare what he said with what actually happened when you did it. Examples: Build a house of cards and ask, "What will happen if I blow on it?" Or, put a cup of milk in the freezer and ask, "What do you think will happen?"
- Describe a scenario (without visual or concrete support) and discuss (predict) what might happen. Ask, for example, "What would happen if I dropped an egg on the floor?"; "if we left ice cream in the sun?"; "if you forgot to wear your jacket outside on a rainy day?"
- Encourage the student to make predictions about events and happenings in real-life; e.g., "what do you think will happen in gym class?" "What do you think Amy has brought for Show and Tell?"

Goal 4: The student will identify what is wrong (absurd) in a situation, picture, and/or spoken sentence (with 80–90 percent accuracy).

Prerequisite: *Understanding of "right" and "wrong"—Chapter 4 (Yes/No), p. 39. Ability to use conjunction "because"—Chapter 10 ("Wh" Questions), Why? Questions, p. 200. Understanding of "no/not"—Chapter 2, Negative Goals, 1–3, pp. 24-27.*

Materials

1. Real objects that can be used to create "wrong" situations; e.g., sock, hat. See list REAL OBJECTS/WRONG SITUATIONS, Table 91, below.
2. Commercial picture card sets that show a deliberate error; e.g., a fish in a bird nest; a girl eating soup with a fork.
3. List WHAT'S WRONG/ABSURD SENTENCES, Table 92, below.

Introduction

Explain to the student that sometimes people do or say silly things and we know that they are wrong (absurd). Today you are going to talk about some silly things. Use some of the real objects to create a "wrong" situation; e.g., put a pair of gloves on your feet. Describe what is wrong/silly and why. Example: "I can't wear gloves on my feet. That's silly! Gloves fit over my hands and fingers. They do not fit over my feet and toes. I wear socks on my feet."

Activity 1 **Receptive** and **Expressive** (with visual)

Step 1: Use real objects from REAL OBJECTS/WRONG SITUATIONS to create wrong (absurd) situations; e.g., put socks on your hands; put a hat on your foot. Have the student identify what is wrong/silly and describe the correct way. Prompt with questions. Examples: "What did I do that was silly?" (e.g., put cereal in shoe). "Why is that silly?" "What should I have done?" "You should put cereal in a bowl and not in a shoe."

Step 2: Use the commercial pictures that show a deliberate error and have the student describe what is wrong/silly (absurd) and why. Example: "What do you see that is wrong?" (a fish in bird nest). "A fish lives in water and cannot fly to a bird nest/a bird lives in a nest and a fish lives in the water."

Encourage the use of full sentence structures.

Activity 2 **Receptive** and **Expressive** (without visual)

Read a sentence to the student from WHAT'S WRONG/ABSURD SENTENCES and have him describe what is wrong. Example: "We go to school at night time—what did you hear that was wrong/silly?" "We go to *bed* at night time and go to *school* in the day time."

Note: *This task requires good auditory processing skills and therefore may be difficult for some students. See Chapter 16 (Listening Skills - Auditory Processing), p. 305.*

Carryover

- Create wrong (absurd) situations during the day and encourage the student to comment on them; e.g., put the trashcan on top of the desk.
- Make absurd statements and have the student correct you; e.g., "we are going to the moon after lunch."

Table 91: REAL OBJECTS/WRONG SITUATIONS

Objects needed: toothbrush, toothpaste, hairbrush, cereal bowl, dry cereal, 2 mittens, pencil with eraser on the end, ball, water bottle, 2 hats, shoe, spoon, slice of bread.

Objects	Situation
Toothpaste and hairbrush	Put toothpaste on the hair brush.
Cereal bowl and cereal	Turn cereal bowl upside down and try to pour cereal into it.
2 identical mittens	Put mittens on your feet.
Pencil	Write with the eraser end.
Ball	Pretend to eat the ball as though it were an apple.
Water bottle	Try to drink from the bottom, not the top.
2 identical hats	Put hats on your hands.
Cereal and shoe	Pour cereal into the shoe.
Toothbrush	Brush your hair with the toothbrush.
Slice of bread and spoon	Try to cut the bread with the spoon.

Table 92: WHAT'S WRONG/ABSURD SENTENCES

Sentence	Response	Correct/ incorrect
1. A cat has two legs.		
2. A cow can bark.		
3. We write with a fork.		
4. Boys wear trees.		
5. I drink soup from a bucket.		
6. Horses wear pajamas.		
7. Dogs ride bikes.		
8. The alphabet goes 1, 2, 3…		
9. Sheep climb trees.		
10. We eat a book.		
11. We go to school at night time.		
12. I brush my hair with a spoon.		
13. Snow is hot.		
14. Bananas are blue.		
15. Children drive cars.		
16. I do up my socks with zippers.		
17. Frogs can fly.		
18. Butterflies swim in water.		
19. The sun is cold.		
20. A stop sign means "go."		

Goal 5: The student will identify what is missing from a picture and/or spoken list (with 80–90 percent accuracy).

Note: *The ability to identify what is missing from a picture requires good visual processing and therefore this goal may not be suitable for all students.*

Prerequisite: *Recognition of the presence or absence of objects in a physical group—Chapter 3 (Same and Different), Goal 3, p. 32. Ability to generate a list of items in a classification or category—Chapter 6 (Classification and Categorization), Goal 5, p. 91.*

Materials

1. 2 identical magnetic or felt scenes with people, animals, and objects to put on the scene.
2. Commercial picture card sets that show objects with parts missing; e.g., bicycle missing front wheel; cow missing ears.
3. Activity WHAT IS MISSING FROM A LIST? Table 93, below.

Introduction

Introduce this goal by saying that sometimes people show us a picture but it does not have everything in it that it should. Some things are missing.

Use 2 of the same magnetic or felt scenes (scenes "A" and "B"). Arrange 3 or 4 people, animals, or objects on them so that they are identical, except omit one item for scene "B." Identify the missing item and discuss; e.g., "the swing is missing from this scene." Present several examples.

Show a commercial picture of an object that has a part missing. Identify the missing part and discuss; e.g., "the bicycle is missing its front wheel—I would not be able to make it move without the wheel."

Following Step 1, introduce Step 2 by saying that sometimes people leave things off a list. Present one or more example(s) from the activity WHAT IS MISSING? and model the appropriate response.

Activity **Receptive** and **Expressive**

Step 1—What Is Missing from a Picture?

a. Arrange a small number of people/animals/items on the 2 magnetic/felt scenes (make the scenes identical). Take turns to remove an item from one or the other of the scenes and describe what is missing.

b. Use the commercial pictures that show a part missing. Have the student describe what is missing; e.g., the house is missing its roof. Encourage him to give lots of details and use full sentence structures.

Step 2—What Is Missing from a Spoken List?

a. Use WHAT IS MISSING FROM THE LIST? Read the name of an activity and the items listed for it. Have the student list additional items. Example: "We are going to the beach. We have towels and snacks—what else do we need?" (sand-toys, sun-block, swimsuits, etc.).

Table 93: WHAT IS MISSING FROM A LIST?

Ask: What else do I/you/we/he/she/it/they need?

Activity and List	Response
1. I need to clean my teeth. I have water and toothpaste….	
2. Kyle wants to make a sandwich. He has a knife and bread….	
3. You want to make an ice cream cone. You have ice cream and a cone….	
4. You want to draw a picture. You have crayons and pencils….	
5. You are getting ready to go to school. You have your lunch bag and jacket….	
6. It's bath time. You have soap and a washcloth….	
7. You have a cut on your hand. You washed it in soap and dried it….	
8. Anna is having a birthday party. There are decorations and presents….	
9. John is going to wrap a gift. He has paper and tape….	
10. Dad wants to fasten two pieces of wood together. He has wood and nails….	
11. You want to paint a picture. You have paper and a brush….	
12. Your family wants to go for a drive. Dad has the car….	
13. Mom is making your bed. She has sheets and a blanket….	
14. Austin is old enough to fix his own breakfast. He has cereal and a bowl….	
15. My dog needs a bath. I have a big tub and shampoo….	
16. It is Halloween and you are going Trick or Treating. You have your costume….	
17. You are going to the public swimming pool. You have money and a swimsuit….	
18. Dad and you are going to wash the car. You have a bucket and a sponge….	
19. Mom wants to make cookies. She has flour and eggs….	
20. The firemen got a call to go to a fire. They have their helmets and coats….	

Carryover

- Create situations in which a key item is missing; e.g., paintbrush in art class; spoon at lunchtime. Have the student identify what is missing and why it is needed.
- Draw a picture but omit a part. Have the student identify the part that is missing and tell you how to complete the picture. Examples: "The horse is missing its ears—you need to draw it ears"; "a chair is missing one of its legs—you need to draw the chair leg."
- Say a familiar rhyme to the student but leave out a key word. Have the student tell you the missed word. Example: "Row, row, row your _____ (boat). Gently _____ (down) the stream."
- Say a short sentence to the student, pause then say it again but leave out a word. Have the student tell you the word that you missed; e.g., "the spider sat on a log." Pause. "The ____ sat on a log (spider)."
- While reading a familiar story to the student, omit a key word from a sentence and have him add the missing word; e.g., "it was a cold rainy _____ "(day); "the two _____ (dogs) raced across the field."

Note: *Step 2 and some of the carryover listening activities listed are excellent practice for short- term auditory memory.*

Goal 6: The student will make inferences from a picture or verbal information (with 80–90 percent accuracy).

Materials

1. Pictures from storybooks and magazines that show an event has happened or suggest that an event is about to happen.
2. Commercial picture card sets for inferences.
3. List EVENTS FOR INFERENCES, Table 94, below.

Introduction

Tell the student that people do not always show us or tell us all that we need to know. Sometimes we need to work it out for ourselves. For instance, if the teacher puts a cloth on the table for art class, I can work out that she did that because she does not want paint to get on the table. We are going to look at some pictures and talk about things that we are not shown in the picture.

Activity **Receptive** and **Expressive**

Step 1—Pictures:
   a. Use materials #1. Have the student describe what is happening in the picture. Then ask questions about information not shown in the picture so that he is required to make inferences; e.g., picture of firemen putting away hoses and ruins of a building in the background. Ask, "What might have happened before this picture?"

Table 94: EVENTS FOR INFERENCES

Ask: What might happen or might have happened?

Event	Response
1. I pour water into a bucket that has a hole in it.	
2. I leave a Popsicle in the sun.	
3. Dad's hair is shorter tonight than it was this morning.	
4. A dog is all wet.	
5. The TV won't work.	
6. There is a different teacher in your classroom.	
7. You open your lunchbox but it is empty.	
8. A boy throws a ball against a window.	
9. You ride your bicycle too fast.	
10. We turn off all the lights.	
11. There is broken glass on the ground.	
12. Susie went to see the doctor.	
13. Some paper plates blow off the picnic table.	
14. Mom comes home carrying a bag of groceries.	
15. Peter is wrapping a present.	
16. The lady with a camera tells Ryan to smile.	
17. Mom picks up something when it rings and she talks into it.	
18. Johnny is still in bed when the school bus comes.	
19. I forgot to bring my library book on library day.	
20. You touch the stove top.	

b. Present commercial picture cards for inferences and ask relevant questions. Use Tim's Game or Magic Bag to add interest.

Step 2—Verbal Information: Use EVENTS FOR INFERENCES. Read a listed event to the student and discuss what might have happened and/or what will happen.

Carryover

- Discuss inferences in everyday events. Examples: "There is trash lying on the ground—what might have happened?" (somebody knocked over the trash can). "We need to shut the window— what might happen if we don't?" (the room will get cold).

Goal 7: The student will answer "How?" questions:

How do you _____? (perform an action); e.g., sharpen a pencil).
How are things the same/different? e.g., an apple and an orange
How do you know/think/can you tell? e.g., know which month it is
How does something look/move/feel/taste/sound? e.g., a bike move
How would you/someone feel if _____? (emotions); e.g., you lost a toy.

Prerequisites: *Knowledge of sequencing—Chapter 13 (Advanced Expressive Language), Goal 2, p. 265). Knowledge of same/different—Chapter 3 (Same and Different), Goal 5, p. 34. Knowledge of classification and categorization—Chapter 6 (Classification and Categorization), Goal 3, pp. 81. Use of descriptors—Chapter 8 (Descriptors), Goal 4, p. 128. Knowledge of emotions—Chapter 8 (Descriptors), Goal 5, p. 130.*

Materials

1. List SEQUENTIAL EVENTS, Table 90, above, p. 267.
2. List SAME/DIFFERENT PAIRED ITEMS, Table 6 from Chapter 3, Goal 5, p. 36.
3. List CATEGORY LISTS, Table 26, from Chapter 6, Goal 3, p. 82.
4. List HOW DO YOU KNOW/THINK/CAN YOU TELL, Table 95, below.
5. List HOW DOES SOMETHING LOOK/MOVE/FEEL/TASTE/SOUND?, Table 96, below.
6. List HOW WOULD YOU/SOMEONE FEEL IF…?, Table 97, below.

Introduction

Introduce this goal by telling the student that he is going to learn to answer questions that begin with "how?" Explain that "how" means "in what way?" Give an example: Your teacher asks me, "How did you get to school today?" She is asking me "in what way did you get to school?" I will tell her that I came in my car. Ask the student, "How did you come to school today?" and help him with his reply; e.g., did you come on the bus or did mom drive you? Give further examples as needed.

To encourage further discussion and ideas in the following Steps, prompt with "how else?" e.g., "how else can you tell that it is hot out?" "How else are these things the same?" Encourage the student to use full sentence structures in all Steps.

Activity **Receptive** and **Expressive**

Step 1—How Do You….? (Perform an Action): Choose an action from the list SEQUENTIAL EVENTS. Ask, "How do you….?" e.g., "how do you brush your teeth?" Encourage the student to include details in 2 to 4 sequential steps.

Step 2—How Are Things the Same/Different?

a. Choose a pair of items from the list SAME/DIFFERENT PAIRED ITEMS and ask, "<u>How</u> are they the same/different?" Example: "<u>How</u> is an apple the same as/different from an orange?" Rephrase the question to "how, *in what way*, are they the same/different?" if he has difficulty understanding what you mean. Start by discussing how the items are the same, then progress to how they are different.

b. Choose a category from CATEGORY LISTS and ask, "<u>How</u> *(in what way)* are they all the same?" e.g., "<u>how</u> are all animals the same?" Prompt with "what?" questions; e.g., "what do they all have?" "What can they all do?"

Step 3—How Do You Know? How Do You Think? How Can You Tell? Choose a scenario from the list HOW DO YOU KNOW/THINK/CAN YOU TELL….? and discuss how you know what has happened/is happening. Prompt with "what?" questions; e.g., "what is it that tells you that….?" "What do you see that tells you that….?"

Step 4—How Does Something Look/Move/Feel/Taste/Sound? Choose a subject from the list HOW DOES SOMETHING LOOK/MOVE/FEEL/TASTE/SOUND? e.g., <u>how</u> does a turtle move? <u>How</u> does a pillow feel? Encourage the use of descriptors.

Step 5—How Would You/Someone Feel If….? (Emotions): Choose a scenario from HOW WOULD YOU/SOMEONE FEEL IF….? e.g., Kate lost her favorite toy— <u>how</u> does she feel? Encourage the use of words that describe emotions.

Carryover

- Ask "how?" questions and model answers throughout the day. Use pictures in books and real-life situations. Example: "How do you know it is hot out?" Response: "The sun is shining; people are wearing shorts." "How can you tell that it is lunchtime?" Response: "I am hungry; people are lining up to go to the cafeteria."
- Ask "how?" questions about stories; e.g., "how does the mom know where the children are hiding?"
- Make a craft or art project such as paper-bag puppets. Discuss, e.g., "how are we going to make the hair?" "How are we going to make the eyes?"
- Use a children's book of magic tricks. Perform a trick that prompts the student to ask, "How did you do that?" Then teach the student to perform the trick for other people so they will ask the same question.
- Play Animal Walk. One player (the leader) will choose the name of an animal (real or imaginary) that the other players are to act like. They will need to ask the leader how they need to walk and sound to be like that animal; e.g., Leader: "You are going to be elephants." Players: "How do we need to walk?" Leader: "Walk with big steps." Players: "How do we need to sound?" Leader: "Make big trumpeting noises" (all the players will walk around using big steps and making trumpeting sounds until told to stop. Then another player will choose an animal).

Table 95: HOW DO YOU KNOW/THINK/CAN YOU TELL....?

Scenario	Student response	Comment
1. That it is going to rain.		
2. That something is on fire.		
3. That a car has a flat tire.		
4. When to get up in the morning.		
5. That a bucket has a hole in it.		
6. That someone is knocking on the door.		
7. When to change a light bulb.		
8. When to buy more food.		
9. That the floor needs sweeping.		
10. That dinner is ready.		
11. When a movie is finished.		
12. That your pencil needs sharpening.		
13. That you have the wrong key for a door.		
14. That someone has used your towel.		
15. Which month it is.		
16. When summer is over.		
17. When a store is open.		
18. That a car is out of gas.		
19. That there are chocolate chips in the cookies.		
20. Which bus to get on to go home.		

Table 96: HOW DO/DOES SOMETHING LOOK/MOVE/FEEL/TASTE/SOUND?

Scenario	Student response	Comment
1. A turtle move.		
2. A pillow feel.		
3. Candy taste.		
4. A bell sound.		
5. A bike move.		
6. Fire feel.		
7. A frog move.		
8. An eraser feel.		
9. Pizza taste.		
10. Flowers look.		
11. An ice cube feel.		
12. A snake move.		
13. Children playing at recess sound.		
14. Toothpaste taste.		
15. New clothes look.		
16. A brick feel.		
17. A lion sound.		
18. A spider move.		
19. A bird sound.		
20. A hug feel.		

Table 97: HOW WOULD YOU/SOMEONE FEEL IF....?

Scenario	Student response	Comment
1. Lost a favorite toy.		
2. Did not sleep well last night.		
3. Went for a ride in a spaceship.		
4. Had your own puppy.		
5. Did not get any time on the computer.		
6. Recess lasted all afternoon.		
7. Someone got hurt.		
8. A friend would not play with you.		
9. Were the principal for a day.		
10. Did not have breakfast.		
11. Sat in the sun all day.		
12. Heard a very loud noise.		
13. Did not have anything to drink.		
14. Had a cough and cold.		
15. Saw your mom on TV.		
16. Did not get any birthday presents.		
17. The teacher said you had done good work.		
18. Someone gave you an ice cream.		
19. Missed the school bus.		
20. Ate a whole bag of chips.		

14.
Listening Skills:
Auditory Discrimination

These goals are appropriate for students with one or more of the following characteristics:

- has difficulty processing information in spoken language, including directions

- is easily distracted by sounds

- mistakes one word for another during listening tasks; e.g., chat–cat, in–on

- has a short auditory attention span

- has difficulty imitating words modeled

- makes articulation errors

- shows an interest in reading but is not yet able to decode

Auditory Discrimination Goals

The student will discriminate between:

Goal 1: noisemakers that are similar or distinctly different from each other in sound and appearance; e.g., squeaker/rattle.

Goal 2: paired single consonants that are the same or different; e.g., p/p, p/s.

Goal 3: paired single-syllable words that differ by one or more than one consonant or vowel; e.g., gate/got, bet/cup.

Goal 1: The student will discriminate between 2 noisemakers that are similar or distinctly different from each other in sound and appearance (with 80–90 percent accuracy).

Prerequisite: *Understanding of concepts "same" and "different"—Chapter 3 (Same and Different), Goal 1, p. 30.*

Materials

1. 4–6 identical pairs of rattles and squeakers (baby rattles or dog toys) that make a distinctly different sound, one pair from another; e.g., rattle, tinkle, squeak.
2. 4–6 pairs of noisemakers that look alike but sound different. (See below for instructions.)
3. Cardboard barrier for Barrier game (p. 7).

Make the noisemakers: *from small containers that the student cannot see inside of; e.g., small tubs with lids. Divide the containers into pairs and place identical small items in each pair so that they will make a noise when the container is shaken; e.g., dry rice, cereal, small jingle bells. Each pair will make a different sound from the other pairs; e.g., a high-pitched rattle, a tinkle, or a dull thud. The noisemakers must be indistinguishable from each other unless they are shaken. Firmly attach the lids so that the student cannot look inside and to avoid spilling the contents!*

Introduction

Tell the student she is going to do some special listening. Encourage her to "put on her listening ears!"

Model the sounds of the rattles and squeakers (materials #1) and discuss how those that look the same sound the same and those that look different sound different. Allow the student to play with the rattles and squeakers so that she becomes familiar with their sounds. Teach her to make two sounds separately rather than at the same time so that she can compare the difference between them. Use the words "same" and "different."

Introduce the noisemakers that look alike but sound different after playing the barrier game below.

Activity **Receptive** and **Expressive**

Barrier Game

Use two of the identical pairs of rattles and squeakers (materials #1). Place the barrier between you and put one of each pair on either side of the barrier (one in front of the student and the other one of the pair in front of you).

Behind the barrier and out of sight of the student, shake or squeeze one of the rattles or squeakers (continue to hold it in your hand). Tell the student to make the same sound.

After she has made the sound lift the barrier so that she can see whether or not she selected the same rattle or squeaker as you did.

Gradually increase to a choice of all 4–6 squeakers and rattles.

Sorting Noisemakers

Use 2 pairs of the noisemakers that look alike but sound different (materials #2). Mix them up and have the student sort them into the pairs that make the same sound. Gradually increase to a choice of all 4–6 pairs of noisemakers. Since the containers are identical, this activity does not lend itself to presentation as a barrier game.

Carryover

- Encourage the student to imitate sounds throughout the day; e.g., percussion or home-made instruments, tapping the table, etc.
- Stand silently somewhere in school or on the playground. Listen to and discuss the sounds that you hear; e.g., door slamming, students talking, paper rustling, coughing, ball bouncing.
- Draw the student's attention to sounds in the environment and discuss whether the sound was like any other sound that she is familiar with. For example, that truck sounds like Daddy's car; that dog's bark is high and squeaky, but your dog's bark is deep.

Goal 2: The student will discriminate between paired single consonants that are the same or different; e.g., p/p, p/s (with 80–90 percent accuracy).

Prerequisite: *Understanding of concepts "same" and "different—Chapter 3 (Same and Different), Goal 1, p. 30.*

Materials

1. List CONSONANTS, Table 98, below.
2. Blank copies of TEACHING DISCRIMINATION OF CONSONANT PAIRS, Table 99, below.
3. List TRACKING CONSONANT DISCRIMINATION, Table 100, below.

Introduction

Tell the student that she is going to listen to pairs of sounds that we make with our mouth when we are talking and decide if the sounds are the same or different.

Select sounds from the list CONSONANTS and model pairs of identical sounds and pairs of non-identical (different) sounds; e.g., p/p (same), p/s (different). Exaggerate the sounds so that they can be more easily distinguished.

Be aware that you are producing *speech* sounds and not *letter* sounds; e.g., "p" is the short explosive sound at the end of "hop" and not "pee" as in the letter "P." Discuss whether the sounds in a pair are the same or different. Begin by presenting sounds that are very different; e.g., "b" contrasted with "sh." Progress to sounds that are more similar to each other; e.g., "b" contrasted with "p."

Have the student imitate the consonant pair after she has identified them as the same or different but only if she is able to imitate accurately. Students who are unable to imitate due to articulation difficulties should be encouraged to listen only.

Activity **Receptive** and **Expressive**

1. Use the list CONSONANTS. Present pairs of consonants and ask if they sound the same or different; e.g., k/k = same; b/s = different.

   Work through each consonant. Begin by presenting the target consonant *after* other consonants (final position) and when the student is able to discriminate in the final position with 80–90 percent accuracy, present the target consonant *before* other consonants (initial position); e.g., target consonant p̲ - f/p̲ (after/final position), p̲/s (before/initial position). It is easier for you to emphasize or elongate a consonant in the final position, which makes it easier for the student to hear. It is also easier for her to remember the last sound that she heard.

2. Repeat the pair of consonants and have the student imitate them if her articulation skills allow.

3. Record each consonant pair that you present on a blank copy of TEACHING DISCRIMINATION OF CONSONANT PAIRS. Note also whether the pair was the same or different, whether or not the student was able to identify the pair as being the same or different, what sounds she used when attempting to imitate the pair and whether her imitation was correct or not. Compare the lists from each teaching session to give an overall view of the student's ability to discriminate consonants in specific positions.

4. Track the student's progress using TRACKING CONSONANT DISCRIMINATION. When she is able to discriminate pairs with the target sound in the initial or final position to 80–90 percent accuracy, put a check mark in the appropriate column next to the consonant; e.g., when "p" occurs before another consonant.

Table 98: CONSONANTS

Consonants are made as they sound in words not as alphabet letters, so "t" is pronounced as "t" in "bat" not "Tee" the letter. Each consonant is listed with an example to show how it sounds at the end of a word.

Important: *keep the sounds in this table in the order and grouping shown.*

Consonants:

p (ho̲p̲)	**t** (ra̲t̲)	**k** (ma̲k̲e)
b (ro̲b̲)	**d** (pa̲d̲)	**g** (le̲g̲)
m (mo̲m̲)	**n** (fa̲n̲)	
ch (mu̲ch̲)	**sh** (pu̲sh̲)	**j** (ora̲ng̲e)
f (kni̲f̲e)	**v** (li̲v̲e)	**th** (ba̲th̲)
s (hou̲s̲e)	**z** (free̲z̲e)	

Of the 40 phonemes in the English language, the 16 listed above are the most suitable for early discrimination activities.

Table 99: TEACHING DISCRIMINATION OF CONSONANT PAIRS

Consonant pair	Same/ Different	Correct/ incorrect	Imitation	Correct/ incorrect
1.				
2.				
3.				
4.				
5.				
6.				
7.				
8.				
9.				
10.				
11.				
12.				
13.				
14.				
15.				
16.				
17.				
18.				
19.				
20.				

Table 100: TRACKING CONSONANT DISCRIMINATION

Consonant	Initial position; e.g., p/s	Final position; e.g., f/p
p		
t		
k		
b		
d		
g		
m		
n		
ch		
sh		
j		
f		
v		
th		
s		
z		

Carryover

- Encourage family and caregivers to draw attention to speech sounds and to carry out this activity in other situations throughout the day so that the student learns to discriminate sounds in spite of background noise; e.g., while driving in the car.
- Play Simon Says, p. 8, to develop general discrimination skills.

Goal 3: The student will discriminate between paired single-syllable words that differ by one or more than one consonant or vowel; e.g., gate/got, bet/cup (with 80–90 percent accuracy).

Prerequisite: *Understanding of concepts "same" and "different—Chapter 3 (Same and Different), Goal 1, p. 30.*

Materials

1. List A: SINGLE-SYLLABLE WORDS THAT DIFFER BY <u>2 OR MORE </u>CONSONANTS OR VOWELS, Table 101, below.
2. List B: SINGLE-SYLLABLE WORDS THAT DIFFER BY <u>ONE</u> CONSONANT OR VOWEL, Table 102, below.
3. Blank copies of TEACHING AND TRACKING WORD DISCRIMINATION, Table 103, below.

Introduction

Tell the student that she is going to listen to pairs of words and tell you if they are the same or different.

Present word-pairs that you create from List A. Repeat a word twice (same) or select two different words (different); e.g., soup/soup (same), push/ball (different). Say the words slowly and clearly. Discuss whether they are the same or different.

Have the student imitate the word-pair after she has identified them as same or different only if she is able to imitate accurately. Students who are unable to imitate due to articulation difficulties should be encouraged to listen only.

Following Step 1 below, model examples of Step 2; and following Step 2, model examples of Step 3.

Activity **Receptive** and **Expressive**

Present Steps 1–3 below.

Use a blank copy of TEACHING AND TRACKING WORD DISCRIMINATION. Record the words that you present in the column "word-pair" and how the pair of words are the same or different in the next columns—by vowel or first or last consonant; e.g., ball/bell differ by vowel; mouse/house differ by first consonant; night/nice differ by last consonant. Record whether the student's response was correct or incorrect.

Compare the lists from each teaching session to give an overall view of the student's ability to discriminate vowels and consonants in specific positions.

Step 1—Discriminate between Words Differing by 2 or More Consonants or Vowels: Use List A: SINGLE-SYLLABLE WORDS THAT DIFFER BY *2 OR MORE* CONSONANTS OR VOWELS.

Present word pairs as described in the Introduction. Repeat a word twice (same) or select two different words from the list (different); e.g., dog/dog = same; cat/mop = different. Have the student identify them as the same or different. Present same and different pairs in random order.

Step 2—Identify a Word Differing by 1 Consonant or Vowel within a List of 3:
Use List B: SINGLE-SYLLABLE WORDS THAT DIFFER BY *ONE* CONSONANT
OR VOWEL.

Present any pair of words from the list and repeat one of the words in the pair
to make a series of 3 words (2 the same and 1 different). Place the word that is different at random in the series Have the student identify the word that is different;
e.g., cat, cat, <u>mat</u>; teeth, <u>tease</u>, teeth; <u>late</u>, light, light.

Use a blank copy of the list TEACHING AND TRACKING WORD DISCRIMINA-
TION for this Step, but ignore the "same/different" column.

**Step 3—Discriminate between Words Differing by 1 Consonant or Vowel
within a Pair:** Use List B: SINGLE-SYLLABLE WORDS THAT DIFFER BY *ONE* CON-
SONANT OR VOWEL.

Present word-pairs that are the same by reading any word from the list twice
and word-pairs that are different by reading the pairs as they are written; e.g.,
jump/jump (same); dog/dig (differ by vowel); chin/chip (differ by last consonant).
Present same and different pairs at random.

Discuss with the student how one word is different from the other in the pair; e.g.,
chin/chip—chin has an "n" sound on the end and chip has a "p" sound on the end.

Carryover

- Draw attention to like-sounding words throughout the day, particularly when reading
  a storybook or during language arts; e.g., "bark" sounds almost like "park."
- Play Make a New Word. Create new words: a) substitute one vowel or consonant for
  another; e.g., dog > dig > dug; call > fall > stall > tall; sip > sit > sing. b) take a
  frequently occurring word ending and go through the sound alphabet to see which letters can be added to make it into a new word. Discuss whether or not you have made a
  real word. Examples: "at" + "b" = bat; "at" + "c" = cat, "at" + "d" = "dat"—is that a
  real word? (no); "ight" + "b" = "bight" (acceptable even though it is spelled differently
  than "bite"); "ight" + "c" = "kite" (again acceptable since you are working on sounds
  not spelling); "ight" + "d" = "dight" (not a real word).
- Use commercial auditory discrimination programs, including computer listening
  programs.

Table 101: LIST A—SINGLE-SYLLABLE WORDS THAT DIFFER BY 2 OR MORE CONSONANTS OR VOWELS

cat	fun	mud
dog	back	teeth
pot	meet	case
soup	hole	game
push	night	snow
safe	bet	shine
lock	shirt	sick
cart	lip	pack
nose	bell	less
moose	beach	bug
fat	boat	side
cup	scarf	tub
head	spin	kid
roll	van	job
soap	fish	judge
jump	house	went
smoke	gas	farm
top	laugh	chair
bake	purse	school
book	path	date

Table 102: LIST B—SINGLE-SYLLABLE WORDS THAT DIFFER BY *ONE* CONSONANT OR VOWEL

Differ by vowel		Differ by first consonant		Differ by last consonant	
Dog	Dig	Cat	Mat	Pot	Pop
Soup	Sap	Lock	Dock	Back	Bag
Fat	Fit	Boat	Coat	Night	Nice
Cup	Cap	Nose	Rose	Sip	Sit
Bed	Bead	Call	Fall	Pan	Pat
Gate	Got	Rope	Hope	Teeth	Tease
Top	Tip	Jump	Bump	Bat	Bath
Meet	Mitt	Bake	Lake	Fork	Fort
Pool	Pull	Shirt	Hurt	Hose	Home
Bet	Bait	Spin	Tin	Cake	Cage
Ball	Bell	Mouse	House	Moon	Moose
Teach	Touch	Boot	Root	Race	Rain
Sick	Sack	Game	Same	Chin	Chip
Light	Late	Tea	Me	Shop	Shock
Bug	Big	Four	Chore	Soap	Soak

Table 103: TEACHING AND TRACKING WORD DISCRIMINATION

Word-pair/series	Same/ Different	Differ by Vowel	Differ by First Consonant	Differ by Last Consonant	Correct/ Incorrect
1.					
2.					
3.					
4.					
5.					
6.					
7.					
8.					
9.					
10.					
11.					
12.					
13.					
14.					
15.					
16.					
17.					
18.					
19.					
20.					

15.
Listening Skills:
Auditory Memory

These goals are appropriate for students with one or more of the following characteristics:

- has difficulty remembering spoken and/or written information (directions, details from stories, new vocabulary, songs, names, etc.)

- processes information better when it is broken into short units

- has difficulty listening for longer periods of time

- watches and copies peers rather than carrying out directions independently

- stumbles when pronouncing multisyllabic words

- is echolalic (spontaneously repeats incidental word series and conversations) but has difficulty with applied listening and remembering

Auditory Memory Goals

The student will remember:

Goal 1: series of sounds made by noisemakers; e.g., squeakers, rattles.

Goal 2: series of nouns with picture support; e.g., apple, bus, pen.

Goal 3: series of nouns without picture support; e.g., house, banana, tree.

Goal 4: number series with and without visual support; e.g., 3, 1, 6.

Goal 5: spoken sentences of 3 words or more; e.g., I like pizza.

Goal 1: The student will remember series of sounds made by noisemakers; e.g., squeakers, rattles (with 80–90 percent accuracy).

Materials

- 4–6 identical pairs of rattles and squeakers (baby rattles or dog toys) that make a distinctly different sound, one pair from another; e.g., rattle, tinkle, squeak (as used in Chapter 14 Auditory Discrimination Goal 1, materials #1, p. 282).

Introduction

Tell the student that he is going listen to and copy series of sounds.

Select any two of the rattles/squeakers and make 2 sounds, pause, and then repeat them. Example: Rattle, squeak (pause), rattle, squeak. Explain that you are copying what you first heard. Give several examples.

Activity **Receptive** and **Expressive**

Use 2 pairs of rattles and squeakers. Give one of each pair to the student and keep the other one of the pair for yourself (provide a choice of more than two noisemakers as the student's ability improves).

Make 2 sounds either by sounding the same noisemaker twice or by sounding 2 different noise makers once each. Have the student repeat the sounds in the same order; e.g., squeak followed by ringing a bell.

Gradually increase the number of sounds in the series by adding other noisemakers or by sounding the same noisemaker more than once; e.g., bell, bell, squeak.

Be careful to avoid frustration. Always end each listening session with a series that is easy for the student; e.g., if working on a series of 4 sounds, end with a series of 2 sounds.

Have the student be the instructor and make series of sounds for you to imitate. If he has difficulty remembering the series that he made, tape record his series as he makes it and imitate the series yourself. Then play back his original and have him compare the sounds you made with the tape recording.

Carryover

- Encourage imitation during music making with a variety of toys and instruments.
- Tap out a rhythm with your hand or foot or use a drum and have the student imitate it; e.g., 1 tap followed by a brief pause, then 2 quick taps.
- Play Clap Like Me—clap a simple rhythm and have the student imitate.

Goal 2: The student will remember series of nouns *with* picture support; e.g., apple, bus, pen (with 80–90 percent accuracy).

Prerequisite: *Ability to follow single-step directions using Listen, Repeat, Do strategy—Chapter 1 (Following Directions), Goal 1, p. 14.*

Materials

- 20 pictures of single toys, objects, and/or animals familiar to the student.

Introduction

Tell the student that he is going to listen to and remember series of words with the help of pictures.

Place 2 single-item pictures side by side, face up on the table. Point to them one at a time from left to right and name them. Turn the pictures face down and tell him that you are going to name them again even though you cannot see the pictures. Point to them and name them again. Then turn them face up and show that you named them correctly.

Use different pictures each time that you present a series. Present a series (e.g., of 3 pictures) 10 times with 80–90 percent accuracy before requesting a higher number of pictures (e.g., series of 4 pictures) or presenting a greater number of choices (e.g., increase from a choice of 4 pictures to 5 or 6 pictures) (Steps 2 and 3).

Model Steps 2 and 3 before presenting them as activities for the student.

Be careful to avoid frustration. Always end each listening session with a series that is easy for the student. For example, if working on a series of 4 pictures, end with a series of 2.

Activity **Receptive** and **Expressive**

Step 1—Name Pictures That Are Face Down: Place 2 pictures *face up* on the table and have the student point to each one and name them (from left to right). Turn the pictures *face down* and have the student name them again. Turn up the pictures to show that he was correct.

If the student *has difficulty remembering both pictures* then have him name them when they are face up on the table and *turn only one face down*. Have him name the one that is now face *down*. Be sure to keep the cards in the same order on the table so that the student can use position as a cue.

Increase to a series of 3 then 4 pictures depending on the student's ability.

Step 2—Name Pictures That Are Face Up (Limited Choice): Instruct the student that he is to use the *Listen, Repeat, Do* strategy. He is going to *Listen* to the series of words, *Repeat* the series, then *Do* (give you the pictures that you name).

Place 2 single-item pictures *face up* on the table and name them in the order that you want him to give them to you. Have him *Listen;* e.g., dog—bus; have him *Repeat;* e.g., dog—bus; have him *Do;* e.g., give you dog and bus pictures in that order.

Note: *The pictures remain face up in this activity.*

After he has given you the pictures that you requested, hold them so that they are still in the order in which you said them but turned away from him so that he cannot see them. Ask him to tell you the names of the pictures again. Example: "What did you give me?" Student: "Dog—bus."

Sample dialog

> **Instructor:** "Give me cup, frog" (student - *Listen*).
> **Student:** "Cup, frog" (*Repeat*).
> **Student:** Gives cup and frog pictures to instructor (*Do*).
> *Instructor holds the pictures in the same order as requested but so the student cannot see them*
> **Instructor:** "What did you give me?"
> **Student:** "Cup, frog."

If the student has difficulty recalling a name, prompt by turning the relevant picture toward him briefly so he has a quick glimpse of it and have him name both pictures in the correct order.

Progress to presenting and requesting 3 (then 4) pictures when he is able to recall 2 pictures with 80–90 percent accuracy without any prompts.

Encourage him to look at the choice of pictures on the table while you request a specific one. This will provide visual support for his auditory memory.

Step 3—Name Pictures That Are Face Up (Choice of More Than Requested): As for Step 2, request 2 pictures in the order that you say them, but have the student select them *from a choice of 3 or more*. The added visual distraction makes it more difficult for the student to remember the target pictures, making this a more challenging task.

Present and request an increased number of pictures (to a maximum of 4) when he is able to recall 2 with 80–90 percent accuracy without any prompts at the same time as you increase the number of picture choices (from 3 to a maximum of 8). Work up in increments—recall 2 pictures from a choice of 3, then 4, then 5, etc. Next, recall 3 pictures from a choice of 4, then 5, then 6, etc.

Keep verbal instructions and prompts to a minimum and end each session with success. For instance, if the student is having difficulty recalling 3 out of 6 pictures, then at the end of the session make a request at an easier level; e.g., 2 out of 4.

Intermediate Step: *Some students find it difficult to progress from remembering 2 pictures to remembering 3, or from 3 pictures to remembering 4. For these students, add this intermediate step:*

Start the session at the student's ability level. For instance, have him give you 2 pictures out of 6; e.g., "car, sun" (from "horse, car, chair, sun, apple, cat"). After the student has repeated, given, and recalled these successfully, *use the same pictures* and the *same words again* but add a third word from the choice of pictures; e.g., "car, sun, chair." The student may work at this level (2 then 2+1) until he is ready to progress to the full step of 3 pictures that are all new.

To make the step from 3 to 4 pictures, work on 3+1; e.g., "apple, cookie, tree," then "apple, cookie, tree, mouse."

Carryover

- Play Echo—take turns repeating everything that the other person says.
- Encourage the student to imitate word series such as nursery rhymes, songs, poems, and lines from stories, particularly those that have a chorus or line that is repeated throughout; e.g., *The Three Little Pigs*—"I'll huff and I'll puff and I'll blow your house down."
- Give the student a password that he has to use throughout the day every time he does a specific activity. For example, each time he enters the classroom, ask him for the password. Change the password and the specific activity daily.

Goal 3: The student will remember series of nouns *without* picture support; e.g., house, banana, tree (with 80–90 percent accuracy).

Note: *Some students find it easier to recall short, meaningful sentences than series of unrelated words. If so, omit this goal and work on Goal 5 (spoken sentences of 3 words or more), p. 300.*

Materials

1. List A: SINGLE-SYLLABLE WORDS THAT DIFFER BY *2 OR MORE* CONSONANTS OR VOWELS, p. 289 (Chapter 14, Table 101).
2. Blank copies of NOUN SERIES FOR VERBATIM REPETITION, Table 104, below.
3. Familiar nouns selected at random from any age appropriate story book.

Introduction

Introduce this goal by telling the student that he is going to listen to and remember series of words just like in Goal 2 but this time he will not have any pictures to help him. Tell him that you are going to say 2 words, then he is going to say them back to you in the same order that you said them. Model some examples: "House, ball" (pause), "house, ball"; "car, table" (pause), "car, table."

Activity **Receptive** and **Expressive**

Step 1—Verbatim Repetition: Read any 2 words from List A: SINGLE-SYLLABLE WORDS THAT DIFFER BY *2 OR MORE* CONSONANTS OR VOWELS and have the student repeat them to you *in the same order* that you read them. Example: "Boat, pan." Response: "Boat, pan." If he forgets a word or reverses the order, read the series again or have him say the words with you as many times as needed until he is able to say them correctly on his own.

Encourage the student to shut his eyes during this activity if it helps him to concentrate.

Record the word series that you present and the student's response on a blank copy of NOUN SERIES FOR VERBATIM REPETITION.

Gradually increase from 2 to 4 words using the intermediate step described in Goal 2, p. 296, if necessary (present 2 words, then the same 2 plus a new word— 2+1). Be careful to avoid frustration.

Increase the level of difficulty by using 2-syllable words selected from any age-appropriate story book.

Step 2—Which Word Was Added? Read any 2 words from List A: SINGLE-SYLLABLE WORDS THAT DIFFER BY *2 OR MORE* CONSONANTS OR VOWELS, pause, then read them again and add another word anywhere in the series. Ask the student which word you added. Example: "Dog, cat" (pause), "dog, cat, horse" ("horse" was added); "nail, door" (pause), "nail, mouse, door" ("mouse" was added).

Gradually increase from a series of 2 words to 3 and then 4.

Carryover

- Play the game "I Went to the Store and Bought…." Player #1 says the introductory sentence and names one item that he bought at the store. Player #2 repeats the sentence and the item and adds another item and so on until a player forgets an item. Items must be listed in the correct order. Example: Player #1—I went to the store and bought an apple. Player #2—I went to the store and bought an apple and a hat. Make the game less competitive by taking turns saying each word in a series or deliberately forgetting a word and having the student help you. Vary the game by using a different introductory sentence, such as: I went to the moon and took… ; Grandma put in her suitcase… ; I made a pizza and on it I put….

Goal 4: The student will recall number series with and without visual support; e.g., 3, 1, 6 (with 80–90 percent accuracy).

Note: *Omit this goal if the student does not know numbers.*

Materials

1. Numerals 1–9 each written separately on a small flashcard.
2. Toy telephones/cell phones (optional).
3. Blank copies of NUMBER SERIES FOR VERBATIM REPETITION, Table 105, below.

Introduction

Tell the student that you are going to play the Telephone (Cell Phone) game. You are going to tell him a phone number, and he is going to repeat it back to you. Model examples: Say a series of 2, 3, or 4 numbers, pause, and then repeat the series; e.g., "8, 4" (pause), "8, 4"; "5, 1, 6" (pause), "5, 1, 6."

Activity **Receptive** and **Expressive**

Play the Telephone game. Say 2 numbers to the student and have him repeat them in the same order that you said them. Encourage him to shut his eyes during this activity if he finds it helpful.

Table 104: NOUN SERIES FOR VERBATIM REPETITION

Noun series	Student response	Correct/ incorrect
1.		
2.		
3.		
4.		
5.		
6.		
7.		
8.		
9.		
10.		
11.		
12.		
13.		
14.		
15.		
16.		
17.		
18.		
19.		
20.		

If the student needs visual support, present written numerals as you say the series, then turn them over and have the student recall them without being able to see them. Fade the support as he becomes more competent.

Gradually increase from 2 numbers to 3 and more using the intermediate step described in Goal 2, p. 296, if necessary (present 2 numbers, then the same 2 plus a new number—2+1). Be careful to avoid frustration.

Record the number series that you present and the student's responses on a blank copy of NUMBER SERIES FOR VERBATIM REPETITION.

Increase the level of difficulty by using numbers above 10, providing the student is familiar with them.

Carryover

● Give the student a magic number that he has to say every time he does a specified task during the day; e.g., he opens his desk. Change the number each day and increase to a series of numbers; e.g., 2, 5, 1.
● Have the student use a combination lock for his locker, a cupboard, or locked box. Change the combination periodically so he must recall new numbers.

Goal 5: The student will remember spoken sentences of 3 words or more; e.g., I like pizza (with 80–90 percent accuracy).

Materials

1. 20 pictures of single toys, objects, and/or animals familiar to the student (but different from those used for Goal 2).
2. 20 pictures of single or groups of people or animals carrying out an action that is familiar to the student; e.g., a man eating; two dogs running.
3. Blank copies of SENTENCES FOR VERBATIM REPETITION, Table 106, below.

Introduction

Tell the student that he is going to learn to remember sentences of 3 words or more.

Select one of the single-item or action pictures. Model a 3-word sentence associated with the picture, pause, and then repeat it; e.g., "I like dogs" (pause), "I like dogs"; "John is jumping" (pause), "John is jumping." Give several examples.

Encourage the student to visualize what the sentence is telling him "like a TV camera."

Activity **Receptive** and **Expressive**

Step 1—repeat unrelated 3-word sentences: Create a 3-word sentence related to a single-item picture or action picture and have the student repeat it. The sentences will be related to the pictures but not related to each other.

Record the sentences that you present and the student's responses on a blank copy of SENTENCES FOR VERBATIM REPETITION.

Table 105: NUMBER SERIES FOR VERBATIM REPETITION

Number series	Student response	Correct/incorrect
1.		
2.		
3.		
4.		
5.		
6.		
7.		
8.		
9.		
10.		
11.		
12.		
13.		
14.		
15.		
16.		
17.		
18.		
19.		
20.		

Step 2—repeat unrelated 4–8 word sentences: When the student is able to repeat 3-word sentences with 80–90 percent accuracy, present the same pictures again and gradually increase to unrelated sentences of 4–8 words. Be careful not to present sentences that are too long and cause frustration.

Step 3—increase the length of a given sentence: Create a 3-word sentence that relates to a picture, and have the student repeat it. Example: "I like dogs." Then add another word to the same sentence; e.g., "I like *brown* dogs," and have him repeat. Continue to add words one at a time, making the sentence longer, and have him repeat after each addition. Example: "I like brown dogs *that*"; "I like brown dogs that *run*"; "I like brown dogs that run *fast.*" This can be played as a turn-taking game in a group situation.

Step 4—repeat related sentences of increasing length: Present sentences of increasing length around a picture or story theme. Use a variety of words for each sentence. Example: for the theme "cats"—"I like cats; cats make good pets; my cat's name is Patches; Patches eats kibble and drinks milk." Have the student repeat each sentence after you.

Carryover

- Play Simon Says as a group activity using Motor Activities without Props (Chapter 1, Following Directions, Goal 1, p. 14.
- Tell the student a joke within his level of understanding. Have him remember it and tell it to someone else.
- Play a variation of "I Went to the Store and Bought…" using a different opening sentence; e.g., "I looked under the bed and found…"; "For breakfast I ate…"; 'In my backpack I put…" (as for Goal 3, p. 297).
- Work on commercial auditory memory programs including computer programs.

Table 106: SENTENCES FOR VERBATIM REPETITION

Sentence	Student response	Correct/ incorrect
1.		
2.		
3.		
4.		
5.		
6.		
7.		
8.		
9.		
10.		
11.		
12.		
13.		
14.		
15.		
16.		
17.		
18.		
19.		
20.		

16.
Listening Skills:
Auditory Processing

These goals are appropriate for students with one or more of the following characteristics:

- has difficulty understanding information presented orally or in writing

- does not know where within a sentence to locate information required to answer a question. Example: The dog is brown. What is brown? The dog (information at the beginning)

- has difficulty staying focused on listening tasks

- needs directions explained or demonstrated

- fails to analyze verbal or written information for truth or accuracy

- has difficulty understanding humor

- avoids conversation and/or makes comments that do not fit the discussion

Auditory Processing Goals

The student will process isolated sentences and answer either a what? who? where? which? or when? question related to information that occurs in a specific position within the sentence:

Question word(s)	Position of information
Goal 1: What?	End of sentence.
Goal 2: What? Who?	Beginning of sentence.
Goal 3: What? Who?	Beginning and end of sentence.
Goal 4: What? Who?	Middle of sentence.
Goal 5: Where?	End of sentence.
Goal 6: Which?	Beginning and end of sentence.
Goal 7: When?	Beginning and end of sentence.

Basic Teaching Plan Common to All Auditory Processing Goals

Prerequisite: *Understanding of "wh" question words—Chapter 10 ("Wh" Questions), Goals What? Who? Where? Which? When?, pp. 179-197. Ability to repeat a sentence (maximum 8 words) —Chapter 15 (Auditory Memory), Goal 5, p. 300.*

Materials

1. Lists of AUDITORY PROCESSING SENTENCES at the end of each goal (2 lists per goal).
2. AUDITORY PROCESSING TRACKING CHART, Table 107, below.
3. Blank copies of AUDITORY PROCESSING SENTENCES, Table 108, p. 312.

Introduction

Introduce each goal by telling the student that she is going to learn how to listen to and answer questions. The answer to the question will be hidden in the sentence and she is going to learn how to find the answer. Give several examples appropriate to the specific goal that you are introducing. Example: The sky is blue—What color is the sky? The answer is at the end of the sentence—"blue."

Instruct the student that when you read a sentence to her she is to *Listen* to the sentence, *Repeat* it back to you exactly as you say it, and then *Answer* the question. This strategy was also used in Chapter 1 (Following Directions), Goal 1, p. 14.

Use the AUDITORY PROCESSING TRACKING CHART as a guide to the progression of how many words occur in the sentence, how many are required for the answer, and the question words involved. Most students find it easiest to recall the most recent information heard, so sentences/questions pertaining to information *at the end* are presented in the first goal.

Activity **Receptive** and **Expressive**

Listen/Repeat/Answer: Read the target sentences one at a time, starting with the example, and have the student *Listen* to the sentence, then *Repeat* it verbatim.

If the student **repeats the sentence correctly,** then ask the accompanying question and have the student *Answer* it (the student does not need to repeat the question).

If the student **is unable to repeat** the sentence, reread it as many times as is necessary for the student to retain it and repeat it correctly. Frequent difficulty repeating even 3–5 word sentences would suggest that the student needs to work on Auditory Memory (Chapter 15) prior to working on Auditory Processing.

If the student **repeats correctly but is unable to answer** the question related to the information:

a. *at the end of the sentence*—use sentence completion to elicit the correct response. Example: John likes chocolate cookies—question: what does John like? John likes chocolate _____ (cookies). John likes _____ (chocolate cookies).

b. *at the beginning or in the middle of the sentence*—repeat the sentence and put emphasis on the answer within the sentence. Example: *Paul* is walking—

question: who is walking? Have the student imitate the sentence and place emphasis as you did. Present the question again and this time, emphasize the question word; e.g., *who* is walking?

Record response: Use AUDITORY PROCESSING TRACKING CHART to record the student's progress through the goals.

Create more sentences: Use an early grade reading book as a guide to create more practice sentences. Record your sentences on a blank copy of AUDITORY PROCESSING SENTENCES.

Create sentences that target specific parts of speech that the student is having difficulty with, such as pronouns; e.g., "the boy rode his bike"—which bike did the boy ride? Or recalling series of descriptors; e.g., the kite has a long, shiny tail. What does the kite have?

Carryover

- Have the student repeat individual sentences while she is listening to an age appropriate storybook. Ask her a question about information that occurs in the same position in the sentence as it does in the sentences that she is working on in structured activities. Example (end position): John and Mary ran down the road. Where did John and Mary run?
- "Spot the Mistake"—while reading a story to the student, make a deliberate error and have her question the mistake and correct the error based on information from the story or general knowledge. Example: You misread, "Felix was a brown dog." Student: "Felix was a *cat*"; You: "Felix barked really loudly." Student: "Felix cannot bark because he is a cat." Similarly, make deliberate errors in familiar rhymes; e.g., Eensy Weensy spider climbed up a pole (water spout). Down came the snow (rain) and washed the froggy (spider) out.
- Play Simon Says.
- Use commercial auditory processing programs including computer programs.

See also: *Chapter 13 (Advanced Expressive Language), Goal 4—identify what is wrong (absurd) in a situation, picture, or spoken sentence, p. 269.*

Table 107: AUDITORY PROCESSING TRACKING CHART

Goal	Question word(s)	Position of answer	Sentence length	Answer length	Date completed and comments
Goal 1:1	What?	End	4	1–2	
Goal 1:2	What?	End	5–7	2–3	
Goal 2:1	What? Who?	Beginning	3–5	1–2	
Goal 2:2	What? Who?	Beginning	5–6	2–3	
Goal 3:1	What? Who?	Beginning and end	3–5	1–2	
Goal 3:2	What? Who?	Beginning and end	5–7	2–3	
Goal 4:1	What? Who?	Middle	4–6	1–2	
Goal 4:2	What? Who?	Middle	6–8	1–3	
Goal 5:1	Where?	End	5–7	3	
Goal 5:2	Where?	End	7–8	3–5	
Goal 6:1	Which?	Beginning and end	5–8	3	
Goal 6:2	Which?	Beginning and end	5–8	3	
Goal 7:1	When?	Beginning and end	5–7	1–4	
Goal 7:2	When?	Beginning and end	6–10	2–5	

Auditory Processing Goals and Carryover

Auditory Processing Goal 1:1 and 1:2:

The student will process isolated sentences and answer a question related to information that occurs at the end of the sentence (sentences of 4–7 words; 1–3 words required in the answer to a "what?" question) with 80–90 percent accuracy.

See: *Basic Teaching Plan Common to all Auditory Processing Goals, above.*
See: *Goal 1:1 and 1:2 AUDITORY PROCESSING SENTENCES, Tables 108 and 109, p. 312 and p. 313.*

Carryover

- Ask "what?" questions about information that occurs at the *end* of a sentence while reading storybooks. Example: The girl carried her backpack. What did the girl carry? (her backpack).

Auditory Processing Goal 2:1 and 2:2:

The student will process isolated sentences and answer a question related to information that occurs at the *beginning* of the sentence (sentences of 4–6 words; 1–3 words required in the answer to a "what?" or "who?" question) with 80–90 percent accuracy.

See: *Basic Teaching Plan Common to all Auditory Processing Goals, above.*
See: *Goal 2:1 and 2:2 AUDITORY PROCESSING SENTENCES, Tables 110 and 111, p. 314 and p. 315.*

Carryover

- Ask "what?" and "who?" questions about information that occurs at the *beginning* of a sentence while reading storybooks. Example: Ann carried a backpack. Who carried a backpack? (Ann).

Auditory Processing Goal 3:1 and 3:2:

The student will process isolated sentences and answer a question related to information that occurs at the *beginning* or *end* of the sentence (sentences of 3–5 words; 1–2 words required in the answer to a "what?" or "who?" question) with 80–90 percent accuracy

See: *Basic Teaching Plan Common to all Auditory Processing Goals, above.*
See: *Goal 3:1 and 3:2 AUDITORY PROCESSING SENTENCES, Tables 112 and 113, p. 316 and p. 317.*

Carryover

● Ask "what?" and "who?" questions about information that occurs at the *beginning* or *end* of a sentence while reading storybooks. Example: Ann carried a backpack. Who carried a backpack? (Ann). What did Ann carry? (a backpack).

Auditory Processing Goal 4:1 and 4:2:

The student will process isolated sentences and answer a question related to information that occurs in the *middle* of the sentence (sentences of 4–8 words; 1–3 words required in the answer to a "what? or "who?" question) with 80–90 percent accuracy.

See: *Basic Teaching Plan Common to all Auditory Processing Goals, above.*
See: *Goal 4:1 and 4:2 AUDITORY PROCESSING SENTENCES, Tables 114 and 115, p. 318 and p. 319.*

Carryover

● Ask "what?" and "who?" questions about information that occurs in the *middle* of a sentence while reading storybooks. Example: Ann gave her backpack to Carl. What did Ann give to Carl? (her backpack).

Auditory Processing Goal 5:1 and 5:2:

The student will process isolated sentences and answer a question related to information that occurs at the *end* of the sentence (sentences of 4–8 words; 3–4 words required in the answer to a "where?" question) with 80–90 percent accuracy.

See: *Basic Teaching Plan Common to all Auditory Processing Goals, above.*
See: *Goal 5:1 and 5:2 AUDITORY PROCESSING SENTENCES, Tables 116 and 117, p. 320 and p. 321.*

Carryover

- Ask "where?" questions about information that occurs at the *end* of a sentence while reading storybooks. Example: Ann left her backpack on the floor. Where did Ann leave her backpack? (on the floor).

Auditory Processing Goal 6:1 and 6:2:

The student will process isolated sentences and answer a question related to information that occurs at the *beginning* or *end* of the sentence (sentences of 5–7 words; 3 words required in the answer to a "which?" question) with 80–90 percent accuracy.

See: *Basic Teaching Plan Common to all Auditory Processing Goals, above.*
See: *Goal 6:1 and 6:2 AUDITORY PROCESSING SENTENCES, Tables 118 and 119, p. 322 and p. 323.*

Carryover

- Ask "which?" questions about information that occurs at the *beginning* or *end* of a sentence while reading storybooks. Example: Ann carried her heavy backpack. Which backpack did Ann carry? (her heavy backpack).

Auditory Processing Goal 7:1 and 7:2:

The student will process isolated sentences and answer a question related to information that occurs at the *beginning* or *end* of the sentence (sentences of 5–7 words; 1–4 words required in the answer to a "when?" question) with 80–90 percent accuracy.

See: *Basic Teaching Plan Common to all Auditory Processing Goals, above.*
See: *Goal 7:1 and 7:2 AUDITORY PROCESSING SENTENCES, Tables 120 and 121, p. 324 and p. 325.*

Carryover

- Ask "when?" questions about information that occurs at the *beginning* or *end* of a sentence while reading storybooks. Example: Ann carried her backpack to school every morning. When did Ann carry her backpack to school? (every morning).

Table 108: Goal 1:1 AUDITORY PROCESSING SENTENCES

Question word(s)	Position of answer	Sentence length	Answer length
What?	END	4 words	1–2 words

Example: I have cold hands. What do I have? Cold hands.

Sentence	Correct repeat	Question—What?	Place	Correct/ incorrect
1. I saw an elephant.		What did I see?	End	
2. John has three dogs.		What does John have?	End	
3. Sue climbed a tree.		What did Sue climb?	End	
4. Jane rode a horse.		What did Jane ride?	End	
5. Paul ate chocolate cookies.		What did Paul eat?	End	
6. I got a present.		What did I get?	End	
7. Kyle drives his truck.		What does Kyle drive?	End	
8. Mom dropped the cup.		What did Mom drop?	End	
9. Kaitlyn drank hot soup.		What did Kaitlyn drink?	End	
10. Lydia has her blanket.		What does Lydia have?	End	
Total: Correct repeat:		**Correct answer:**		

Table 109: Goal 1:2 AUDITORY PROCESSING SENTENCES

Question word(s)	Position of answer	Sentence length	Answer length
What?	END	5–7 words	2–3 words

Example: Tom likes playing with his black dog. What does Tom like playing with? His black dog.

Sentence	Correct repeat	Question—What?	Place	Correct/ incorrect
1. The teacher asked for <u>my homework</u>.		What did the teacher ask for?	End	
2. Four children decided to <u>play tag</u>.		What did four children decide to do?	End	
3. After school Kate read <u>a funny story</u>.		What did Kate read after school?	End	
4. My favorite drinks are <u>milk and juice</u>.		What are my favorite drinks?	End	
5. Birds are sitting in <u>the trees</u>.		What are the birds sitting in?	End	
6. On the rocks there are <u>green turtles</u>.		What are on the rocks?	End	
7. Tom and Ben rode <u>their new bikes</u>.		What did Tom and Ben ride?	End	
8. At the zoo I saw <u>an elephant</u>.		What did I see at the zoo?	End	
9. Today I wore <u>the yellow raincoat</u>.		What did I wear today?	End	
10. Sharp scissors cut <u>straight lines</u>.		What do sharp scissors cut?	End	
Total: Correct repeat:		**Correct answer:**		

Table 110: Goal 2:1 AUDITORY PROCESSING SENTENCES

Question word(s)	Position of answer	Sentence length	Answer length
What? Who?	BEGINNING	3–5 words	1–2 words

Example: Susie likes pizza. Who likes pizza? Susie.

Sentence	Correct repeat	Question—What Who?	Place	Correct/ incorrect
1. <u>Doors</u> have handles.		What have handles?	Begin	
2. <u>Toothbrushes</u> clean teeth.		What clean teeth?	Begin	
3. <u>My pillow</u> is soft.		What is soft?	Begin	
4. <u>The ocean</u> tastes salty.		What tastes salty?	Begin	
5. <u>Dad</u> drove to the store.		Who drove to the store?	Begin	
6. <u>Fire</u> burns wood and paper.		What burns wood and paper?	Begin	
7. <u>A clock</u> tells time.		What tells time?	Begin	
8. <u>Horses</u> gallop around the field.		What gallops around the field?	Begin	
9. <u>Sally</u> is very friendly.		Who is very friendly?	Begin	
10. <u>Robbie</u> has dirty boots.		Who has dirty boots?	Begin	
Total: Correct repeat:		**Correct answer:**		

Table 111: Goal 2:2 AUDITORY PROCESSING SENTENCES

Question word(s)	Position of answer	Sentence length	Answer length
What? Who?	BEGINNING	5–6 words	2–3 words

Example: The hot drink tasted good. What tasted good? The hot drink.

Sentence	Correct repeat	Question—What Who?	Place	Correct/incorrect
1. Blue birds fly in the sky		What flies in the sky?	Begin	
2. Three dogs ran down the road.		What ran down the road?	Begin	
3. The tall tree fell down.		What fell down?	Begin	
4. A black horse ate grass.		What ate grass?	Begin	
5. Chocolate chip cookies are yummy.		What are yummy?	Begin	
6. My babysitter gave me a present.		Who gave me a present?	Begin	
7. The blue car went fast.		What went fast?	Begin	
8. A big plate broke in pieces.		What broke in pieces?	Begin	
9. Hot soup can hurt your mouth.		What can hurt your mouth?	Begin	
10. The soft blanket keeps me warm.		What keeps me warm?	Begin	
Total: Correct repeat:		**Correct answer:**		

Table 112: Goal 3:1 AUDITORY PROCESSING SENTENCES

Question word(s)	Position of answer	Sentence length	Answer length
What? Who?	BEGINNING or END	3–5 words	1–2 words

Example (beginning): Charlie eats hot dogs and mustard. Who eats hot dogs and mustard? Charlie.

Example (end): Cindy is wearing blue jeans. What is Cindy wearing? Blue jeans.

Sentence	Correct repeat	Question—What Who?	Place	Correct/ incorrect
1. <u>Ann</u> sleeps in bed.		Who sleeps in bed?	Begin	
2. I like <u>white cats</u>.		What do I like?	End	
3. George pulls <u>a wagon</u>.		What does George pull?	End	
4. <u>The teacher</u> shut the door.		Who shut the door?	Begin	
5. <u>Ryan</u> put on his shoes.		Who put on his shoes?	Begin	
6. Sally picked up <u>the book</u>.		What did Sally pick up?	End	
7. <u>Mom</u> went to her bedroom.		Who went to her bedroom?	Begin	
8. David ate <u>an apple</u>.		What did David eat?	End	
9. Melanie watched <u>TV</u>.		What did Melanie watch?	End	
10. <u>Chris</u> blew out the candles.		Who blew out the candles?	Begin	
Total: Correct repeat:			**Correct answer:**	

Table 113: Goal 3:2 AUDITORY PROCESSING SENTENCES

Question word(s)	Position of answer	Sentence length	Answer length
What? Who?	BEGINNING or END	5–7 words	2–3 words

Example (beginning): Ann and Jane like to walk together. Who like to walk together? Ann and Jane.

Example (end): Up on the roof is a brown bird. What is up on the roof? A brown bird.

Sentence	Correct repeat	Question—What Who?	Place	Correct/ incorrect
1. Dan and Peter like scrambled eggs.		Who likes scrambled eggs?	Begin	
2. Yesterday I saw a black dog.		What did I see yesterday?	End	
3. Karl climbed a tall tree.		What did Karl climb?	End	
4. Jane's family went on a long trip.		Who went on a long trip?	Begin	
5. Two boys ate chocolate ice cream.		Who ate chocolate ice cream?	Begin	
6. Jay blew up six red balloons.		What did Jay blow up?	End	
7. Mom and Dad cleaned out the garage.		Who cleaned out the garage?	Begin	
8. Kyle dropped the glass star.		What did Kyle drop?	End	
9. Ben stepped in a deep hole.		What did Ben step in?	End	
10. A brown horse jumped over the fence.		What jumped over the fence?	Begin	
Total: Correct repeat:		**Correct answer:**		

Table 114: Goal 4:1 AUDITORY PROCESSING SENTENCES

Question word(s)	Position of answer	Sentence length	Answer length
What? Who?	MIDDLE	4–6 words	1–2 words

Example: John is walking in the park. What is John doing in the park? Walking.

Sentence	Correct repeat	Question—What? Who?	Place	Correct/ incorrect
1. I will give <u>Jessica</u> the ball.		Who will I give the ball to?	Middle	
2. Take <u>Ann</u> to the playground.		Who will you take to the playground?	Middle	
3. Put <u>the trucks</u> away.		What will you put away?	Middle	
4. Babies <u>cry</u> when they are hungry.		What do babies do when they are hungry?	Middle	
5. I buy <u>apples</u> at the store.		What do I buy at the store?	Middle	
6. Wear <u>warm pajamas</u> in winter.		What should you wear in winter?	Middle	
7. Cut <u>the paper</u> with scissors.		What do you cut with scissors?	Middle	
8. Put <u>the bags</u> in the truck.		What shall I put in the truck?	Middle	
9. Phone <u>the doctor</u> in the morning.		Who will I phone in the morning?	Middle	
10. Take <u>a shower</u> after supper.		What will I take after supper?	Middle	
Total: Correct repeat:			**Correct answer:**	

Table 115: Goal 4:2 AUDITORY PROCESSING SENTENCES

Question word(s)	Position of answer	Sentence length	Answer length
What? Who?	MIDDLE	6–8 words	1–3 words

Example: Eddy gave the ball to Ann. What did Eddy give to Ann? The ball.

Sentence	Correct repeat	Question—What? Who?	Place	Correct/ incorrect
1. Paul wears <u>his jacket</u> at recess.		What does Paul wear at recess?	Middle	
2. Mom said "<u>hurry up</u>" to my brother.		What did Mom say to my brother?	Middle	
3. I can <u>walk backwards</u> with my eyes closed.		What can I do with my eyes closed?	Middle	
4. Tom eats <u>a green apple</u> every day.		What does Tom eat every day?	Middle	
5. At lunch time <u>John and Jack</u> sit together.		Who sits together at lunch time?	Middle	
6. I mailed a <u>birthday card</u> to Grandma.		What did I mail to Grandma?	Middle	
7. Open <u>the door</u> before you go out.		What should you open before you go out?	Middle	
8. Blow out <u>the candles</u> on the cake.		What should you blow out on the cake?	Middle	
9. Write <u>numbers</u> on the board with chalk.		What should you write on the board with chalk?	Middle	
10. Liam carried <u>the big flag</u> into the school.		What did Liam carry into the school?	Middle	
Total: Correct repeat:			**Correct answer:**	

Table 116: Goal 5:1 AUDITORY PROCESSING SENTENCES

Question word(s)	Position of answer	Sentence length	Answer length
Where?	END	5–7 words	3 words

Example: The children played on the swings. Where did the children play? On the swings.

Sentence	Correct repeat	Question—Where?	Place	Correct/ incorrect
1. The rabbit ran <u>around the field</u>.		Where did the rabbit run?	End	
2. A cat crawled <u>between two chairs</u>.		Where did the cat crawl?	End	
3. The bug is <u>on the flower</u>.		Where is the bug?	End	
4. The pencil rolled <u>off the table</u>.		Where did the pencil roll?	End	
5. The block dropped <u>onto the floor</u>.		Where did the block drop?	End	
6. Sally climbed <u>over the fence</u>.		Where did Sally climb?	End	
7. John slept <u>under the blanket</u>.		Where did John sleep?	End	
8. The sun shone <u>above the clouds</u>.		Where did the sun shine?	End	
9. The fish swim <u>in the pond</u>.		Where did the fish swim?	End	
10. Mom left her cup <u>beside the couch</u>.		Where did Mom leave her cup?	End	
Total: Correct repeat:		**Correct answer:**		

Table 117: Goal 5:2 AUDITORY PROCESSING SENTENCES

Question word(s)	Position of answer	Sentence length	Answer length
Where?	END	7–8 words	3–5 words

Example: Liz put the flowers beside the TV. Where did Liz put the flowers? Beside the TV.

Sentence	Correct repeat	Question—Where?	Place	Correct/incorrect
1. A silver plane flew <u>up in the sky</u>.		Where did the silver plane fly?	End	
2. A black squirrel hid <u>under a log</u>.		Where did the black squirrel hide?	End	
3. A big duck sat <u>beside the lake</u>.		Where did the big duck sit?	End	
4. Three horses galloped <u>around the field</u>.		Where did the three horses gallop?	End	
5. The sugar cookies are <u>on the table</u>.		Where are the sugar cookies?	End	
6. Mom left her purse <u>in the car</u>.		Where did Mom leave her purse?	End	
7. A spotted frog jumped <u>over a leaf</u>.		Where did the spotted frog jump?	End	
8. The car was parked <u>in front of a store</u>.		Where was the car parked?	End	
9. My Dad poured coffee <u>into his coffee mug</u>.		Where did my Dad pour coffee?	End	
10. The little cat slept <u>behind the couch</u>.		Where did the little cat sleep?	End	
Total: Correct repeat:		**Correct answer:**		

Table 118: Goal 6:1 AUDITORY PROCESSING SENTENCES

Question word(s)	Position of answer	Sentence length	Answer length
Which?	BEGINNING or END	5–8 words	3 words

Example (beginning): The big rabbit ate the lettuce. Which rabbit ate the lettuce? The big rabbit.

Example (end): The elephant reached the long leaf. Which leaf did the elephant reach? The long leaf.

Sentence	Correct repeat	Question—Which?	Place	Correct/ incorrect
1. A fat bird sat on a branch.		Which bird sat on the branch?	Begin	
2. The boy climbed the short ladder.		Which ladder did the boy climb?	End	
3. Mom drank the hot tea.		Which tea did mom drink?	End	
4. The first girl got to choose a balloon.		Which girl got to choose a balloon?	Begin	
5. Jordan ate the big cookie.		Which cookie did Jordan eat?	End	
6. The wet dog rolled on the grass.		Which dog rolled on the grass?	Begin	
7. The new car was parked in the garage.		Which car was parked in the garage?	Begin	
8. Anna slept in the soft bed.		Which bed did Anna sleep in?	End	
9. The happy boy swam in the pool.		Which boy swam in the pool?	Begin	
10. Dad told me to wear my old shoes.		Which shoes did Dad tell me to wear?	End	
Total: Correct repeat:		**Correct answer:**		

Table 119: Goal 6:2 AUDITORY PROCESSING SENTENCES

Question word(s)	Position of answer	Sentence length	Answer length
Which?	BEGINNING or END	5–8 words	3 words

Note: *Same level of difficulty as Goal 6:1*

Example (beginning): The hot drink tastes good. Which drink tastes good? The hot drink.
Example (end): The teacher called to the noisy children. Which children did the teacher call to? The noisy children.

Sentence	Correct repeat	Question—Which?	Place	Correct/ incorrect
1. The red flower is in a pot.		Which flower is in a pot?	Begin	
2. The girl climbed over the brick wall.		Which wall did the girl climb over?	End	
3. Sam drank the cold juice.		Which juice did Sam drink?	End	
4. The tall girl got to choose a book.		Which girl got to choose a book?	Begin	
5. Kyle wore the dirty shirt.		Which shirt did Kyle wear?	End	
6. The narrow road is long.		Which road is long?	Begin	
7. The heavy bag fell on the floor.		Which bag fell on the floor?	Begin	
8. Mom listened to the quiet music.		Which music did Mom listen to?	End	
9. The empty box is on the shelf.		Which box is on the shelf?	Begin	
10. I throw the ball with my right hand.		Which hand do I throw the ball with?	End	
Total: Correct repeat:		**Correct answer:**		

Table 120: Goal 7:1 AUDITORY PROCESSING SENTENCES

Question word(s)	Position of answer	Sentence length	Answer length
When?	BEGINNING or END	5–7 words	1-4 words

Example (beginning): At lunchtime I ate spaghetti. When did I eat spaghetti? At lunchtime.

Example (end): Brett drinks water when he is thirsty. When does Brett drink water? When he is thirsty.

Sentence	Correct repeat	Question—When?	Place	Correct/ incorrect
1. Snow comes in the winter.		When does snow come?	End	
2. Before recess we do math.		When do we do math?	Begin	
3. Mom reads a story after bath time.		When does Mom read a story?	End	
4. The sun is hot in summer.		When is the sun hot?	End	
5. Dad will be home at supper time.		When will Dad be home?	End	
6. When it's dark I go to bed.		When do I go to bed?	Begin	
7. During a movie I eat popcorn.		When do I eat popcorn?	Begin	
8. I nap when I am sleepy.		When do I nap?	End	
9. Yesterday Todd ran fast in the race.		When did Todd run fast in the race?	Begin	
10. On her birthday Ann got a present.		When did Ann get a present?	Begin	
Total: Correct repeat:		**Correct answer:**		

Table 121: Goal 7:2 AUDITORY PROCESSING SENTENCES

Question word(s)	Position of answer	Sentence length	Answer length
When?	BEGINNING or END	6–10 words	2–5 words

Example (beginning): After lunch the children go out to play. When do the children go out to play? After lunch.

Example (end): The teacher drives to school every morning. When does the teacher drive to school? Every morning.

Sentence	Correct repeat	Question—When?	Place	Correct/ incorrect
1. The stars shine brightly <u>at night</u>.		When do the stars shine brightly?	End	
2. <u>When something is funny</u> I laugh.		When do I laugh?	Begin	
3. My dog is scared <u>when he hears thunder</u>.		When is my dog scared?	End	
4. I get my hair cut <u>when it is too long</u>.		When do I get my hair cut?	End	
5. <u>At bedtime</u> I brush my teeth.		When do I brush my teeth?	Begin	
6. <u>When I drink soup</u> I use a spoon.		When do I use a spoon?	Begin	
7. Jason eats cereal <u>at breakfast time</u>.		When does Jason eat cereal?	End	
8. <u>When it gets dark</u> I turn on the lights.		When do I turn on the lights?	Begin	
9. We are quiet <u>during a movie</u>.		When are we quiet?	End	
10. <u>When Amber hurt her knee</u> she cried.		When did Amber cry?	Begin	
Total: Correct repeat:		**Correct answer:**		

Table 122: AUDITORY PROCESSING SENTENCES

Question word(s)	Position of answer	Sentence length	Answer length

Sentence	Correct repeat	Question	Place	Correct/ incorrect
1.				
2.				
3.				
4.				
5.				
6.				
7.				
8.				
9.				
10.				
Total: Correct repeat:		Correct answer:		

17.
Whole Word Reading Program

Goal: The student will learn to read sight words using the Whole Word Reading Program.

This *whole word reading program* is based on teaching the student to visually match whole words to whole words using a grid and flashcards. The method was adapted with permission from the book *Teaching Reading to Children with Down Syndrome* by Patricia Logan Oelwein (Woodbine House, 1995).

The student who will benefit from this goal is one who:

VERBAL	NONVERBAL
Communicates in single words, phrases, or sentences	Uses PC symbols or other nonverbal system to communicate

Has a good visual memory.
Is able to match identical single-item pictures.
Is unable to decode written words using phonics.
Is interested in looking at books and listening to stories.

Teach a nonverbal student to read in order to:

- Open the possibility of developing spoken language through the visual rather than the auditory channel.
- Develop the student's ability to use spelling or pointing to written words to enhance his or her communication system.
- Provide the student with a means to acquire general knowledge, enrich his leisure time, and increase his independence.

Prerequisite for verbal and nonverbal students: *Ability to match object to object, object to picture, and picture to picture (not covered in this manual).*

BEFORE YOU BEGIN

Teaching Procedures

- Present the whole word reading program *3 times each day* to provide short, frequent periods for learning.
- Present *each* step up to the current level of learning *3 times* during each teaching session.
- Do not progress to a subsequent step until the student has reached 100 percent accuracy on the current step.
- Follow each step as described and use Sub-steps and Alternate Methods (see end of chapter) as needed:

  Step 1: MATCH
  Step 2: SELECT
  Step 3: NAME

Materials:

1. 8 x 11 sheets of white or pale blue cardstock.
2. Black marker pen or computer-generated printing.

Preparation:

1. Choose 4 target words that are *important* to the student, such as the student's name (e.g., Ryan); the name of a family member (e.g., Dad); the name of something that the student likes (e.g., pizza). Use the word "likes" as the fourth word.
2. Divide two 8 x 11 pieces of cardstock into 4 equal quadrants. Write or type each target word in a quadrant in large letters/font on both cards (the cards will be identical).

pizza	Dad
Ryan	likes

3. Cut one of the prepared cards into 4 single-word cards.

likes	**Dad**	**Ryan**	**pizza**

You now have 1 solid grid card and 4 single cards that match the words on the grid card.

WHOLE WORD READING PROGRAM

Verbal and nonverbal students will follow the same program for Step 1 (Match) and Step 2 (Select). Verbal students will then follow Step 3 below for the third Step (Name), Step 3 (Name) for nonverbal students is on p. 330.

Step 1—MATCH

Introduce this step by telling the student that he is going to learn to match words to the same words on a grid.

Use the single word cards and the matched grid card and sit so that the student can see your face:

a. Place the grid card face up on the table in front of the student.

b. Hold up a single word card close to your mouth so that it faces the student and say the word on the card.

c. Have the student place the word card on the matching word on the grid card (present the words in random order).

d. Repeat these steps until all 4 words are placed on the grid (leave each one in place after it has been matched).

e. Remove the cards from the grid card and repeat these steps 2 more times for a total of 3 times during that session. This will end your teaching session.

f. Repeat this teaching session 2 more times during the day.

Note: *To prevent the student from memorizing the position of the words on the grid and therefore not actually matching the words, prepare other grids using the same words but in different locations. Alternate grid cards during your sessions.*

When the student is **able** to match the word cards to the words on the grid with 100 percent accuracy, go to **Step 2**.

If the student is **unable** to match the word cards to the words on the grid, repeat **Step 1—MATCH** later in the day (up to 3 times during the day) and continue to practice 3 times each day on subsequent days until the student can match with 100 percent accuracy.

If, after 3 days (9 sessions), **MATCH** is still not mastered, go to **Sub-steps and Alternate Methods** at the end of this chapter.

Step 2—SELECT

Introduce this step by telling the student that he is going to give you the word that you read.

Before starting this Step present Step 1—MATCH 3 times at the beginning of every teaching session in order to reinforce learning and increase the student's confidence with written words.

Use the same 4 single-word cards from Step 1 and spread them face up on the table in random order.

   a. Remind the student that he is to give you the word that you say. Say the word on one card; e.g., "pizza." *Say only the word on the card (do not precede it with "Give me."*

   b. After the student has given you the word that you requested, replace the card on the table so that there is always a choice of 4 cards on the table. Acknowledge his *correct* choice by saying the word on the card again in a positive tone (avoid saying extra words such as "good' or "yes" because you do not want these to become associated with the word card). If his choice is *incorrect*, read the word on the card to him and replace it on the table then request the original word again.

   c. Request each word in random order.

   d. Repeat **Step 2—SELECT** two more times for a total of 3 times per session. Do both Step 1 and Step 2 during 3 sessions each day.

When the student is *able* to select the 4 single-word cards as named with 100 percent accuracy, progress to **Step 3—NAME**.

If the student makes an error, then give assistance by covering the card that he mistakenly gave you so that he only has a choice of 3 cards from which to choose the one that you say. If he makes many errors and is obviously *unable* to select the word cards consistently, repeat **Step 1—MATCH 3** times each session before trying **Step 2—SELECT**. If difficulty continues, go to **Sub-steps and Alternate Methods** at the end of this chapter.

Step 3—NAME (for Verbal Students)

Introduce this step by telling the student that now he is going to read the words by himself.

Begin your teaching session by presenting **Step 1—MATCH** and **Step 2—SELECT**. Then use the same 4 single-word cards for **Step 3—NAME,** and proceed as follows:

   a. Place each word card on the table in front of the student one at a time in random order and have the student say the word. If at first he does not respond, provide a model. Gradually fade the model (by first whispering and then mouthing the word) so eventually he is able to read each word independently with no prompts.

   b. Repeat **Step 3—NAME 2** more times for a total of 3 times per session. Repeat all 3 Steps during 3 sessions each day.

When the student is *able* to read the 4 words with 100 percent accuracy and no prompts, progress to **Teaching More Words** (see below).

If the student is *unable* to read the words independently after 3 days (9 consecutive sessions), go to the **Sub-steps and Alternate Methods** at the end of this chapter.

TEACHING MORE WORDS

When the student is able to read the 4 target words presented at random with 100 percent accuracy, choose 4 new target words (involve him in the choice). Choose words that can later be included in sentences; e.g., names of family/friends/pets, names of places ("store," "home," "library"), verbs ("goes," "has," "wants"). The words *must be meaningful* to the student.

Teach these new words using Steps 1 to 3 and review the original 4 words frequently so the student does not forget them. Only teach 4 new words at one time.

Play games:

- Tim's game—use the student's word cards. Have him pick up each card with the magnetic wand and read the word on the card.
- Lotto—when the student has learned at least 8 words, use the grid cards and matching words.
- Memory and Go Fish—use pairs of matching word cards (at least 8 words).

BUILDING SENTENCES FOR VERBAL STUDENTS

When the student is able to read 16–20 words, that include both nouns and verbs, you are going to create sentences for him using those words.

Materials:

1. Sentence board made from corrugated plastic or heavy cardboard. Attach 2 strips of plastic or cardboard to make pockets that word cards can slot into.

> ---
> ---

2. Write each word that the student is now able to read on 2 single, identical cards:

Ryan	Ryan

Reading sentences:

a. Build a sentence of 3–4 words in the top pocket using one set of the word cards.
b. Have the student use the duplicate cards to create the same sentence in the bottom pocket.
c. Have him read the words; e.g., Ryan likes pizza. Since he is already able to read these words when presented in isolation, he should have no difficulty reading them in a sentence.

When he is able to read words arranged in sentences on the sentence board with 100 percent accuracy, progress to **Sentence Cards,** below.

SENTENCE CARDS

Materials (as for Step 1—Match):

    1. 8 x 11 sheets of white or pale blue cardstock.
    2. Black marker pen or computer-generated printing.

Preparation:

Use the sentences that the student was able to copy and read in Building Sentences (above).

As for **Step 1—Match**, prepare 2 matching grid cards and write one sentence in each quadrant. Cut up one card into single-sentence cards.

Ryan likes Dad	**Dad likes pizza**
Dad likes Ryan	**Ryan likes pizza**

Ryan likes Dad	**Ryan likes pizza**	**Dad likes Ryan**	**Dad likes pizza**

Match, Select, Name:

Work through the original Steps 1–3. Have the student **MATCH** each sentence card to the sentence on the grid; **SELECT** the sentence read to him; **NAME** (read) each sentence without a model.

MAKE BOOKS

The student is now ready for his first "I like" book. Use cardstock and the words that he has learned. Illustrate each sentence with a photo or picture; e.g., "Ryan likes Dad" (photo of Ryan and his father together); "Dad likes pizza" (photo of father eating pizza). Fasten the pages together with staples or spiral binding.

Have the student read the book at school and at home to consolidate knowledge of these sentences and "show off" his new accomplishment. The book will be a treasured possession!

Expand to other titles as his reading word-bank expands (each word will be taught through the same original steps). For example: Make "I play," "I have," and "I want" books.

MAKE OTHER PATTERN BOOKS

Buy 2 copies of a book on a topic of interest to the student; e.g., trucks or Disney movies. Blank out or cover over the writing in the book and paste in simple sentences made up of words from his word bank. Include some new words and teach these through the original steps (MATCH, SELECT, NAME).

Step 3—NAME (for Nonverbal Students)

Introduce the program and work through **Step 1—MATCH** and **Step 2—SELECT** exactly as for the verbal student, as described above. When you get to **Step 3—NAME**, proceed as described below.

Materials:

1. Large piece of cardboard or corrugated plastic or a metal cookie sheet.
2. Cardstock to use to make word cards.
3. Adhesive Velcro (for cardboard and plastic) or 8 metal juice-can lids and adhesive magnetic tape (juice-can lids are ideal because they are firm, rugged and easy to hold/manipulate).
4. Real photos, pictures, or Picture Communication Symbols (PCS) that match the target words—e.g., word "mom" + photo of mom; word "likes" + PC for "likes."

Preparation:

1. Use the large piece of cardboard/corrugated plastic or metal cookie sheet as a work-board and draw a line down the center of it.
2. Use the target words that the student has already learned during **Step 1—MATCH** and **Step 2—SELECT**.
3. Write the target words on individual cards and either mount them on adhesive Velcro (for the cardboard or plastic work-board) or attach one to the front of each juice-can lid (for the cookie sheet). Attach magnetic tape to the back of the juice-can lids.
4. Prepare the work-board made of cardboard or plastic by attaching Velcro down each side between the center line and the edge (one side of the line for the words and the other side for the pictures). The cookie sheet needs no further preparation, as the magnetic strip on each lid will attach to the sheet.
5. Mount the photos, pictures, or PCSs that match the words onto adhesive Velcro (for the cardboard or plastic work-board) or onto juice can lids attached to magnetic tape (for the cookie sheet work-board).

Ryan	Photo of Ryan
Dad	Photo of Dad
Pizza	PC symbol for pizza
Likes	PC symbol for likes

Demonstrating reading ability:

Since the student has already worked on these words through Steps 1 and 2, he is able to match them word to word and can identify them when they are read to him. To demonstrate that he understands their meaning:

- *Match pictures to words*—place the *words* on the work-board and have the student match the *pictures* to the words.
- *Match words to pictures*—place the pictures on the work board and have the student match the words to the pictures.

Repeat 3 times each session.

Play games:

- Memory—use word cards and matching photos, pictures, or PCS.
- Lotto—when the student has learned at least 8 words, put the words on 2 work-boards (one for you and one for the student). Then take turns drawing a matching picture from a stack and see who can fill up his card first.

Progression:

Expand the nonverbal student's reading word-bank following the same steps as for verbal students.

Sub-steps and Alternate Methods

Use the following steps as sub-steps or alternate teaching methods for students who are experiencing difficulty with the main teaching method.

1. **Simplify Step 1—MATCH.** Present only 2 words and work through Step 1a-f, as for 4 words.

2. **Work on single-word matching.**
   a. Choose 1 target word. Write the word on 2 cards and have an identical card that is blank. Have the student match the target word to the same word given the choice of a target word card and a blank card.
   b. Write the target word on 5 cards and a very different looking word on 5 cards; e.g., target word "Ryan" and different word "elephant." Show the target word and have the student find all the word cards that are the same.

3. **Work on written word-to-picture association through fading a written word.** Choose 2 target words. Make a word + picture card for each word (a picture of the word with the word printed below); e.g., a picture of a dog with the word "dog" printed below it; a picture of mom with "mom" printed below it. Also prepare a card for each target word showing only the word; e.g., "mom," "dog."

   Step 1: Present the 2 word + picture cards and the corresponding single words. Have the student match the single word to the correct word + picture card (matching the written words). Progress to step 2 when the student is able to match with 100 percent accuracy.

   Step 2: Present one of the word + picture cards already used. Cover the word with a layer of tissue paper so that the word is slightly obscured. Present a choice of the 2 word cards already used. Have the student match the correct word card to the word + picture card.
   When the student is able to match with 100 percent accuracy, add another layer of tissue on top of the word and have him match again from the same choice of 2 words. Continue to add layers until the word under the picture is completely obscured and the student is matching word to picture.
   Increase the level of difficulty by presenting a choice of more word cards from which the student is to find the correct one to match the word + picture card.

   Step 3: Work on new single target words in the same way.
   The student may eventually be able to follow the Whole Word method or he may need to continue learning through fading the word.

For more suggestions on techniques to teach reading and fuller explanations of the steps described here, see *Teaching Reading to Children with Down Syndrome* by Patricia Logan Oelwein (Woodbine House, 1995).

Appendix 1: TRACKING GOALS and PREREQUISITES

Note: Goal descriptions are in an abbreviated form to save space—for full descriptions see Table of Contents.

GOALS	PREREQUISITES	DATE/COMMENTS
1. FOLLOWING DIRECTIONS		
Goal 1: body parts with/without props	**Goal 1:** none	
Goal 2: selected prepositions	**Goal 2:** none	
Goal 3: color and prepositions	**Goal 3:** colors – Ch. 8 (*Descriptors*), Goal 1, p. 120	
2. NEGATIVE – NO/NOT		
Goal 1: names of objects, people, animals	**Goal 1:** none	
Goal 2: concrete/visual parts	**Goal 2:** none	
Goal 3: attributes/actions/places	**Goal 3:** none	
3. SAME/DIFFERENT		
Goal 1: identical/non-identical objects	**Goal 1:** match object to object (not in manual)	
Goal 2: identical/non-identical by color	**Goal 2:** colors – Ch. 8 (*Descriptors*), Goal 1, p. 120	
Goal 3: presence/absence in physical group	**Goal 3:** none	
Goal 4: same name but varied features	**Goal 4:** descriptors – Ch. 8 (*Descriptors*), Goals 2–4, pp. 125, 127, 128	
Goal 5: different name but shared features	**Goal 5:** categories – Ch. 6 (*Classification and Categorization*), Goal 3, p.81; noun function – Ch. 5 (*Nouns*), Goal 2, p. 58	
Goal 6: pictures vary by one feature	**Goal 6:** no/not – Ch. 2 (*Negative No/Not*), Goals 1–3, pp. 24-27	
Goal 7: picture scenes vary by several features	**Goal 7:** none	
4. Yes/No		
Goal 1: name of object, person, or animal	**Goal 1:** no/not – Ch. 2 (*Negative No/Not*), Goals 1–2, pp. 24, 25	
Goal 2: action by person or animal	**Goal 2:** action – Ch. 7 (*Verbs*), Goal 2, p. 103	
Goal 3: color of object or animal	**Goal 3:** colors – Ch. 8 (*Descriptors*), Goal 1, p. 120	
Goal 4: position of object, person, or animal	**Goal 4:** prepositions – Ch. 1 (*Following Directions*), Goal 2, p. 18	
Goal 5: general knowledge	**Goal 5:** none	
Goal 6: personal information	**Goal 6:** none	

GOALS	PREREQUISITES	DATE/COMMENTS
5. NOUNS **Goal 1:** basic vocabulary **Goal 2:** object function **Goal 3:** association **Goal 4:** classification and categorization **Goal 5:** define nouns using a Word Web	**Goal 1:** none **Goal 2:** none **Goal 3:** Association 4: Ch. 5 (*Nouns*) Goal 2, p. 58 **Goal 4:** Ch. 6 (*Classification and Categorization*), pp. 77-97 **Goal 5:** none	
6. CLASSIFICATION AND CATEGORIZATION **Goal 1:** shape sorting **Goal 2:** exclusion shape sorting **Goal 3:** category name **Goal 4:** exclusion from category **Goal 5:** generate items in category **Goal 6:** generate items in subcategories	**Goal 1:** same/different – Ch. 3 (*Same and Different*), Goals 1–5, pp. 30-38; color – Ch. 8 (*Descriptors*), Goal 1, p. 120 **Goal 2:** no/not – Ch. 2 (*Negative No/Not*), Goals 1–3, pp. 24-27 **Goal 3:** none **Goal 4:** no/not – Ch. 2 (*Negative No/Not*), Goals 1–3, pp. 24-27 **Goal 5:** none **Goal 6:** none	
7. VERBS **Goal 1:** imitate/name modeled actions **Goal 2:** action in picture **Goal 3:** different people/animals same action **Goal 4:** perform action in picture **Goal 5:** name actions that can be carried out **Goal 6:** reason for action **Goal 7:** define verbs using a Verb Word Web	**Goal 1:** none **Goal 2:** none **Goal 3:** none **Goal 4:** none **Goal 5:** who? which? questions – Ch. 10 (*"Wh" Questions*), Goals who? p. 184, which? p. 193; no/not – Ch. 2 (*Negative No/Not*), Goals 1–3, pp. 24-27; yes/no –Ch. 4 (*Yes/No*), Goal 2, p. 42 **Goal 6:** why? questions – Ch. 10 (*"Wh" Questions*), Why? Goal B, p. 203; Why? General Suggestions, pp. 200-01 **Goal 7:** none	

8. DESCRIPTORS

Goal	Reference
Goal 1: primary colors	Goal 1: same/different – Ch. 3 (*Same and Different*), Goal 1, p. 30
Goal 2: size big/little	Goal 2: none
Goal 3: color and size together	Goal 3: none
Goal 4: variety of descriptors	Goal 4: none
Goal 5: feelings and emotions	Goal 5: none
Goal 6: opposites (antonyms)	Goal 6: none

9. CONCEPTS

Goal	Reference
Goal 1: position (prepositions)	Goal 1: prepositions – Ch. 1 (*Following Directions*), Goal 2, p. 18
Goal 2: quantity	Goal 2: no/not – Ch. 2 (*Negative No/Not*), Goal 2, p. 25
Goal 3: inclusion/exclusion	Goal 3: none
Goal 4: time	Goal 4: none
Goal 5: before/after (time)	Goal 5: before/after (position) – Ch. 9 (*Concepts*), Goal 1, p.149; 2-step directions – Ch. 1 (*Following Directions*), Goals 1–3, pp. 14-22

10. "WH" QUESTIONS

WHAT?

Goal	Reference
Goal 1: question "What is it?"	Goal 1: none
Goal 2: variety of "What?" questions	Goal 2: none

WHO?

Goal	Reference
Goal 1: question "Who is it?"	Goal 1: none
Goal 2: variety of "Who?" questions	Goal 2: none
Goal 3: contrasted "What?" and "Who?"	Goal 3: none

WHERE?

Goal	Reference
Goal 1: "Where?" place names and positions	Goal 1: prepositions – Ch. 1 (*Following Directions*), Goal 2, p. 18
Goal 2: "What/where?"; "Who/where?"; and "What/who/where?"	Goal 2: none

WHICH?

Goal	Reference
Goal: "Which?" choices	Goal: none

GOALS	PREREQUISITES	DATE/COMMENTS
WHEN? **Goal:** "When?" daily activities, calendar, seasons, conditions, and clock time	**WHEN?** **Goal:** concepts of time – Ch. 9 (*Concepts*), Goals 4–5, pp. 165 and 168	
MIXED QUESTION WORDS—1 **Goal:** "Who?" "What?" "Where?" "When?"	**MIXED QUESTION WORDS—1** **Goal:** none	
WHOSE? **Goal:** "Whose?" ownership (nouns and possessive pronouns "my," "your," "his," "her")	**WHOSE?** **Goal:** possessive "s" – Ch. 11 (*Word and Sentence Structure*), Goal 7, p. 230; possessive pronouns – Ch. 12 (*Pronouns*), Goals 4-5, pp. 254 and 257	
WHY? **Goal A:** function **Goal B:** action **Goal C:** association **Goal D:** categorization **Goal E:** cause and effect **Goal F:** absurdity	**WHY?** **Goal A:** object function – Ch. 5 (*Nouns*), Goal 2, p. 58 **Goal B:** review Ch. 7 (*Verbs*), Goal 6, p. 114 **Goal C:** review Ch. 5 (*Nouns*), Goal 3, pp. 61-69 **Goal D:** generate lists – Ch. 6 (*Classification and Categorization*), Goals 3–4, pp. 81-89 **Goal E:** none **Goal F:** absurdity – Ch. 4 (*Yes/No*), Goals 1–4, pp. 40-45; Ch. 13 (*Advanced Expressive Language*), Goal 4, p. 269	
MIXED QUESTION WORDS—2 **Goal:** "What?" "Who?" "Where?" "Which?" "When?" "Whose?" "Why?"	**MIXED QUESTION WORDS—2** **Goal:** none	
11. WORD AND SENTENCE STRUCTURE **Goal 1:** subject + is/are + "ing" verb **Goal 2:** article + is/are + "ing" verb **Goal 3:** article + is/are+ "ing" verb + article + object or place	**Goal 1:** verbs + ing ending – Ch. 7 (*Verbs*), Goals 1–3, pp. 100-108 **Goal 2:** articles – Ch. 9 (*Concepts*), Goal 2, p. 157 **Goal 3:** prepositions – Ch. 1 (*Following Directions*), Goal 2, p. 18; "Wh" questions – Ch. 10 ("*Wh*" *Questions*), What? Who? Where? Goals, pp. 179-192	

Goal	Reference
Goal 4: subjective and possessive personal pronouns	**Goal 4:** Ch. 12 (*Pronouns*), p. 245
Goal 5: present, past, and future verb tenses	**Goal 5:** time – Ch. 9 (*Concepts*), Goals 4–5, pp. 165 and 168; sequence – Ch. 13 (*Advanced Expressive Language*), Goal 2, p. 265
Goal 6: noun plurals	**Goal 6:** none
Goal 7: possessive "s" marker	**Goal 7:** possession – Ch. 10 (*"Wh" Questions*), "Whose?" Goal, p. 199
Goal 8: descriptors (adjectives and adverbs)	**Goal 8:** Ch. 8 (*Descriptors*), p. 119
Goal 9: conjunction "and"	**Goal 9:** "and" – Ch. 1 (*Following Directions*), Goal 1, p. 14
Goal 10: comparative "er" and superlative "est"	**Goal 10:** descriptors – Ch. 8 (*Descriptors*), Goals 2 and 4, pp. 125 and 128; no/not – Ch. 2 (*Negative No/Not*), Goals 1–3, pp. 24-27

12. PRONOUNS

Goal	Reference
Goal 1: gender (boy/girl)	**Goal 1:** none
Goal 2: personal "he," "she," "it," and "they"	**Goal 2:** sort people/things – Ch. 6 (*Classification and Categorization*), Goal 3, p. 81; subject+is/are+ing – Ch. 11 (*Word and Sentence Structure*), Goal 1, p. 211
Goal 3: personal "I," "we," and "you"	**Goal 3:** What? questions – Ch. 10 (*"Wh" Questions*), What? Goals 1–2, pp. 179-180
Goal 4: possessive "his," "her," "its," and "their"	**Goal 4:** none
Goal 5: possessive "my," "your," and "our"	**Goal 5:** none
Goal 6: personal "me" and "you" and possessive "mine" and "yours"	**Goal 6:** none

13. ADVANCED EXPRESSIVE LANGUAGE

Goal	Reference
Goal 1: picture scene	**Goal 1:** none
Goal 2: sequence story	**Goal 2:** time – Ch. 9 (*Concepts*), Goals 4–5, pp. 165-68
Goal 3: predict	**Goal 3:** none
Goal 4: identify what is wrong (absurd)	**Goal 4:** right/wrong – Ch. 4 (*Yes/No*), p. 40; "because" – Ch. 10 (*"Wh" Questions*), Why?, p. 200; no/not – Ch. 2 (*Negative No/Not*), Goals 1–3, pp. 24-27

GOALS	PREREQUISITES	DATE/COMMENTS
Goal 5: identify what is missing **Goal 6:** make inferences **Goal 7:** answer "How?" questions	**Goal 5:** presence/absence of objects – Ch. 3 (*Same and Different*), Goal 3, p. 32; generate lists – Ch. 6 (*Classification and Categorization*), Goal 5, p. 91 **Goal 6:** none **Goal 7:** sequencing – Ch. 13 (*Advanced Expressive Language*), Goal 2, p. 265; same/different – Ch. 3 (*Same and Different*), Goal 5, p. 34; categorization – Ch. 6 (*Classification and Categorization*), Goal 3, p. 81; descriptors – Ch. 8 (*Descriptors*), Goal 4, p. 128; emotions – Ch. 8 (*Descriptors*), Goal 5, p. 130	
14. LISTENING SKILLS: AUDITORY DISCRIMINATION **Goal 1:** noisemakers **Goal 2:** paired single consonants **Goal 3:** paired single-syllable words	**Goals 1–3:** same/different – Ch. 3 (*Same and Different*), Goal 1, p. 30	
15. LISTENING SKILLS: AUDITORY MEMORY **Goal 1:** series of noisemakers **Goal 2:** series of nouns with picture support **Goal 3:** series of nouns without picture support **Goal 4:** number series with/without support **Goal 5:** spoken sentences	**Goal 1:** none **Goal 2:** 1-step directions – Ch. 1 (*Following Directions*), Goal 1, p. 14 **Goal 3:** none **Goal 4:** knowledge of numbers (not in manual) **Goal 5:** none	
16. LISTENING SKILLS: AUDITORY PROCESSING Information that occurs: **Goal 1:** What? End **Goal 2:** What? Who? Beginning **Goal 3:** What? Who? Beginning/end **Goal 4:** What? Who? Middle	**Goals 1–7:** question words – Ch. 10 ("*Wh*" *Questions*), pp. 179-98; repeat a sentence – Ch. 15 (*Auditory Memory*), Goal 5, p. 300	

Goal 5: Where?	End	
Goal 6: Which?	Beginning/end	
Goal 7: When?	Beginning/end	
17. WHOLE WORD READING For verbal and nonverbal students		Ability to match object to object, object to picture, and picture to picture (not in manual)

Appendix 2
Materials

The materials used for the activities in this manual are **small toys and real objects, pictures of toys, objects and animals, and commercial picture cards** (e.g., action pictures, association cards purchased from a supplier such as those listed at the end of this appendix). You can also use pictures downloaded from the Internet or take your own photos (photos of people should only be taken with permission).

The toys and real objects should be familiar to the student and easy for him or her to manipulate. Since similar materials are used in many of the goals, you will need a varied collection of toys, objects, and animals (singles and in groups of identical and non-identical items) so that whenever possible the materials that you use are unique to each goal. This will prevent the student from taking the target response that he associates with one group of materials to a new goal and thus becoming confused about the new response required.

Some students find manipulatives distracting, and should therefore work with pictures only.

Pictures of toys, objects, people, and animals should be:
- Realistic and clear (not in cartoon style)
- Easy to handle (at least 3 inches or 7.5 centimeters high)
- Black and white or colored
- Photographed or drawn on an uncluttered background with no additional features

Action pictures should show one person or animal or a group of people or animals (as stated in the list of materials for that goal), carrying out the action(s).

Picture and magnetic/felt/vinyl scenes should show several people and/or animals carrying out a variety of activities in a familiar setting; e.g., in the park; at the mall.

Commercial games and activities are often suggested in "Carryover" activities at the end of each goal. Be careful not to use commercial games and activities, computer games, and apps that are above the student's level of language and cognition.

> **Note:** *Review the names of the objects or pictures that will be used for teaching prior to each activity. Replace any that the student does not know with ones that he does (except when working on activities where the goal is vocabulary development).*

Materials can be purchased from:

Attainment Company, Inc.
504 Commerce Parkway
P.O. Box 930160
Verona, WI 53593-0160
www.attainmentcompany.com

LinguiSystems
3100 4th Avenue
East Moline, IL 61244
www.linguisystems.com

Silver Lining Multimedia, Inc
P.O. Box 544
Peterborough, NH 03458
www.silverliningmm.com

Super Duper Publications
P.O. Box 24997
Grenville, SC 29616
www.superduperinc.com

Wintergreen Learning Materials
3075 Line B, RR2
Bradford, ON L3Z 2A5
www.wintergreen.ca

Appendix 3
References

Arnold, L. A. *The Source for Aphasia Therapy.* East Moline, IL: LinguiSystems, 1999.

Barton, J. B., J. R. Lanza, and C. C. Wilson. *SCOR Sequential Communication Objectives for Remediation.* East Moline, IL: LinguiSystems, 1984.

Boehm, A. E. *Boehm Test of Basic Concepts.* New York: The Psychological Corporation/ Harcourt Brace Jovanovich, 1983.

Dodwell, T. *Teaching Reading and Mathematics to Children with Autism and Developmental Disorders.* Conference presentation by Algonquin and Lakeshore Catholic District School Board, May 2004.

Eckenrode, L., P. Fennell, and K. Hearsey. *Tasks Galore.* Raleigh, NC: Tasks Galore, 2003.

Freeman, S., and L. Dake, *Teach Me Language.* Langley, BC: SKF Books, 1997.

Goldberg, R., and V. Rothstein. *BESST 1: Book of Exercises for Successful Semantics Teaching.* East Moline, IL: LinguiSystems, 1986.

Goldberg, R., and V. Rothstein. *BESST 2: Book of Exercises for Successful Semantics Teaching.* East Moline, IL: LinguiSystems, 1986.

Golick, M. *Deal Me In!* Madison, CT: Jeffrey Norton Publishers.

Gonzalez, A. X., L. J. Brady, and J. Elliott. *Speech in Action: Interactive Activities Combining Speech Language Pathology and Adaptive Physical Education.* London: Jessica Kingsley Publishers, 2011.

Hamaguchi, P. M. *Childhood Speech, Language, and Listening Problems.* New York, NY: John Wiley & Sons, 2001.

Jeffries, J. H., and R. D. Jeffries. *All In One.* Youngtown, AZ: ECL Publications, 1997.

Lazzari, A. M., and P. M. Peters. *HELP 1: Handbook of Exercises for Language Processing.* East Moline, IL: LinguiSystems, 1987.

Lazzari, A. M., and P.M. Peters. *HELP 2: Handbook of Exercises for Language Processing.* East Moline, IL: LinguiSystems, 1987.

Lazzari, A. M., and P. M. Peters. *HELP 3: Handbook of Exercises for Language Processing.* East Moline, IL: LinguiSystems, 1988.

Lazzari, A. M., and P. M. Peters. *HELP 4: Handbook of Exercises for Language Processing.* East Moline, IL: LinguiSystems, 1989.

Lazzari, A. M., and P. M. Peters. *HELP Elementary Handbook of Exercises for Language Processing.* East Moline IL: LinguiSystems, 1993.

Leaf, R., and J. McEachin. *A Work in Progress.* New York, NY: DRL Books, 1999.

Martin, L. *Think It – Say It.* Tucson, AZ: Communication Skill Builders, 1990.

Maurice, C., G. Green, and S. C. Luce, Eds. *Behavioral Intervention for Young Children with Autism.* Austin, TX: Pro-Ed, 2002.

Oelwein, P. L. *Teaching Reading to Children with Down Syndrome: A Guide for Parents and Teachers.* Bethesda, MD: Woodbine House, 1995.

Pepper, J., and E. Weitzman, E. *It Takes Two to Talk.* Toronto: The Hanen Program, 2004.

Plummer, D. *Helping Children Improve Their Communication Skills.* London, U.K: Jessica Kingsley Publishers, 2011.

Prater, R., and K. Stefanakos. *Memory Language Comprehension.* Austin, TX: PRO-ED, 1982.

Prater, R., and K. Stefanakos. *Auditory Rehabilitation.* Tigard, OR: C.C. Publications, Inc., 1982.

Quill, K. A. *Do-Watch-Listen-Say.* Baltimore: Paul H. Brookes Publishing, 2000.

Quill, K. (1996) *Teaching Children with Autism and PDD.* Ontario Association of Speech-Language Pathologists and Audiologists (OSLA) Conference. Toronto, Ontario, Oct. 25, 1996.

Quill, K. A. *Teaching Children with Autism.* Albany, NY: Delmar Publishers, 1995.

Semel, E. M., E. H. Wiig, and W. Secord. *Clinical Evaluation of Language Fundamentals - Revised (CELF-R).* San Antonio, TX: Psychological Corporation, 1987.

Shahzade, A. *Oral Language Development: A Systematic Activities Approach.* Allen, TX: DLM, 1982.

Sigafoos, J., M. Arthur-Kelly, and N. Butterfield. *Enhancing Everyday Communication for Children with Disabilities.* Baltimore: Paul H. Brookes Publishing, 2006.

Smith, S. M. *SPARC Picture Scenes.* East Moline, IL: LinguiSystems, 1992.

Thomsen, S., and C. Sander. *SPARC Stimulus Pictures for Assessment, Remediation, and Carryover.* East Moline, IL: LinguiSystems, 1982.

Warr-Leeper, G. *Assessment and Programming for School-age Children.* Workshop Ontario Association of Speech-Language Pathologists and Audiologists. Renfrew County Chapter. Arnprior, Ontario, May 3, 2003.

Wise, D., and S. Forrest. *Great Big Book of Children's Games.* New York, NY: McGraw-Hill Publishers, 2003.

Young, E. C. *Language Approach to Open Syllables.* Tucson, AZ: Communication Skill Builders, 1981.

Zachman, L., C. Jorgensen, M. Barrett, R. Huisingh, and M. K. Snedden. *MEER Manual of Exercises for Expressive Reasoning.* Moline, IL: LinguiSystems, 1982.

Appendix 4
Terminology

Absurdities—pictures that show unreal situations or sentences that give obviously incorrect information so they seem nonsensical (silly). For example, a picture of a chicken in a bathtub or the sentence "sheep climb trees."

Carryover—activities that are presented at the end of each goal to encourage students to use the target word, sentence, or concept in less structured settings, in order to help develop generalization.

Choice—to help the student say the target word or select the target picture, offer him the target in a choice of 2 words or pictures. Be aware of where you place the target word/picture in the choice. It may be easier for him to respond if he hears or sees the target word/picture consistently *first* in the choice; e.g., "is this a <u>dog</u> or a horse?" Or he may respond correctly more often if he hears the word/sees the picture *last* in the choice; e.g., "is this a horse or a <u>dog</u>?" Work toward having him select the correct choice when it is presented in either position at random.

Directions—verbal instructions (commands) often beginning with "point to," "show me," or "give me."

Elicit—draw out the target response from the student by providing choices and other prompts as needed.

Established/Generalized—refers to a skill that the student is able to appropriately use spontaneously (such as using a target word or structure in spontaneous language).

Expressive language—the use of spoken or written language to communicate.

Fade the support—as the student becomes more proficient at producing the target response with the help of verbal or written prompts, gradually reduce your support (help) over subsequent practice periods. Examples: Allow a longer time for him to respond before you provide the support; point to the picture when it is still face down on the table rather than show it to him directly; give him only the first *sound* of the word if you previously gave him the first *syllable*.

Listen, Repeat, Do strategy—have the student *Listen* to what you say, *Repeat* what you say, and then *Do* it (carry out the direction).

Model—provide the student with an example of what you want him to do or say. Examples: Demonstrate and say, "This is 'put the ball in the cup.'" Or, say the target question, "What is it?" and have him imitate (copy) you.

Process—think in order to understand. Students with developmental challenges often take longer to process language than typical students. Their delays in responding to your directions or questions may be because it takes them *longer* to understand the question, as opposed to not understanding it all. (That is, the student's receptive language is good, but his ability to process is slow.)

Prompt—help the student who is having difficulty making or saying a target response. Examples: Start the word for him using the initial sound or syllable; e.g., "f…." [frog]; "frrr…."[frog]; give him a description of the target word; e.g., "it jumps in the water" [frog]; provide the beginning of a relevant sentence and have him complete it; e.g., "I saw a big green _____"[frog]; provide a picture of the target, or, for students who can read, show the target word written on a cue card.

Receptive language—the understanding or comprehension of spoken or written language.

Sub-stepping—going back to an easier task; e.g. going back from Goal 2 in an activity to Goal 1, or going back to using picture support to elicit a target word.

Appendix 5
Index of Tables

17	Object-to-location association	64
18	Object-to-occupation association	66
19	Object-to-activity association	68
20	Part-to-whole association	70
21	Sample objects that have parts	71
22	Word web level 1	73
23	Word web game level 1	73
24	Word web level 2	74
25	Word web game level 2	75

6. Classification and Categorization

26	Category lists	82
27	Sort person and thing	84
28	Identify the category	86
29	Identify the category	87
30	Identify the category	88
31	Category exclusion	90
32	Add to the category	93
33	Categorization and classification	94
34	Subcategories	97

7. Verbs

35	Early developing verbs for imitation & naming	101
36	Tracking early developing verbs	102
37	Tracking later-developing verbs	105
38	What can a person, animal, or object do?	112
39	Who or what can do it?	113
40	Why? Questions related to actions	115
41	Verb word web	117
42	Verb word web game	118

Index

About the Author:

Caroline Lee graduated from the Oldrey-Fleming School of Speech Therapy, London, England, in 1968 and emigrated to Canada two years later. Her long career working with children as a Speech-Language Pathologist in public health, school boards, and private practice included seventeen years with the Renfrew County District School Board in Ontario. She managed assessments and planned programming for students with a broad range of speech/language delays and developmental challenges, and had a particular interest in children on the autism spectrum. She supervised the implementation of the programs by communicative disorders assistants, educational assistants, and other support personnel. Following retirement in 2011, she wrote the book that she wishes she had had on her desk all along!